The New Topiary

Imaginative Techniques
from
Longwood Gardens

The New Topiary

Imaginative Techniques
from
Longwood Gardens

Patricia Riley Hammer

Garden Art Press

ISBN 1 870673 03 4

Published by Garden Art Press Ltd, Northiam, East Sussex TN31 6NH

Artwork by Jane Porteous, England

Illustrator: Joan Messick Frain
Photographer: Larry Albee

British Library CIP Data
Hammer, Patricia Riley
    The new topiary: imaginative techniques from Longwood
    Gardens
    I. Title
    715.1

Frontispiece: These colorful topiary peacocks were part of the 1990 Chrysanthemum Festival at Longwood.

Printed in England by the Antique Collectors' Club Ltd., Woodbridge, Suffolk

Contents

Introduction by Penelope Hobhouse 7

Photographic Credits and Illustrations .8

Foreword by Katy Moss-Warner .9

Acknowledgements and Credits 10

Preface 11

Part I	History 13
	1. American Topiary History 15
	2. Topiary at Longwood Gardens 28
Part II	Topiary Techniques 37
	1. Cascading Chrysanthemum Topiaries 38
	2. Tabletop Topiaries 55
	3. Large-Scale Stuffed Topiaries 89
	4. Standards 97
	5. The Wreath 118
	6. Specialty Topiaries 128
	7. Good Ideas from Others 152
Part III	Application 160
	1. Festival Topiaries 161
	2. Topiaries for Children 186
	3. Interiorscaping, Outdoor and Turn-About Topiaries 196
Part IV	Elements of Topiary 214
	1. Topiary Frames .215
	2. Plants for Topiary 226
	3. Plant Chart 230
	4. Ivy Chart 242

Sources 252

Bibliography 256

Index 263

To Alex and Bill

A background of blossom for the topiary at Longwood Gardens.

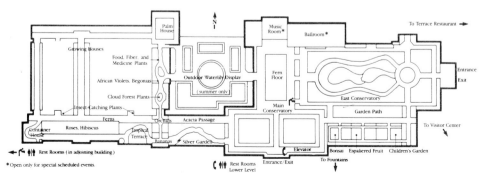

Plan of the Conservatories at Longwood Gardens.

Introduction

Topiary, the art of training and manipulating plants into prescribred shapes, has been 'in' and 'out' of garden fashion since we first hear of Pliny the Younger's gardeners, in the 1st century AD, cutting their own as well as their master's initials in box. Predictably it has always provided a rich subject for debate between the priorities of art and nature; an argument between those who feel that plants can be bent and trimmed to man's will and those who believe strongly even fanatically that plants in gardens should be grown with freedom to make their own natural shape. Over the centuries as we have 'grown' as gardeners these distinctions seem no longer to be so emotive; you don't have to be a French-style fanatic to mould plants to become decorative adjuncts to the garden or ornaments in house or conservatory. Most gardeners recognise the special value of topiary art forms which by geometry and precision hold a design together and by contrast with nature's shapes give variety and interest. In fact the 'new-style' topiary has a much more relaxed air. Now, with the skills to make brilliantly decorative self-contained topiaries which can be moved at will and placed outside or indoors, we can add other dimensions to these old traditions. Classical obelisks, cubes and drums, cones and finials, monsters, birds and whimsical animals, all dressed in living greens, are equally attainable. Some, grown in containers, are trimmed as specimens or more specifically trained on prefabricated frames. Given mobility these topiary features can be sheltered in winter and can be moved around to adjust to the changing garden appearance during summer months. The most exciting option, and to me a new American and very practical adaptation, is to stuff imaginatively designed frames with sphagnum moss in which suitable evergreen plants, such as ivy and creeping figs, actually grow and thrive, surviving for many years as 'living' ornaments.

In **The New Topiary,** all these techniques, traditional and modern, (as well as how to plan for and achieve Japanese-inspired cascading chrysanthemum blooms) are discussed and elaborated in careful detail. Pat Hammer is a topiary 'Queen'; she plans and executes the towering fantasies which decorate the great Conservatory at Longwood Gardens. Her book is an eye-opener to a world of rich invention and dedication; her instructions so practical that you feel in the safest of hands. The list of suitable plants with details of habits, growth patterns and appearance is invaluable revealing a new range of possibilities. Topiary styling is no longer confined to traditional woody subjects such as long-venerated box and yew but is extended to include quick-growing twiners and perennials which introduce softer outlines and textures to please the eye. Topiary, instead of being tight and geometric as of old, expands to give more gentle curves.

Longwood itself has an aura of excellence and even of grandeur; in the book Pat Hammer retains Longwood's authority but scales her advice to a human level introducing the reader to charming possibilities for both outdoor and indoor decoration.

Penelope Hobhouse.

Photographic Credits

Photographs by **Larry Albee,** Longwood Gardens except for:

Thomas J. Brinda: 80 bottom, 228 top, 229 top.

Edward Broadbent: 73 top, 175 right.

Rachel Cobb: 17 top, 25, 54 top right, 58 top left, 68, 69, 115 bottom, 123, 188 bottom left and right, 220 top right, 229 bottom right, 240 top.

The Walt Disney Company©. Furnished by Katy Moss Warner: 72.

Sharon Fisher: 19 top right, 20 bottom left, 21 bottom left.

Bud Gahs: 200 top.

Garden Art Press: 49 bottom right, 76, 77, 82, 87 top and bottom left, 103 middle, 115 top right, 116, 208 top right, 209 top right, 212.

Robert E. Gardener: 196.

Edmund B. Gilchrist Jr.: 24 bottom left.

Patricia R. Hammer: 14 top, 15, 17 bottom middle and right, 27, 119 top right, 127, 200 bottom, 205 bottom.

Ken C. Hardcastle: 220 bottom right, 221 top left.

Mia Hardcastle: 142 bottom right, 220 bottom left, 221 top right.

Dick Keen: 32 top, 34, 47 top right, 50 bottom, 59, 62, 65, 87 bottom right, 126 left, 168 top, 169 top, right, and bottom, 186.

Dale A. Lauver: 38.

Longwood Gardens File: 28, 30, 31, 41, 51, 85, 88, 148, 151

Richard Lyon: 199.

James T. Mason: 16.

Billings M. McArthur: 24 top right.

McGuire Topiary and Sculptural Designs: 201.

Michael S. Owen: 189 bottom.

Julie A. Padrutt: 217.

Library, Pennsylvania Horticultural Society: 22, 23.

Suzanne Pierot, courtesy of: 24.

Deborah Reich: 155 top left, 197 top left.

Jim Roberts: 155 top left, 189 top.

Topiary Inc: 220 top left and right, bottom left.

Debbie Turner Rogers: 154.

Landon Scarlett: 32 bottom left, 164 bottom left, 216.

Courtesy of the Office of Horticulture, Smithsonian Institution, Washington, D.C.: 19 top left and middle, bottom left and middle, 20, 21 top and bottom left.

Ernie G. Wasson: 17 bottom left.

Tom Woodham: 134 top row.

Time-Life Encyclopedia of Gardening: Herbs. Photograph by Marina Schinz. ©1977 Time-Life Books Inc., 24 top left.

Illustrations

Illustrations by **Joan Messick Frain** except for:

Mary Mizdail Allinson and Catherine Eberbach: The Childrens' Garden Plan, 1990; 194.

Mary Mizdail Allinson: animal drawings for The Childrens' Gardens 194, 195.

Thomas J. Brinda: Design for Turn-About Garden; 206.

George W. Earle Jr.: Drawing for Pagoda, 185.

Karl Grieshaber: 31.

James T. Mason: Study for the topiary at the Deaf School Park, Columbus, Ohio, 16.

Gerry Simboli: 1986 Penguins and Reindeer, 170, 171, 174.
　　　　　　1987 Carousel animals, Swan and Ostrich, 162.

Frank Sipala: Dragon, 178.

Foreword

Fun. Fantasy. Magic. Just imagine…a garden full of plants that tickle our fancy, make us laugh. Just imagine a garden where plants are fun. Just imagine a garden full of topiary characters.

A bright green lawn stretches out before us. Great branches from giant trees arch overhead. Shrubs enclose our space in soft, billowy walls of many shades of green. Brightly colored flower beds attract our attention. It is serene and beautiful. And then all of a sudden, we chuckle. Is that dancing hippopotamus really wearing a tutu of pink begonias? Can that seal balancing on a circus ball really be made out of plants? Is that a ''bush'' elephant waving at us? The fanciful green characters have made the garden fun. It is for this joy that the creative art of topiary deserves attention.

In my experience, topiary can touch people in powerful ways. It can capture the heart and lift the spirit. Imagine a place where families with terminally ill children come for a special and magical vacation…a place where a playful sea serpent topiary wriggles across a lawn surrounded by gingerbread houses. Imagine a very sick little girl with only a few days to live who spots this sea serpent, regains her strength and lives for many more months. This really happened. The little girl was named Amanda. It is incredible to think that topiary might have this power.

There are a number of exceptional collections of topiary in the world. In each, the topiary characters more than any other plants in the garden have the ability to transport us into a wonderful world of fun and fantasy, inspiration and magic. It is hoped that with the information and ideas in this book, you might be transported to this wonderful, magical world with your own topiary creations.

Katy Moss Warner

Katy Moss Warner
General Manager
Parks Horticulture
Walt Disney World Company

Acknowledgements and Credits

The following people made direct contributions to this book.

American Topiary History
Tovah Martin
James Buckler
James Moritz
Samuel Phillips

Longwood History
Joe Carstens
Joe Hannas
Bob Pyle
Bob Brown
Landon Scarlett
Dave Thompson

Cascading Chrysanthemums
Wayne Barber
Jack Kopczynski
Dale Lauver

Tabletop Topiary
John Testorf

Large-Scale Topiary
Ed Broadbent

Standards
John Testorf
Herbert Bejamin
David Cox
Jimmy Paolni
Allen Haskell

Wreaths
Bob Pyle
Joe Parrett
Dave Frampton

Topiary and Flowers
Sharon Fisher
Drew Gruenburg, SAF

Moss Topiary
Ed Broadbent

Dried Topiary
Ed Broadbent
Elizabeth Varley

Cut Green Topiary
Bob Pyle
Ken Barker

Festival Topiary
Landon Scarlett
Chrysanthemum Festival Committee
Mel Crossen
John Yoder
Roy Simmers
Dave McCleary
Barney Thompson
Mary Mizdail Allinson
Gibby Bahel
Dick Minner
Ferrell Pierson
Bruce Gentry
Jack Carrigan
Phil Hertzog
Elizabeth Varley
Ed Broadbent

Topiary Frames
Bob Nead
Bob Rowe
Jack Carrigan

Plants for Topiary
Robert Herald
Elizabeth Varley
Ed Broadbent

Special Acknowledgements
Joe Carstens
Enola Teeter
Judy Campbell
Julie Padrutt
Suzanne Knowles
CKM Enterprises

Preface

I had only recently heard of an extraordinary lady who was running all over the world collecting every detail of how and why people grow topiary. She was coming to Longwood to see our topiary, and her reputation was one of contagious, non-stop energy and enthusiasm. Little did I know where that rainy day visit would lead. Thank you, Geraldine Lacey Andrews, for offering me the opportunity to share my love of topiary. Your support and guidance throughout this project will always be appreciated.

Thanks to my Longwood friends and colleagues for encouraging and assisting with my topiary work. None of the displays would have materialized without the combined vision and efforts of the entire staff. I am particularly appreciative of my editing team – Sally Meeting, Colvin Randall, Claire Sawyers, Robert Herald and Elise Everhardt. Special thanks go also to artist Joan Frain and photographer Larry Albee, for their contributions of talent and friendship.

During the past two years, I have gained many new friends-in-topiary all over the United States and in England. You were all so generous with your knowledge, expertise, and even your homes. I hope we will go on sharing in the future.

Heart-felt gratitude goes to fellow members of The American Ivy Society. Thank you, Tom, for your guidance, often-needed kind words, sometimes-needed stiff criticism, and for your treasured friendship. Thank you, Mom and Dennis, for your constant love and support. I am sorry that Dennis did not get to see the book completed. Thank you, Sean and Tina, for bringing me Alexzandria in the middle of this project. What a cherished gift!

It is my husband, Bill Hammer, who deserves the highest commendation. He assumed all my household and family duties, managed The Tree Farm single-handedly, looked after my herd of cats and the dogs, and even took care of my ivy greenhouse for two years. You are the best husband ever, and I shall never forget that your love and support has never faltered.

Patricia Riley Hammer

Patricia Riley Hammer
27th June 1990

The main conservatory at Longwood Gardens decorated with wreathes, swaggs, and cut greens for Christmas 1971.

Part I
History

1. American Topiary History

2. Topiary at Longwood Gardens

Part of the topiary garden at the Governor's Palace, Colonial Williamsburg in Virginia.

Specimen topiary including the now-famous Lyre bird at Ladew Gardens, Monkton, Maryland.

1. American Topiary History

Topiary Gardens

The art of shaping plants into ornamental or fanciful shapes by training and pruning has long been part of the American landscape and decorative tradition. The origin of American topiary can be seen in the reconstruction of the eighteenth-century gardens of Colonial Williamsburg in Virginia where almost every garden contains topiary of some sort. Traditional topiary can be found on almost every residential street in the country. Often it is not thought of as topiary; a pair of square- or cone-shaped yews flanking an entrance is seen as part of the basic garden structure.

Several of America's most celebrated gardens feature topiary. Although Filoli, in Woodside, California, is better known for its magnificent oaks, hundreds of camellias, rhododendrons, roses, and magnolias, it has many clipped shapes and plant walls. Its colorful beds are surrounded and separated by formally pruned plantings including a spectacular dark green allée of Irish yew columns.

Ladew Gardens in Monkton, Maryland, is famous for topiary. Among the creations are a topiary fox hunt, a privet Chinese junk, many whimsical specimens including a Buddha, and massive garden walls of hemlock with swag-topped windows framing a vast meadow.

The Hunnewell Estate in Wellesley, Massachusetts, near Boston, was started by Hollis Hunnewell about 1850. This garden has a terraced slope along the shore of Lake Waban filled with trees and shrubs clipped into geometric shapes which include globes, cones, and pyramids carved from white pine, hemlock, and larch.

Boxwood parterres and formal hedging at Filoli in Woodside, California.

Frame and growing yew
depicting the couple in the
foreground of the drawing
below.

Green Animals, the privet zoo in Portsmouth, Rhode Island, was started in 1893 by Thomas Brayton. The garden now belongs to the Preservation Society of Newport County, and there are eighty topiary pieces including a giraffe, elephant, donkey, wild boar, mountain goat, rooster, sailboat, and policeman.

Vizcaya, in Miami, Florida, was formerly the winter home of James Deering, once vice-president of the International Harvester Company. The mansion and surrounding gardens were built between 1914 and 1916 along Biscayne Bay and were inspired by 16th-century Italian villas and gardens. Topiary and classic sculpture have been produced from subtropical plants such as eugenia, myrtle, and jasmine which have been masterfully substituted for traditional topiary plants.

In addition to these well-established examples, current interest has given rise to the creation of new topiary gardens. A new forty six acre theme park called Hecker Pass in Gilroy, California, is being developed by Michael Bonfante and will include the cherished Circus Trees developed by Axel Erlandson during the 1920s and 1930s which have become giant specimens of horticultural wonder. Bonfante is also growing topiary animals which will be planted throughout the park especially in areas planned for children.

Another current topiary project is developing at Deaf School Park in Columbus, Ohio. This unique garden will bring Georges Seurat's famous painting *A Sunday Afternoon on the Island of La Grande Jatte* to life in topiary. Sculptor James T. Mason has designed metal frames for 46 plant figures. Yews have been planted and the shaping has begun for a scheduled opening in 1992.

Study for the topiary project at the Deaf School Park, Columbus, Ohio.

Simple, dark-green topiary forms contrast with the elaborate stonework at Vizcaya, in Miami, Florida.

By examining topiary design and its function today and during colonial days, we realize that it is more than simple decoration; it was, and is, used to set boundaries, to create intimate little gardens, and to draw attention to special garden features. It is also prized as a horticultural art expressing skill and imagination.

Sitting bear from the privet zoo at Green Animals, Portsmouth, Rhode Island.

Two topiary dogs to be seen at the Hecker Pass theme park in California.

Some of the elaborate circus trees at Hecker Pass.

The Victorians and Portable Topiary

Today's interest in portable topiary can be traced back to the first plants used to embellish the parlor during the Victorian era when hardy, half-hardy, and perennial plants were brought indoors to extend their display time. Among the first to be moved inside were primroses, violets, carnations, roses, and ivies. Once the Victorians brought plants indoors, shaping followed. The noted garden writer Tovah Martin, in *Once Upon A Window Sill,* describes what was done with roses:

> Having mastered the basics, many gardeners went on to dabble in more difficult rose-related feats. Rose plants were often coaxed into fanciful shapes as they grew. In the spirit of the era, women were encouraged to develop their hobby into a fine art. Topiary, standard and espaliered indoor roses were quite frequently attempted by ladies who used their plants as a means of self-expression. Most often, roses were shaped into cones. After pruning, the new growth was drawn to the edges of the pot and pinned in place with hairpins. From that point, the branches were allowed to ascend upward until they met at the cone's tip. More ambitious gardeners tried coaxing their roses into half globes, fans, pyramids and standards.

Accounts and illustrations from the late 1800s display plant-filled front parlors and sitting rooms. As the rooms became brighter, the number of plants increased. With more sunlight, plants grew with exuberance. Ivies were trained up and around windows, archways, and even on indoor trellises, eventually into fanciful and often useful shapes with wire and frame-like structures.

One such popular indoor plant structure mentioned about 1870 was the ivy privacy screen, a frame fastened to an ornate container and used as the growing trellis. This quick and easy-to-grow vine soon adorned more ornate shapes and figures in keeping with the style of the era.

The Victorian interest in ivy topiary and the transformation of the art from outdoors to indoors is best summarized by Tovah Martin:

> Ivy inspired further creative caprices. The plant's willing adaptability lends itself to sculpting fanciful shapes and forms. Hence, ivy became a likely subject for the age-old art of topiary. Formerly, that art had found most of its applications in the garden outdoors, although trained roses frequently adorned the parlor in winter. Ivy provided another venue for exercising the tonsorial arts inside the home. Vines were fashioned into pyramids and coaxed into globes, they wound their way around every geometric shape known to man. Best of all, anyone could experiment with topiary. Although the art of training plants demands time and skill, it requires little monetary investment. An ivy topiary was a horticultural feather in the cap of any gardener, and it was within everyone's reach, regardless of their position on the socio-economic ladder.

During the mid 19th-century, according to James Moretz, Director of the American Floral Art School in Chicago, Illinois, the first true commercial florists began to appear in larger cities. The early shops were a combination of florist and garden supply centers offering all the horticultural needs in one location. Florists were developing the concept of the floral "set piece". Set pieces were usually funeral designs developed to pay tribute to the deceased and to their special interests or affiliations during life.

Wire work exhibits at the Centennial
International Exhibition, 1876, at the
Horticultural Hall, Philadelphia.

"The Presidential Chair," Washington Park,
Chicago.

An empty chair depicting
sorrow.

"The Blessing," April 14, 1903.

"Gates Ajar," Washington Park, Chicago.

Frame for "Gates Ajar."

Among the more popular were emblems for every known organization such as "Odd
Fellow Links," "Masonic Lodge Symbol," and "Elk's Head Symbol." Each was
covered in detailed color designs using flowers. Other designs were to honor the dead
and mark the passing from one life to the next such as "Gates Ajar." Sorrow was
depicted by the "Broken Heart" or the "Empty Chair." Occasionally set pieces
honored happier occasions such as weddings by using bells, love knots, and even the
wedding ring.

The set piece was made by adding flowers to sphagnum moss-filled frames. In larger
cities the florist could both obtain flowers and order his wire frame from the wire
worker found at the flower market. Each frame was virtually custom designed, but,
later, extensive wire work catalogs began to appear so florists could order frames in
advance and have a supply on hand.

Floral frame, Swan, ''A Victorian Horticultural Extravaganza'' for the Victorian Horticultural Exhibition at the Smithsonian Institution, Washington, D.C.

Growing plants on wire shapes and adding fresh flowers and cut greens to moss-filled frames eventually developed into what we now call stuffed portable topiary. In several accounts of materials used in set pieces, ivy was mentioned; since it roots quickly in damp sphagnum moss, it is possible that florists discovered another use for the floral display frame by accident!

Some of the early wire frame catalogs also carried numerous designs for ornamental plant stands, indoor arbors, and trellises. M. Walker and Sons in Philadelphia carried these items and a line of one-dimensional plant supports ranging from 12 to 42 inches high, very similar to today's one-dimensional topiary frames, and in several styles including fans, shields, and a musical lyre. Each had prongs at the base used to anchor the frame to the plant container. Thus the portable and stuffed topiary pieces so popular today seem closely related to the horticultural practices of the Victorian era.

Reconstruction of the Weber Train for the Victorian Horticultural Exhibition at the Smithsonian Institution, Washington, D.C.

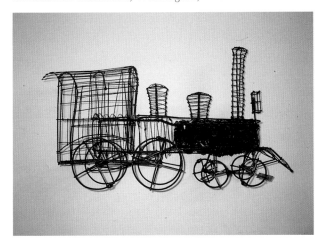

Wire frame for Weber Train.

Creations on frames, Smithsonian Institution, Washington, D.C., 1980.

A topiary by Mrs Clark at the Philadelphia Flower Show.

An elegant spiral of dwarf myrtle by Mrs. Reath.

The cone of rosemary was exhibited by Mrs. Keith at the Philadelphia Flower Show, 1974.

The Role of Horticultural Societies

Over the years, plant trends have been greatly influenced by organized horticultural groups. The Horticultural Society of New York, started in 1818, and the Pennsylvania Horticultural Society, started in 1827, were established to promote horticulture. The first members were generally professional plantsmen, but by the 1880s, groups of garden hobbyists including women had begun to form. Today's topiary can be traced through the history of these organizations.

Topiary appears in numerous photographs that record the celebrated Philadelphia Flower Show since 1929. Azalea and ivy standards can be found in the records of 1929 and 1932. The 1933 show included floral-type standards with tops of carnations. In 1934, the Settlement Garden Club displayed wicker baskets apparently planted with vines that covered the handles. In the early 1940s, geranium standards appeared regularly, and a few years later an ivy wreath grown in a pot was featured. The first moss-stuffed portable wire frame, in a bird-like shape, appeared in the background of a photograph taken at the Philadelphia Flower Show in 1955. The bird forms have wire legs and the plants are incorporated into the body, **not coming up from a pot.** Stuffed topiary does not show up again in photographs of the Philadelphia Flower Show until the early 1960s.

An eagle was among the first trained-up, pre-formed topiary as we know it today. It was designed and started in 1957 by Grace Machall, then National Chairperson of the Horticultural Committee for The Garden Club of America, for an exhibit in the 1959 New York Flower Show. She planned a competitive exhibit of the diverse merits of *Hedera helix* to include ivies as ground covers, pot plants, trailing plants, hanging baskets, and topiary. Her group spent three years growing ivies and preparing for this display, which received the Best Horticultural Exhibit Medal.

The following year (1960), Dorothy Keith brought the eagle design to the Philadelphia Show. She also chaired a committee to design and grow these eagles in honor of the Garden Club of America's 50th-year anniversary to be celebrated in Philadelphia in 1963. Each member of the committee was directed to make an eagle, but those who recall the 1963 event remember only the perfectly trained ivy eagle done by Mrs. Keith. Hers was trained up from a pot and over a frame. Another of Mrs. Keith's specialities was training and pruning woody plants into perfect shapes. Her work won numerous ribbons and awards across the country, and she was featured in several horticultural books and magazines. Fellow enthusiasts considered her a genius.

Two excellent examples of topiary work: on the left, Mrs. Clark's decorative tree; right, a myrtle bird by Mrs. Reath.

After topiary eagles appeared in New York and Philadelphia, interest in portable topiary developed rapidly. During the 1960s and 1970s topiary of every style, shape, and form appeared at the Philadelphia Flower Show each March. Myrtle *(Myrtus communis)* and rosemary *(Rosmarinus officinalis)* were grown and pruned to perfection, and the competition became fierce. Mrs. Keith's passion for trained plants won her the Pennsylvania Horticultural Society's Sweepstakes Trophy more than once.

Two Philadelphians of note in the field of portable topiary are Sally Reath and Cecily Clark. Mrs. Reath has been exhibiting award-winning container topiary in flower shows for over twenty-five years. She pays particular attention to how the plant grows and works with natural forms on many pieces. Occasionally, she even uses a pair of electric shears! Two of her best-known works, myrtle spirals, are pictured in *The Time-Life Encyclopedia of Gardening: Herbs.* Mrs. Clark, armed with nail scissors and tiny paint brushes, prefers the concentrated proportions of specimens of Victorian-rosemary *(Westringia rosmariniformis),* rosemary, myrtle, and ivy. Her greenhouse is filled with prize-winning topiaries.

An assortment of topiary exhibits at the Philadelphia Flower Show, 1955.

Right: From THE TIME-LIFE
ENCYCLOPEDIA OF GARDENING:
Herbs. Photograph by Marina Schinz.®
1977 Time-Life Books Inc.

Mrs. Reath's granddaughter peering out at
Grandmother's pair of myrtle spirals.

This rabbit covered with creeping fig was
created by Mrs. Ballard.

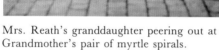

This won Mrs. Haas the Edith Wilder Scott
Award at the Philadelphia Flower Show.

An excellent example of a pot-grown ivy
trained over a frame by Suzanne Pierot.

In 1964, Dorothy Haas created a trend for stuffed topiary without a pot by entering
an ivy-covered seal balancing a striped beach ball of variegated and green ivy in the
Philadelphia Flower Show. She won the Edith Wilder Scott Award.

Ernesta Ballard, former President of the Pennsylvania Horticultural Society, has
been growing topiary since the early '60s and displays it prominently in her garden.
In 1963, her work with pre-formed tabletop topiary was featured in a newspaper article
and, in 1968, she published an article describing how to build a topiary. This brought
the craft to hobbyists nationally.

In 1974, one year after starting the American Ivy Society, Suzanne Warner Pierot

Skilfully planted, this giant cake topped by Mickey Mouse is an eye-catching example of stuffed topiary at Walt Disney World Resort® in Florida.

wrote *The Ivy Book,* subtitled *The Growing and Care of Ivy and Ivy Topiary.* She describes stuffed topiary, ivy wreaths, and ivy ball trees. Instructions are included on how to make frames and on building techniques. It is one of the first books to discuss pre-formed and portable topiary.

In the 1970s, small topiary businesses emerged: Maryvale Garden Shop in San Francisco; Topiary Inc. in Tampa, Florida; McGuire's Topiary in Baltimore, Maryland; Irene's Topiary in Sanger, California; and Topiary by Lucky in Danville, Kentucky.

Large-scale stuffed topiaries appeared throughout the United States in 1984;

amazingly, the individual creators were unaware of one another. Rockefeller Center in New York City displayed larger-than-life-sized animal topiaries in the Channel Gardens on Fifth Avenue to millions of passers-by. Simultaneously, Deborah Reich and Barbara Gallup were collaborating on stuffed topiaries for New York's World Trade Center. While Jeff Brees was creating his first topiary frame in California, Jim Silvia was welding together a people-sized owl, rabbit, and a deer in Middletown, Rhode Island. Jim's ivy-covered frames appeared in the December 1984 issue of *House and Garden* magazine. It was also Longwood's first year for large specimens.

In the last decade, portable topiary has appeared everywhere including in botanical gardens, zoos, and private gardens. It has even taken on political significance in the 1990s. A Republican topiary elephant resides in the garden of the First Lady, Mrs. George Bush.

The Ivy Bear

Another historically important topiary is the Ivy Bear, a 30-foot vine-covered bear that stood next to the Alder Creek Cafe in Oregon and was the creation of Gerald Weir, a man who trained real dogs and bears.

The bear was originally constructed around an old cedar stump covered with ivy. Weir added hand-split cedar boards to create the head, body, arms, and legs. He fastened burlap bags to the wood frame, and the ivy began to cling to the shape. In 1984, a windstorm badly damaged the bear. Three years later, several "Friends of the Bear" organized and started its reconstruction and today the Ivy Bear is well on the way to recovery.

Rear-Admiral Neill Phillips

The name of the late Rear-Admiral Neill Phillips and his estate, Heronwood, were legendary in topiary circles. In 1955 he purchased Heronwood, located in Upperville, Virginia, restored the extensive boxwood plantings, and created many classic topiaries. Few people, however, associate the Admiral with stuffed and pre-formed topiary. An article he wrote for the *Bulletin* of the New York Horticultural Society in 1960 included a brief description of what he classified as "Short Cuts" in topiary. He made stuffed forms from hardware cloth with $\frac{1}{4}$ to $\frac{1}{2}$-inch mesh. The forms were set into the garden and wintercreeper euonymus was planted around the forms and trained to grow onto the moss-filled frames.

The frames were unique in style; although stuffed, they appeared more as a silhouette. A Washington, D.C., newspaper, *The Sunday Star,* featured photographs and an article about these topiaries and described the process as follows:

> Using rat wire, head gardener Richard Wines cut two silhouettes of a rabbit, joining them with a four-to-six-inch-wide strip stapled every few inches with copper pig rings. The bottom is left open so the frame can be stuffed with sphagnum peat moss, then also closed with rings.

Probably Admiral Phillips designed this system to create "instant topiary." The frame was filled with damp moss to encourage the euonymus to climb and cover the shape. After the character was filled in with foliage, the shape would easily serve as a pruning guide. The 1960 articles revealed that Neill Phillips made several shapes including swans, geese, porter pigeons, armillary spheres, obelisks, and ball-on-balls.

Decorative topiary at Lotusland in California.

Lotusland

The earliest known mention of outdoor wire-frame topiary appeared in the *Los Angeles Times*, 1959. This article gave a glimpse of a topiary garden at the Montecito estate of Mme. Ganna Walska, Santa Barbara, California. The garden is called Lotusland and the gardeners are restoring some of the early ivy-covered animals and whimsical creatures. Apparently the ivy was planted directly into the ground and trained over the wire and bamboo frames.

The Walt Disney Company

When it comes to portable topiary, everyone immediately thinks of Disneyland Park® in California and Walt Disney World Resort® in Florida. Walt Disney himself developed the idea of growing his fictional characters in green plants. His plan first came off the drawing board around 1960, and the first pruned-to-shape characters appeared in Disneyland Park's® Fantasyland area in 1963. Now there are over one hundred topiary figures at Walt Disney World Resort® in Florida and numerous forms at the California location.

Many of Disney's topiaries are woody plants such as podocarpus, holly, and juniper growing inside a frame and planted into a large container. They are grown in a "topiary nursery" until perfect and only then moved into the park for display. A favorite is Mary Poppins made of holly and pyracantha.

Disney also makes stuffed topiary. One exceptional example was the giant birthday cake that was located in front of Cinderella's Castle to celebrate the fifteenth anniversary of Walt Disney World Resort® in Florida. The cake, 7 feet tall and 41 feet in circumference at the base, was made of wax begonias and alternanthera.

2. Topiary at Longwood Gardens

Fancifully shaped plants have delighted visitors to Longwood Gardens in recent years, but topiary is just one gem in Longwood's horticultural crown. Longwood is one of America's most historic and theatrical gardens. The property was purchased from William Penn in 1700 by the Peirce family. In 1798 brothers Joshua and Samuel Peirce began planting ornamental trees, and by the mid-19th century, Peirce's Park, as it was then known, ranked among the country's finest arboretums. Industrialist Pierre S. du Pont (1870-1954) bought the property in 1906 to save the trees from destruction and developed it into a horticultural showplace.

Mr. du Pont personally designed Longwood's features, beginning with a six hundred foot long flower garden in 1907. Annual garden parties were so successful that he continually looked for new ways to delight his guests and the always-welcome public. In 1913, an outdoor theatre was constructed; in 1914, a house conservatory; in 1921, a huge greenhouse complex (now totalling nearly four acres); in 1927, an Italianate water garden with six hundred fountain jets and, on the theatre stage, illuminated fountains with seven hundred and fifty jets; and, in 1931, a large fountain garden with lighted jets rising as high as 130 feet. These unusual attractions, recalling the celebrated gardens of Italy, France, and England as well as the great world's fairs, have been well cared for over the years and now attract eight hundred thousand people each year. Longwood cultivates more than eleven thousand types of plants.

Traditional outdoor topiary first appeared at Longwood in 1936 in what was called the Yew Garden. A giant, 37-foot-wide analemmatic sundial was built, backed with a horseshoe hedge and complemented with four cones and eleven large mounds, all of yew. In 1958, thirty topiary figures were purchased from the Bismark Estate in Bayville, Long Island, New York, and the area was renamed the Topiary Garden. Shortly thereafter, the large yew mounds were embellished with additional growth to enhance the geometric feeling. In 1962, eight pieces were imported from the Charles Fiore Nursery in Prairie View, Illinois. Two topiary urns from the Taylor Arboretum in Chester, Pennsylvania, were incorporated into the garden in 1971. Jack Hamilton, who groomed the garden for two decades, created a number of novelty pieces in the 1970s, including a rabbit and an armchair with table. In 1980, five new pieces created by Hamilton in Longwood's nursery were moved into the display.

A chrysanthemum table and two chairs; one of the first displays at Longwood Gardens in the early 1960s.

During the late 1960s a dog was added to the display. The frame was made in two halves.

A view of the famous topiary garden at Longwood.

The mid-1980s brought a new gardener, David Thompson, and a new direction to the garden. Renovation started on several figures, and new shapes including birds and a crown were developed. Accent points were added to the balls and cylinders flanking the garden's entrance. A progression of gardeners continues to maintain some of the best examples of geometric forms in the United States.

In the conservatories, the growing of plants into specific shapes has been an ongoing practice since the 1920s. Large, single-stem laurel standards (*Laurus nobilis*) were the first topiary forms displayed indoors. Over the years, hundreds of portable specimens, including many rare and unusual plants, have been grown in containers. From the start, the indoor plants were shaped like outdoor garden topiary, and although other designs are tried, the classic garden shapes have always been favored.

Cascading chrysanthemums were grown in ball shapes before 1958, but one of the first imaginative topiary displays was developed for a chrysanthemum celebration in 1964 when a table and two chairs in full bloom were positioned on the lawn of the main conservatory. A few years later a dog was grown, in two parts, each part one half from nose to tail. For display, the two halves were joined together and the containers recessed into the conservatory lawn. Today, Longwood's chrysanthemum displays include many shapes which are grown and trained for almost a year to present a spectacular November exhibit.

1967, Christmas display showing ivy bells.

In 1971, forms were made representing 6 running boys. Cuttings of ivy and creeping fig were rooted and planted into sphagnum-filled frames which were displayed in several locations in the conservatories. Two of the original 6 were dismantled after fifteen years and have recently been reconstructed. Although new ivy varieties have been used, the planting method has remained the same.

For a 1975 display, cones as large as 6 feet high and balls 4 feet wide were exhibited around pools in the conservatory. To produce these, the wire forms had been filled with moss. Long, unrooted ivy cuttings were stuck directly into it, and the remainder of each runner was pinned to the form. To encourage quick rooting, an overhead mist system was installed in the production greenhouse.

Three small animals using baby's-tears and creeping fig for a topiary display in 1980 at
Longwood Gardens.

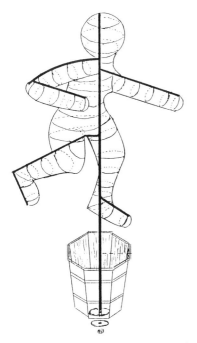

Longwood frame design for a running boy.
Drawing by Karl Grieshaber.

The running boy, stuffed and covered by
creeping fig.

The Rockefeller Center giraffe on display at Longwood, 1984.

Rockefeller giraffe in New York.

The large elephant and the hippo in the pool were part of the 1987 Animal Safari.

During the 1960s and 1970s, other topiary styles developed. Cut greens were added to classically shaped styrofoam forms and decorated with fruit. Christmas wreaths became a tradition. Beginning in the late 1970s, reindeer frames were stuffed with cut greens and decorated with lights for the holiday season. These have become annual favorites.

In the mid-1970s when small topiary frames became commercially available, a collection of small rabbits, squirrels, dogs, and birds covered in baby's-tears *(Soleirolia soleirolii)* was started. These creatures were an immediate success and their popularity has continued. Visitors may not know the names of the plants or understand how they grow, but everyone can recognize a dog, cat, or frog. Most importantly, the magical world of topiaries is something adults can explore with their children while visiting the garden.

The first large-scale topiary display in Longwood's conservatories with a unifying theme was for a Chrysanthemum Festival in November 1984. The idea was to place topiary creatures throughout the greenhouses as a drawing card for visitors and to spread the crowd around. The staff humorously suggested ''Chicken Little'' made of chickweed, ewe-sized ''Lamb Chop'' made of spreading yew, and ''Popeye'' made of spinach. In the end, a ''Harvest Magic'' theme was realized, with thirty-two topiary animals ranging from tiny 6-inch ducklings to a 14-foot giraffe and life-sized gorilla. The animals were displayed in appropriate settings: ducks were placed in or near water, and a bat inhabited a sausage tree *(Kigelia pinnata)* – appropriate because in the wild bats are the only known creatures to pollinate it. In some cases a small drama was enacted: a cat stalked a mouse who was about to steal some cheese. Unfortunately, Dutch cheese made of golden baby's-tears later turned into Swiss when cultural problems caused brown spots to appear just in time for the festival!

''Popeye.''

''Chicken Little.''

''Lamb Chop.''

Headlining the exhibit were extraordinary life-sized topiary animals on loan from New York's Rockefeller Center where they had been the stars of the Channel Gardens just weeks before. A lion, rhinoceros, elephant, and camel, all 5 to 8 feet tall, 6 to 8 feet long, 3 to 6 feet wide, and made from creeping fig *(Ficus pumila)*, were overshadowed just a bit by everyone's favorite, the gigantic giraffe.

Not everything that year was a success, A tiger built in a stalking position collapsed from the weight of its moss and soil stuffing. Rebuilt and replanted, the topiary suffered when new *Sagina* plants wilted and died in unseasonably hot weather. A third planting never came up to Longwood standards, and a few days after the display opened, the tiger was replaced with a sign that read ''ESCAPED.''

The 1985 Carousel which was designed to fit over the octagonal pool in the East Conservatory for the Chrysanthemum Festival.

With each success and failure, much was learned, especially the need for detailed and accurate record-keeping. A check list with thirty two drawings was handed out so visitors could go on a plant-animal hunt, but many wanted to know details. How many plants? How much time to build? How long to grow in? How big? What color and what plants? The same questions came again and again from thousands of guests passing through the gardens that fall.

In 1985 for "The World Around," a topiary carousel with a camel, lion, goat, reindeer, and four prancing horses surrounding a fountain took center stage. It was one of the most popular topiaries ever assembled at Longwood Gardens.

Ever more elaborate themes have been conjured up in the years since. "The Wonderful Garden of Oz" was featured in 1986 with a Yellow Brick Road leading past all the favorite characters in topiary. For Christmas that year, topiary reindeer "ladies" in evening dresses and "gentlemen" in black tie, a topiary penguin waiter, and a penguin pianist and a violinist celebrated the holidays in Longwood's elegant Music Room for all to behold.

The 1987 Chrysanthemum Festival was an African safari, with fifty-seven topiary animals, snakes, insects, and birds. Most exciting was a life-sized elephant squirting water from his trunk into a pool. "In the Dragon's Garden" in 1988 marked the Chinese Year of the Dragon with creatures of all types, including a 28-foot-long living topiary monster that rested, serpent-like, in a pool. A 20-foot-high topiary pagoda stood nearby. Outdoors, a 75-foot-long Fire Dragon of cut greens and dried grasses spewed spectacular fireworks once a week.

The huge topiary pagoda outlined in lights, built for "In the Dragon's Garden."

A brontosaurus standing among the palms and tree ferns for 1989's "Where Dinosaurs Dwell."

Dinosaurs visited Longwood in 1989, when ninety thousand visitors came to enjoy the largest topiaries yet constructed. Conceived and designed by David Murbach of Rockefeller Center for display in New York's Channel Gardens, the three ivy-covered giants were 20 feet tall and up to 41 feet long. The frames were made by Stefan Przystanski of Topiary Art Works in Clearwater, Kansas, and were planted at the Julius Roehrs Company, Farmingdale, New Jersey. After a stay in New York, the dinosaurs were loaned to Longwood where they joined other prehistoric topiaries in the conservatory. Special emphasis was given to plants from the days of the dinosaurs, and each week was capped by an outdoor eruption of a huge 100-foot-wide fountain volcano with fireworks. The dinosaurs eventually made their way to Callaway Gardens in Georgia for an extended visit.

"Birds in Paradise" was an appropriate title for a 1990 exhibit showcasing more than thirty avian topiaries nestled throughout the greenhouses. Garnering the most attention were two 9-foot-tall peacocks fanning 20-foot-wide tails of yellow, purple, and bronze-colored mums with a fern fringe. The upright bodies were ivy-covered, but the horizontal fan tails had a metal framework with rings to hold pots of mums and ferns. A spaghetti-tube watering system fed each pot individually.

From simple formal standards to elaborately themed specimens, topiaries of one style or another have been featured at Longwood Gardens for seventy years. Recently, whole festivals have been built around topiary, and attendance has risen dramatically. Details of some of Longwood's more unusual topiary creations are discussed in "Festival Topiaries" on page 161.

Part II
Topiary Techniques

1. Cascading Chrysanthemum Topiaries

2. Tabletop Topiaries

3. Large-Scale Stuffed Topiaries

4. Standards

5. The Wreath

6. Specialty Topiaries

7. Good Ideas from Others

1. Cascading Chrysanthemum Topiaries

Japanese Influence

During October, chrysanthemum displays are held in almost every city and town in Japan. Animal creations such as monkeys, deer, kangaroos, and sea turtles have evolved from a two-hundred-year-old display tradition known as *kiku-ningyo,* in which life-sized dolls are decorated with living chrysanthemums. These dolls depict stories from Japanese history, and the color of the bloom helps to interpret the characters from each story.

The doll frames are shaped from bamboo and tatami-mat straw; the face and hands are constructed of papier-mâché made from sawdust. The chrysanthemums are often grown in damp sphagnum moss but once the plants are in flower the roots are washed clean and the plants are wrapped and tied over the bamboo frame. Usually all the roots are centrally located inside the frame to make watering easier, which may be required as often as twice a day. Plants are changed regularly to maintain a perfect display. This Japanese artistry has influenced the Longwood Chrysanthemum Festival topiaries.

Finishing touches being added to a Japanese doll which is decorated with living chrysanthemums.

This Japanese male doll has a cloak of flowering chrysanthemums. Such chrysanthemum fantasies can be found in Japanese cities during October.

Huge white balls suspended over two yellow, cloud-shaped chrysanthemums, November 1988, Longwood.

Longwood Chrysanthemum Topiary

Bells, balls, arches, and columns are among the cascading mum topiaries exhibited at Longwood Gardens. Two gardeners spend almost the entire summer in the chrysanthemum field preparing the plants for the November festival. Cascading chrysanthemums are commercially available and specialist growers can supply newly rooted cuttings. Young, virus-free plants are also available from commercial tissue culture laboratories, so if propagating the plants in-house is inconvenient, they can be ordered for a specified date.

Chrysanthemum Propagation

Each year some of the chrysanthemums that have finished blooming are trimmed back and reserved as stock plants for next year's display. The plants are pruned just above the soil surface, leaving enough dormant buds for new growth. They are stored at 35 - 50° F. for four to eight weeks. In the first week of January they are transferred to a greenhouse with night temperatures of 60° F. After three to four weeks new shoots about four inches long appear. Tip cuttings are made in late January to early February but can be taken a few weeks earlier if a longer cascade is required. The cuttings are put into any well-drained propagation mix, such as 50% charcoal and 50% vermiculite in flat trays with a constant bottom heat of 78° F.

Initially, the cuttings need light spraying with water four to five times per day. More frequent spraying is needed in sunny weather. The propagation mix must not be allowed to dry out. After about two weeks roots will appear.

To encourage vegetative growth, chrysanthemums need fourteen hours of daylight, so in February artificial light is necessary to extend the short days. The artificial light is controlled by a time clock set to come on from 4:00 pm until 9:30 pm; however, it is possible to interrupt the night at any time as long as the minimum amount of light hours per day is met.

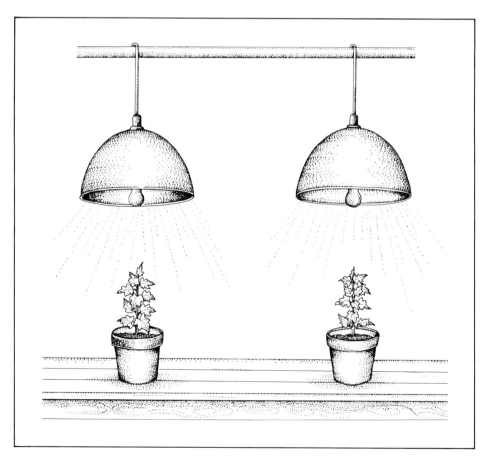

Suspend lights 2 feet above the plants.

Hanging the collars for the November Chrysanthemums Festival 1978.

The lighting need not be elaborate or scientifically designed. A rack suspending ordinary light fixtures above the plants will work adequately. Incandescent 60-watt light bulbs, 2 feet apart and about 2 feet above the foliage, are adequate. A basic timer to turn the lights on and off each day helps, but they can be controlled manually. The routine should be followed daily.

The newly rooted cuttings are potted into 3-inch clay pots about six weeks after propagation. The plants grow rapidly and need to be transplanted into the final container after three weeks. Longwood's growers often plant the new cuttings straight into the final container, bypassing the smaller pot. If the 3-inch pots are skipped, careful watering is needed; new plants must not be over-watered.

Longwood uses a well-balanced soil mix that drains readily and ideally contains some garden soil. The mix is two parts milled peat moss, one part garden loam, ¼-part 4-grade charcoal, and ¼-part medium grade vermiculite by volume. One-half pound of ground dolomitic lime (powder form) is added per bushel of mix. The lime provides the calcium and magnesium needed by chrysanthemums.

The plants need full sun. If grown in shady greenhouses, they will stretch. Optimum temperatures for chrysanthemums are 58° F. at night and 75° F. during the day. (In the Longwood area, days are long enough by May 1 to stop using the artificial lights.) Once the danger of frost has passed, the plants can be moved to a sunny position outside.

Balls, columns, and cascades growing outside at Longwood.

Close-up of white ball with separate arms clearly visible.

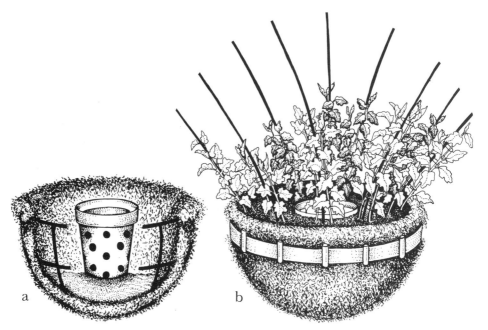

a) Add a perforated pot to the center of the basket to reduce soil volume.
b) Plant eighteen chrysanthemums evenly spaced around the basket, two at each leg.
Stake plants angled outward for early stages in the greenhouse.

Balls

The large spheres measuring 4½ feet to 5 feet in diameter are grown from 16-inch hanging baskets. The cultivars used are 'Megumi', 'Anna', 'Jean Hart', 'Golden Pinwheel', 'Biko', and 'Tsubaki Hime'. Each of the baskets has a collar that holds nine wire legs.

The stainless steel wire basket is lined with between 1 and 2 inches of wet sphagnum moss. The moss is tightly packed and built up the sides and over the rim. The rim should be well padded with moss to prevent the plant stems from becoming damaged. The moss-lined basket will hold the soil and plants for eight months or more so tight packing is very important. There should be no unintentional pockets in the moss.

Three inches of soil should be added to the lined basket. A 6-inch white plastic azalea pot should be placed into the middle of the basket. White reflects sunlight and keeps the roots cooler. The pot sides should be pierced with several holes. This

White balls,and golden collars on display at Longwood, November 1988.

Longwood technique reduces the soil volume during the early stages and ensures that young plants are not overly watered. A particularly rainy year could be harmful to young plants.

After the pot has been added and before the soil is filled in, 18 chrysanthemum plants should be transplanted, two plants for each leg, one on either side of each of the brackets on the collar. Then the basket is filled with soil around the plastic pot. The soil level, pot rim, and basket rim should all be about the same. While the chrysanthemum baskets remain in the greenhouse, the plants should be staked. Later the stems will be turned downward and attached to the legs. For this reason, while the chrysanthemums are growing indoors, stakes should be positioned in the pots at an outward angle to protect the stems from breaking and to help train them straight.

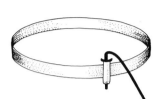

The collar showing one of the nine legs in position.

Pinch out lateral shoots as they develop along the chrysanthemum stem.

Secure each runner along the leg wire with green clips as the plant grows.

a) The hanging basket is positioned onto the tripod base.
b) Long runners are still staked in an upright position as they were while still indoors.
c) Once outside, these stakes are carefully removed and the plants tied down onto the legs immediately.
d) The rope is tied around the legs to stabilize them and limit movement.
e) The tripod is securely anchored into the ground.

Plants should be moved outdoors on a cloudy day or even during light rain to help prevent sunburn. In sunny weather the plants should be shaded for the first two days with shade cloth or newspapers (or the move can be made gradually — under a tree and then into full sun). Never move cascading chrysanthemums outdoors on a windy day; long stems could be broken. Baskets should be moved outside one at a time, anchored, and the nine legs tied down immediately.

The wire baskets are positioned on a specially built 5-foot-tall tripod anchored into the ground. Each of the nine 5-foot legs (made of 8-gauge wire) is attached to the basket collar. About 15 inches below the collar, a rope (any type of sash cord) is tied around each leg at equal distance, circling once around the entire form, thus stabilizing the legs and limiting movement. Independent, sharp movements can cause stem breakage.

With the legs in position, stakes can be removed and each stem turned downward and attached to the leg. There will be two stems per leg, one on each side. If the plants are slightly dry during this step, the stems will be limp and easier to turn down. The stem should be tied at the beginning of the leg and every 3 to 6 inches along the stem to establish a straight form.

Although lightweight green string had been used in the past, we now use a green, plastic-coated, 20-gauge single-strand wire, cut into 3-inch pieces and shaped into a "C" clip, to tie the plants to the legs. The stem is held to the wire by loosely pinching the clip around both. The wire should never restrict the stem too tightly; the wire ends must not be twisted together.

The plant will need tying or clipping about every ten days. Each leader (main stem) should continue down the leg until it reaches the bottom. Lateral shoots developing along the main stem should be pinched back to two nodes or two sets of leaves. When the plant runners reach the rope 15 inches down from the basket, two laterals from each main stem are allowed to grow, trained outward in both directions along the rope to the next leg. By allowing one to come in either direction from each stem, there will

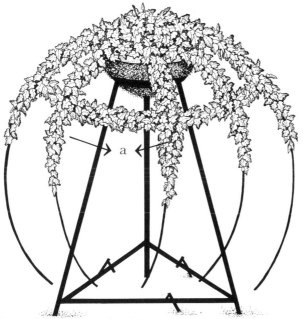

The plants growing well. Clipping and training continues until the stems reach the bottom. Two side shoots, one from either side, are trained along the stabilizing rope.
a) The two will eventually cross in the middle of the rope.

Shear chrysanthemums after individual pinching becomes impossible.

To replace a broken terminal shoot, take a nearby lateral and clip down into the new position.

be two plants crossing each rope.

The white 6-inch azalea pots are removed in mid-June after the plants are well rooted and begin to need watering twice per day. The "pot" cavity should be filled about three-quarters of the way up with soil mix leaving a small depression for a water reservoir. The chrysanthemums will require plenty of water; the reservoir should be filled until it leaks out of the bottom.

The now well-established plants growing down the legs will have developed many lateral shoots. Pinching becomes impossible so hand-held grass shears are used for trimming. Much care should be taken to try to leave two nodes on each lateral. The terminal end of any of the eighteen main stems coming down the legs must not be cut off until it reaches the bottom. All terminal ends should be located before shearing commences.

If a terminal end is damaged before it reaches the bottom, a strong lateral nearby can be trained into position as a new terminal. Breakage does happen, particularly on cool crisp mornings when the chrysanthemums are turgid and brittle. Losing a tip and starting a new one will set back the final length of the plant. The goal is to reach the bottom of each leg during the growing season.

Gradually, with repeated shearing, the top will fill in and become a solid mass. The plants are fastened down and sheared repeatedly all summer. In the first week of September they are treated with a growth retardant (see page 51) and left outdoors until ready for display.

These large baskets should be moved carefully, ideally on a warm day, as the stems are woody and become particularly brittle when it is cool. **If hangers were not added to the baskets when they were first planted, they should be attached before the chrysanthemums are hiding the basket frames.** When the basket is removed from the stand and is hanging up, the nine legs are pulled together at the tips and tied together to form a ball. The wire legs generally overlap about 3 to 4 inches to permit secure fastening.

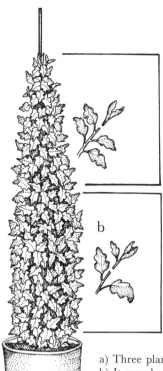

Columns are grown outside at Longwood until just before the November display begins, when they are brought into the conservatories.

a) Three plants are planted around a stake in a 12- to 14-inch container.
b) It may be necessary to pinch harder near the bottom and leave more breaks near the top to achieve uniform size.
c) Another column method uses a wire tube. Six to eight plants are planted evenly around the tube and trained up the wire.

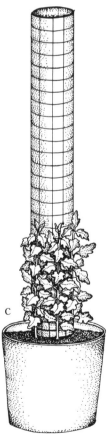

Columns

After young chrysanthemum plants have been in 3-inch clay pots for about three weeks and have become established, they are transplanted into a 12- or 14-inch container. Three plants are planted around a 5½-foot-tall, ½-inch diameter stainless steel stake securely anchored in the middle of the tub. (See staking standards page 98.) Use a sturdy stake that is not too flexible. The pots should be secured to prevent them from falling over or being disturbed by the wind.

The three plants are trained up the stake and tied regularly with green wire clips as used on the balls. During growth, all lateral shoots should be pinched as described for the basket arms. Well-established plants can be sheared.

Special attention is needed to obtain a uniform size for the entire length of the column. It may be necessary to pinch harder near the bottom and leave more nodes and breaks closer to the top. The finished column circumference should be the same bottom to top. Only after the terminal tips have reached the top should the ends be pinched out to encourage side branching.

Another method for developing a column is to use a wire tube 5½ feet tall and 6 inches wide anchored into the middle of the tub. Six or eight plants can be planted evenly around the tube and each terminal leader trained up and tied until it reaches the desired height, then pinched. Side shoots are pinched or sheared back to two breaks. It may be necessary to adjust the number of lateral breaks to obtain the proper shape of the column.

Columns can be any height but shorter columns are a good idea for first-time growers. Leaders can be pinched from each plant when the desired height is established. Longwood's natural growing season

White columns leading up to the golden Taj Mahal. All the plants are cascading chrysanthemums. 1988 Chrysanthemum Festival at Longwood.

Detail from the 1977 chrysanthemum display showing a white screen and an arch.

is May until early September, and the entire season is required to achieve 5½-foot columns. Other climates may need a shorter or longer growing period.

Taller columns can be grown by using the Callaway Gardens method (page 152) or by modifying the frame to hold a hanging basket or tub planted with chrysanthemums at the top so as to have plants both growing down from the top and up from the bottom to join in the middle, thus filling in the entire column in a normal growing season.

When the young plants are first planted into tubs, the volume of soil is considerable compared to the new root systems of the plant. Over-watering must be avoided, and young columns, particularly the tubs with only three plants, should be given about half the fertilizer recommended during the first half of the growing season. By mid-July, Longwood's columns have developed enough roots to be fertilized on the same schedule as for basket chrysanthemums. See General Care and Fertilizer Recommendations.

Arches

Arches are grown the same way as columns. The frame is shaped to fit the final display location. Each arch should be grown in two parts, each frame secured to its tub and bent over in preparation to meet at the center of the finished arch. When displayed, the halves are fastened together at the top, thus appearing as one unit.

To make an arch, each column is bent over to form half an arch. When the plants have grown the two columns are joined together.

47

Watering the balls, with clouds in the foreground still growing outside at Longwood.

Collars being positioned on pillars.

Cloud-Form

Cloud-form topiary chrysanthemums at Longwood have five stems radiating from the base, angled outward, and terminating in cloud-like shapes. Each cloud is a different height, the stem length from 18 inches to 3½ feet, and 4½ inches to 5 inches apart. The five clouds are asymmetrically balanced around the central axis.

The frame is made from five different lengths of 1/2-inch stainless steel rod, each heated and shaped to curve outward with an 8-inch circle at the top to guide the cloud shape. The five rods are welded together at the bottom. The base of the frame bolts through the bottom of the tub (see standards, page 100.) The frames are painted a sandy color to blend in with the plant stems.

One plant (five in all) is trained up each rod until it reaches the top, then the terminal is pinched out. All lateral shoots on the stem are removed as the plant grows, but the primary foliage remains until the stem reaches the top and the cloud begins to form. (These large leaves feed the growing plant.) The big, rather tattered leaves can then be removed.

To form a cloud, the terminal tip should be pinched out and laterals allowed to develop in the top 4 to 6 inches. These shoots should be pinched back to two nodes, keeping the cloud head compact. Any shoots below this area should be removed weekly, thus avoiding woody secondary stems, unsightly scars, or stubs along the main stem. With this routine, a bouquet of bloom will eventually develop at the top of each main stem.

Curtains and Collars

Each year over 100 tubs of chrysanthemums are trained over frames to form a living curtain for Longwood's Exhibition Hall. Among the cascading forms are chrysanthemums that are hung around the huge pillars in the Main Conservatory to form extraordinary collars of yellow, white, or bronze.

The Curtain

One plant is trained along each metal stem and allowed to develop a head at the top of the frame.

Four plants are planted on one side of each container and later trained down onto a wire form. Each of the four plants is pinched at planting time and encouraged to form two leaders. Six to eight leaders are trained from each tub and fastened down the wire frame with green wire clips as used for the balls. These clips must be removed each week and moved down the wire as the terminal shoot grows. (If a new clip were used

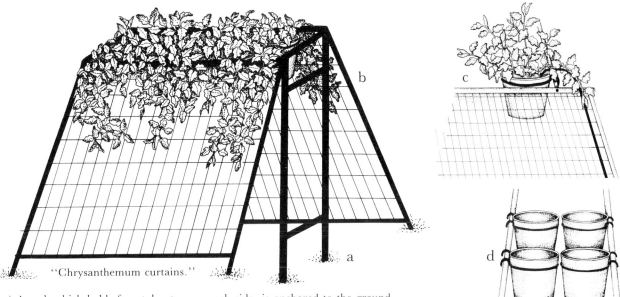

"Chrysanthemum curtains."

a) A rack which holds four tubs, two on each side, is anchored to the ground.
b) Two screens, one on each side of the rack, are angled outwards and then anchored to the ground.
c) The extra wire hoop in the pot is attached to the frame so that when the plants grow down the wire hoop onto the frame, shoulders will form and make the final curtains square.

d) Four tubs are suspended on the 1-inch aluminium pipe of the rack.

each week, there would be thousands to remove at the end of the season.) Unlike the other shapes described, these plants are removed from the frame when ready for display.

As the terminal leader grows and is trained down, lateral shoots are pinched or sheared back to two nodes or to the point that achieves the effect of an evenly filled, flat curtain 4 to 5 feet long. The twenty-four tubs grown for the curtain each year have an extra hooped wire running from the tub to the frame, and a plant is trained onto this hoop to give the shape "shoulders" and make the final display square and uniform in appearance.

The framework for a developing curtain consists of three parts: a rack that holds four tubs, and 5-foot 8-inch by 5-foot screens on either side. The rack is 5 feet high, 3 feet 4 inches long, and 2 feet wide and is made of 1-inch aluminium pipe. The aluminium-framed, 5-foot-square screen is attachable at an angle, to provide maximum sunlight for the plants as they grow. The wire mesh covering is 1 inch by 2 inches. Two tubs face each side, and the chrysanthemums grow from one side down the frame. The frames are A-shaped when fitted together in the production field.

Chrysanthemum curtains on the screens outside, almost ready for display outdoors.

Side view of the curtains on stands, the pots clearly visible.

Yellow chrysanthemum clouds with balls in the background, November 1988, Longwood.

Golden collars in position on the pillars in the conservatory at Longwood.

Arches, balls, bells, and curtains for Longwood's 1977 Chrysanthemum Festival.

The 1981 Chrysanthemum Festival at Longwood.

General Care and Fertilizer Recommendations

In July or when needed, removal of old and unsightly large primary leaves on the main stems can commence. The plants should not be stripped bare but the leaves that are damaged or yellowing should be removed. This will encourage better air circulation and discourage insects and diseases like powdery mildew. Insects often hide in the old foliage. This grooming will also enhance the appearance of the plant, which is so important for display.

Crown buds occasionally develop during the normal growing season, which makes the terminal leader stop vegetative growth to set flower buds on the long stems. Because the day length requirements are not correct, these crown buds will never flower. If they do develop, the terminal should be pinched back to the last node. When new shoots develop at the node, one should be selected and trained as the new leader.

Chrysanthemums are generally heavy feeders, particularly the cascading varieties trained into topiary forms. The fertilizing program should be consistent and followed faithfully. A rate of 600 ppm (parts per million) of nitrogen per week from the first potting until the first of September can be applied in one weekly watering or as three waterings a week. A general purpose liquid fertilizer should be used, following the directions on the package. The amount of fertilizer used at the beginning of September should be reduced to half during September and, finally, applied only enough to keep the foliage green. Flowering chrysanthemums do not need fertilizer.

The last pinching or shearing should be done as quickly and as thoroughly as possible in the first week of September. A growth retardant should be applied simultaneously. When there is less than thirteen and a half hours daylight, the plants will begin to set flower buds. This is a critical time and should be carefully managed. The immediate application of growth retardant keeps the flower buds close to the plant, avoiding long, floppy flower stems. A second application is made three weeks later. This schedule should be kept as closely as possible. The growth retardant B-Nine used as a foliar spray has proved satisfactory at Longwood, but there are other brands and formulations. All manufacturers' directions should be followed and the formulation must be suitable for chrysanthemums. Longwood's chrysanthemums are still outdoors during these applications.

Chrysanthemums that have been grown outdoors all season will tolerate light frost but should be protected from a hard freeze. When possible we leave the topiaries out until required for display. By that time, a few buds will be coloring up. Longwood recently has extended the outdoor period, since the colors become more vibrant with cool nights and fewer disease problems occur due to better air circulation outdoors.

All the dates and scheduling for cascading chrysanthemums will depend on geographic location and should be adjusted accordingly. Plans and dates should be determined in advance to ensure a display of bloom at the desired time.

Crown bud. Pinch off terminal bud to encourage vegetative growth.

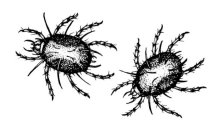

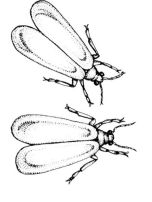

Green Peach Aphid

Small, green, fleshy body usually found on the new plant tips. Ladybugs are the aphids' natural predators but they can be chemically controlled with insecticidal soap and horticultural oil.

Black Aphid

Small, black, fleshy body usually found on the new plant tips. Control as for Green Peach Aphids.

Whitefly

Small, white, winged insect generally found on the underside of the foliage. They will fly about when the plant is disturbed. They can build to large populations in the greenhouse. A few natural predators can be used for greenhouse control, or whitefly can be chemically controlled with insecticidal soap and horticultural oil.

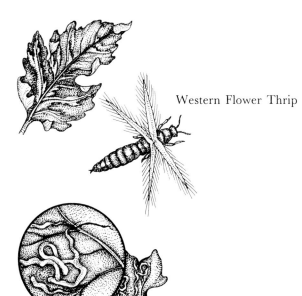

Western Flower Thrip

Microscopic, long, thin and green insect found down inside the unopened terminal bud, usually undetected; but it can cause slightly deformed leaves and yellow streaking on new shoots. Control can be difficult; chemical treatment should be a specific formulation labeled for chrysanthemums. Follow label directions.

Chrysanthemum Leaf Miner

Larval stages of a flying insect tunneling between layers of plant tissue causing irregular pale yellow tunneling patterns visible on the upper leaf surface. This can become a serious problem both in the greenhouse and outdoors. There are chemically controlled formulations specifically labeled for Chrysanthemum Leaf Miner. Follow label directions carefully.

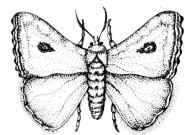

Cabbage Looper

Larval stages of a flying insect ranging from
¼ inch in size. Adults are white moths about
1½ inches wide, often with dark spots on the
wings. The larva hides around base of plant
during daylight hours but chews on the leaves
at night. Damaged leaves and insect droppings
are evidence of this insect. Easily controlled by
Bacillus thuringiensis. Follow label directions.

Virus

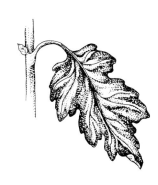

Virus symptoms – loss of plant vigour and
yellow-red streaking – are often the same signs
for other problems so can be hard to diagnose.
Consult an agricultural diagnostic laboratory if
a virus is suspected because it is a serious
problem and can be transmitted plant-to-plant
by mechanical practices and insects. Confirmed
cases should be isolated until the plants can be
destroyed. Do not add virused plants to
compost. Virus-free plants are produced
commercially by tissue culture.

Powdery Mildew

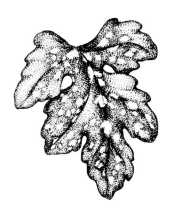

Light gray mold on the upper foliage surface.
Although mildew occurs occasionally in early
spring in the greenhouse, most often it appears
in August and September. Damp nights and
high humidity encourage mildew. When the
plants have much foliage, air circulation is
restricted. Mildew spreads rapidly and can be
difficult to control. Plants must be kept clean of
old and brown foliage. Some growers use
a preventative chemical program recommended
for chrysanthemums. Follow all directions
on the fungicide label and be sure it
is suggested for chrysanthemums.

Stuffed flamingo covered with *Hedera helix* 'Tussie Mussie'.

Silhouette pig frame covered in sheet moss with creeping fig growing up from the pot.

Tools and supplies needed for a stuffed topiary.

The Calico Cat, aptly named as the plant material used is *Hedera helix* 'Calico'.

Elegantly proportioned frame for this ivy-covered cock.

2. Tabletop Topiaries

Tabletop topiaries are simple and quick to make and, with minimum maintenance, are easy to keep attractive. Most homes have a place for some decorative and amusing plant fantasies.

A popular choice for tabletop topiary is a simple wreath that can be used on the patio all summer, decorated for holidays, and kept as the base for more elaborate centerpiece arrangements. Many people have a favorite animal or a preferred design for a topiary subject. How about a herd of mini-elephants as decoration for your party table or a 6-inch turtle for a sunny bathroom? Instead of a hanging basket, how about a ball or a bell, or maybe a bird or an airplane? Whatever your choice, it can be made in a few hours yet will last a long time, possibly years.

Simple frames can easily be made at home and a wide variety of frames is readily available in garden centers or by mail order (see source list). You may need as few as one or two plants or several rooted cuttings, according to the size of the frame and how long you are willing to wait for finished results.

A few tools and supplies will enable you to make most styles of tabletop topiary. Some items you may already have if you're an amateur gardener. The others are usually available from your local garden center, florist, or garden catalog. You will need plants, frames, sphagnum moss, fern pins, pruners, and a tray.

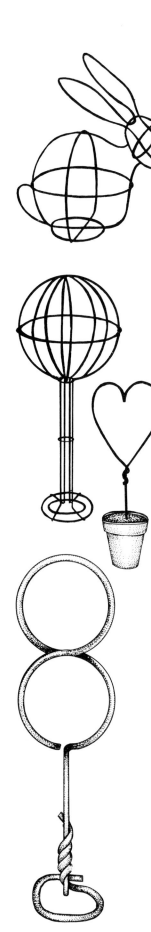

If the leaf size is too large, the topiary characteristics are soon lost in a mass of foliage.

Choose the frame first. Try a simple shape if you are a beginner, avoiding thin legs and tails until you feel confident with the procedures. If you are making the frame at home, keep to a simple shape, avoid sharp edges, and fasten all joints securely. Purchased frames should be examined for faulty welds, poor stability, and sharp edges. Most wire frames should be painted to retard rusting.

If you have a used frame, remove all old plant material, moss, rust, and chipping paint by using a wire brush. Apply a rust proofing or a damp-proof primer and when completely dry, apply a coat of paint. The thinner the frame wire, the faster it will rust through.

Remember when choosing the frame for a stuffed topiary that it will be covered with a ½- to 1-inch coat of plant material. If the shape is too complex, the plant covering may hide the fine detailing needed to give a dramatic and fanciful effect.

Finding the correct plant material to complement your topiary character cannot be over-emphasized. If the frame is only 6 inches tall, you will need a small plant with tiny leaves, such as baby's-tears or miniature creeping fig (*Ficus pumila* 'Minima').

The plant's growth habit is extremely important. Choose a plant that is trailing but has closely spaced leaves and sends out new breaks readily along the vine. Such plants will fill in and cover the topiary rapidly.

Plants that have miniature leaves and are readily self-branching but do not trail will not define the outlines of the topiary, which will end up as a well-covered, undefined puffy ball. Plants that are upright in growth should also be avoided, since they will not follow the form of the frame, and the character's features will be lost.

The dried sphagnum moss you purchase for topiaries should be in its natural state, long and stringy and not finely milled and powdery. Live green sphagnum moss (which keeps its green color for a short while) can be used just as successfully. For most of us, however, dried moss is the only type readily available. Be sure the moss has not

An assortment of plants for topiary including baby's-tears, creeping fig, cotula, and ivy.

An ivy wreath above and a selection of frames below and opposite.

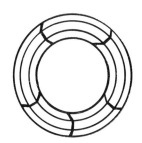

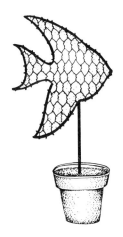

been in storage for a long time since the quality deteriorates with age.

Fern pins are commercially available but hair pins or small pieces of thin wire bent into a U-shape will also work. The pins hold everything together in the building stages and are essential for the continual maintenance of the topiary.

There are many styles of tabletop topiary construction, but the types discussed here are most often used at Longwood. These styles are: pruned, trained-up, and stuffed. The style you choose will depend on how it fits your home or business. Always consider the basic requirements for successful maintenance, such as light, humidity, watering needs, and, of course, your time.

If your finished topiary is for an area where you cannot water by spraying, consider the more conventional "Pruned to Shapes," "Free-Form," or "Trained-Up" methods. These all originate from the pot and allow you to water in the normal manner in the pot. If you can shower over the topiary or move it readily, then you can choose any style.

Watering and humidity are often the major concerns with any topiary, especially with sphagnum-stuffed types. In a house or office area that is very dry, a shallow tray filled with pebbles can be placed under the topiary. Adding water to the tray on a regular basis will raise the humidity in the immediate area. As with most house plants, the topiary (stuffed or potted) should never sit in water for any length of time, as the soil will over-saturate. If this happens, the air spaces around the roots fill with water, the roots cannot breathe, and they begin to die. This condition can occur easily with sphagnum moss because the moss absorbs water like a sponge.

All types of topiary require upkeep and repair. Generally, the type stuffed in a frame may need to be taken apart after two or three years and redone. Trimming the top growth and the roots of a pruned or trained-up topiary could extend its life for several years.

A charming, lopsided rosemary heart designed and planted by Carole Guyton of Topiary Inc.

Ivy growing up from the urn to cover a three-dimensional swan frame in the Meadowbrook Farm of Liddon Pennock.

Pruned or Free-Form Topiaries

Pruning and clipping are the traditional methods used for shaping and maintaining topiaries permanently planted out in the garden. Tabletop-size topiaries can be trained in the same manner. Choose plants that have stiff, self-supporting trunks but branches that are flexible and self-branching.

An outline frame can be used as a pruning guide without actually attaching or training the plant to the frame. Choose the desired shape, select a plant whose form is best-suited for that shape, and use a sturdy support in the early stages of development. In cases where wire forms are used as pruning guides, construct or

A well-defined, free-form, two-tiered myrtle standard at Longwood.

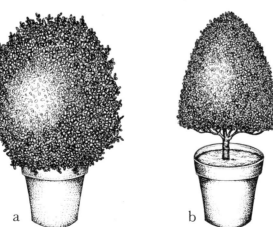

a   b   c

"Pruning."
a) Start with a woody upright plant.
b) Prune into desired basic shape.
c) Shape can then be altered with specific pruning.

Mantlepiece decoration, pot-grown ivy trained up and over frames.

purchase pre-formed frames. Continued pruning and pinching are needed to achieve the final shape.

In many ways, the free-form or pruned topiary in tabletop size follows the basic ideas used in shaping bonsai. Pruning of top growth should be done according to the target shape, and after the desired form has been accomplished, careful pruning will help to maintain it. Root pruning will also help to maintain the desired size.

Pruning skills are important for this style, and it is critical to understand what growth will take place as a result. Be familiar with the plant chosen. Know its growth habits and cultural needs before committing it to topiary.

Using a frame for a guide is very helpful. The plant can either grow up into a frame and then be pruned to fit, or the frame can be a one-dimensional structure used as an outline. As with bonsai, the plant can be temporarily manipulated by wire to train individual branches. Later the wire can be removed. Maybe the shape of your free-form is not a bird, dog, or horse but just an attractive arrangement of branches. This is a style which permits you to create any shape you visualize. Study your subject plant and prune carefully. There is no limit to the imagination with this approach to topiary.

Left: Three-dimensional cone covered in ivy, *Hedera helix* 'Eva'.
Centre: A dramatic effect created by growing an ivy over a simple silhouette frame. The candles add a festive touch to the decoration.
Right: Another simple frame with the ivy following the wire outline.

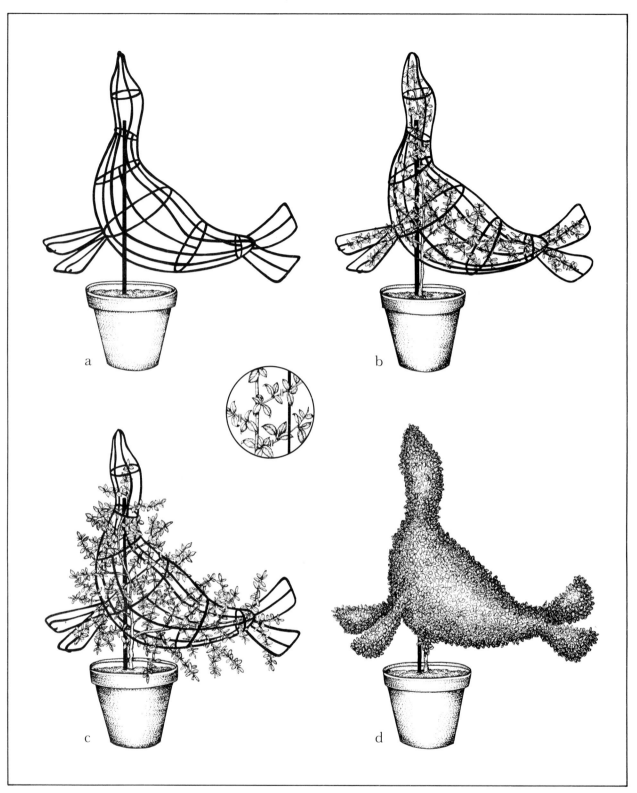

a) Start with an empty three-dimensional frame. Anchor it into the container.

b) Centrally locate a woody, upright plant into the container and allow it to grow up inside the frame. Guide leader stems through the frame to legs and wings to develop the structural skeleton of the topiary.

c) Use the frame as a pruning guide.

d) When the frame is filled, prune regularly to maintain the shape.

(spot) Prune each lateral shoot to one or two leaf nodes to encourage the shape to fill in.

Trained-Up on a Frame

Choosing the right plant material is the most important factor for the trained-up style. A vining or trailing type of plant is required. Self-branching is necessary, but it is not nearly as critical as with other topiary styles. An evergreen groundcover, tropical trailing house plant, or even a deciduous flowering vine is suitable. If you choose a deciduous vine, be sure it will put out new growth each year from the stem and not die back to the soil surface.

The trailing plant is tied to or wrapped around a rigid frame. Eventually the plant will cover the frame. It could, however, be pruned to follow the frame and retain the skeletal effect, which can give a light, open, airy appearance. It may also work well as an accent in a dark corner or in front of a garden wall.

Some suitable plants for the trained-up method:
Evergreen ground covers: Ivy, Juniper (Groundcover or Prostrate), Wintercreeper euonymus
Tropical, trailing house-plants: Jasmine, Creeping fig, Trailing abutilon
Deciduous vines: Honeysuckle, Grape

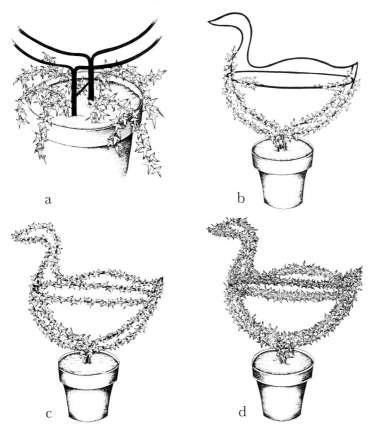

a) Plant vines at the base of the frame.
b) Lead each plant runner up and around the frame, tying the vines along the way.
c) Train the vines along the wires until the frame is completely covered.
d) When the frame is filled, prune to maintain the outline.

Three completed, medium-sized swans on exhibit at Longwood.

Three stages in creating a medium-sized stuffed topiary swan.
a) Empty frame.
b) Moss, soilless mix, and plants.
c) Completed swan.
(spot) The stems should not be planted any deeper into the topiary than they would be planted into a normal pot.

a

b

c

Stuffed

The most popular topiary style is the wire frame stuffed with moss and planted with rooted cuttings. As home projects, these are easy to make. Use well-soaked sphagnum moss. If you are going to use a large amount, soak it overnight if possible; if not, for at least several hours. If the moss is not wet, soft, and pliable before you start, it will be difficult to pack tightly into the frame and almost impossible to saturate once inside the frame. You do not want the moss to change shape, shrink, or allow too much air space into the root area, injuring the plants. Dry moss will be in constant competition with the plants for whatever moisture is available.

Think where you will be putting this topiary when it is finished. Should it be placed on a tray? Will it stand by itself? Secure the topiary to a tray, if desired, before you begin to stuff it.

Start building the topiary with a layer of well-squeezed moss at the bottom of the frame. The first layer should be slightly thicker than the remaining layers to provide a sturdy foundation. Arrange plants around the perimeter of the moss. Do not plant too deeply; allow the base of the plant to be at the surface of the planting medium. Continue layering moss and plants until the topiary is complete. Always pack the sphagnum firmly with continual hand manipulation as if you were kneading bread. As you plant each layer of plants, it may be helpful to alternate the plant row location. This will help you space evenly so that coverage is adequate in all areas.

How can one tell how many plants will be needed and how far apart they should be spaced? These decisions both depend on availability of material. If the plants are vining and self-branching, they will cover more area faster. Try to allocate the plants so you don't use most of them before you get to the topiary head only to discover there

Buy good quality, dry sphagnum moss. Soak before use.

A well-constructed frame.

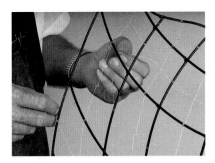
Large gaps between frame wire can be decreased by tying in fish line.

Soil being added to moss-lined body.

The neck being stuffed and tied. No soil is added to thin areas.

Six long runners from nearby body plants being pinned around the neck.

Detail showing wing building.

Nearly finished, but head plants still need to be pinned down.

John Testorf with completed swan.

JOHN TESTORF OF LONGWOOD BUILDING AND PLANTING A SWAN.

are only one or two plants left to cover a large area. If this happens, the whole character will look unbalanced. Judge how to space plants like ivy by studying the length of the runners. If they are 3 to 5 inches long, space the plants 5 inches or more apart. They will break and send out runners in many directions, covering the bare area surrounding the original plants.

Even though using lots of plants will give you a well-covered, instant topiary, it is not always the preferred solution. The figure will soon become over-planted and hard to keep in shape. Competition for water and fertilizer may cause plant stress. Working with fewer plants can be beneficial. You will certainly learn more about training and pinning, and you will quickly become aware of the growth habits of the chosen plants. When the frame is finally covered, there is much satisfaction.

On the other hand, if you are having a party tomorrow and you want a finished topiary as the centerpiece, use lots of plants, pin them down, and pinch off the excess foliage and runners. After the party, be prepared to prune.

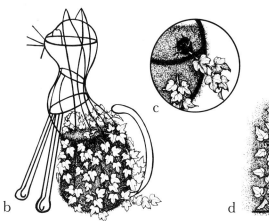
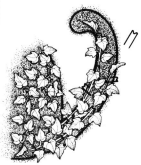

a b c d e

a) Start with a sturdy and properly prepared frame.
b) Build from the bottom up, layering moss and plants.
c) (spot) Do not plant too deeply, positioning the plants below the wire to avoid breaking the stems when packing the next layers of moss and plants.
d) Use long runners for appendages too thin to plant.
e) When planting in thin areas tie moss and plants in with string.

Pin down carefully.

Careless pinning creates loops that are often cut in two.

With most shapes, there are difficult areas to plant and keep watered. Use the long runners near appendages that are narrow and difficult to plant. These areas should be stuffed with moss. The growing parent plant must be located in a more substantial area nearby and the runners allowed to grow out and around, pinned onto the appendages as growth proceeds.

If areas such as tails, ears, and legs are too difficult to pack with sphagnum, plant the longer plants in the main body of the topiary near these appendages and train the vine out and around the frame. Secure the plant with green string, since there is no moss to pin into.

Arms, legs, and tails that can be stuffed may need to be tied after planting to hold the plants and moss in place. Most of the vining plants, such as ivy and wintercreeper euonymus, will form roots along their runners and eventually hold everything together.

When the topiary is first planted, it will look shaggy. Pin all loose runners down. Start pinning at the bottom and continue up. Follow a pattern to help cover the topiary evenly. Always begin pinning a runner near the base of the plant. Do not allow any loops or arches in stems to develop in the pinning procedure. These loops spell disaster later when you prune the runner in two by mistake.

When runners have reached the desired length, pinch out the tips to encourage side growth or lateral branching. If the runners are the same length as the spacing of the plant, pinch them immediately. This will encourage the topiary to fill in evenly all around.

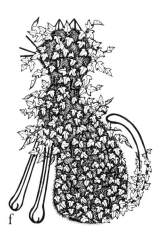
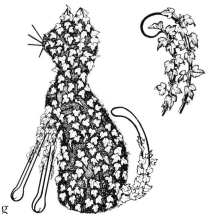

f g h

f) Pin all runners down after planting is completed.
g) Tie at appropriate intervals to keep the form.
h) After the topiary is completed, pin and prune it regularly.

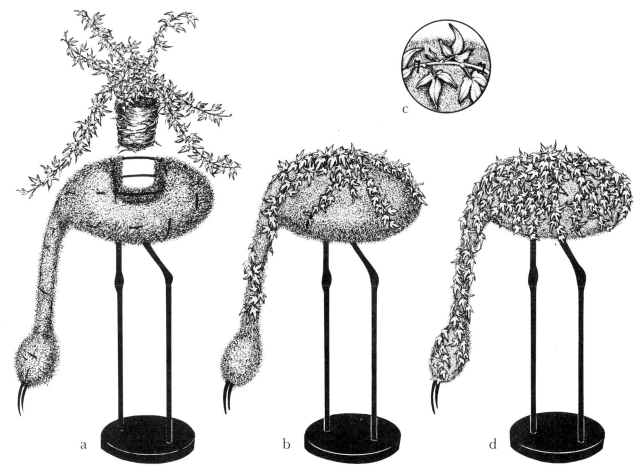

a) Stuff the frame with wet moss leaving a centrally located opening for one well-established plant and add the plant.
b) Direct and space the runners evenly.
c) (spot) Pin the runners close to the surface to allow them to root into the moss.
d) After the character is covered completely, continue to pin and clip for good definition.

One-Plant Stuffed

It is possible to make a topiary using only one plant. It will take more time for the plant to grow and fill in, but there are some advantages to using one well-established plant. Plan the topiary carefully. Choose a frame that is not too large and does not have too many long arms and legs. The best figures are birds, turtles, and creatures that have a main body section. Choose the plant species remembering that one plant will have to cover the entire subject. Often it is not convenient to root cuttings at home or possible to purchase several plants of the cultivar you favor. If you have one or two specimen pots of ivy that you would like to use in a small topiary, then try this style. An ivy that sends out self-branching runners is ideal; 'Greenfeather' is one that has been used successfully.

The beginning steps are much the same as for the stuffed topiaries. Soak sphagnum moss until soft. Fill the frame with it, leaving just enough space to plant one plant in a central spot. Insert the plant in the spot provided in the moss. Leave as much of the soil and root ball undisturbed as possible. Fill the remaining area of the root ball with moss. Be sure the top of the root ball is thinly covered with moss. This prevents it from drying out too often, but remember never to plant too deeply.

When the topiary is stuffed and planted, start pinning the runners down onto the surface of the moss. Pin evenly around the surface. Training only one plant to cover all areas can take time. Always pin to get the runners growing in one direction.

Planted but not yet pinned down.

Completed bird.

65

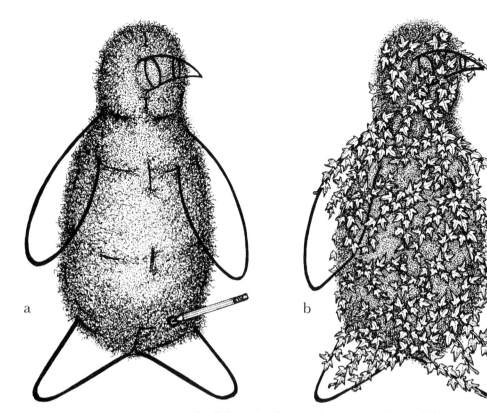

a) Stuff the entire frame with wet moss. Use a dibble or pencil to make a hole in the moss. Use two or three cuttings in each hole. At least one or two leaf nodes should be stuck into the moss.

b) Space the cuttings evenly over the entire stuffed form. Pin the runners against the moss to encourage lateral rooting. Keep newly planted topiary misted.

c) Train runners along extremities that are too thin to stuff with moss. As the vines begin to grow, tie and prune to maintain form.

Dibble or pencil.

Two or three cuttings for each hole.

At least one or two leaf nodes.

Unrooted Cutting

It is possible to take a short cut by planting unrooted cuttings in a topiary. A word of caution: do not attempt this unless you are able to mist over several times a day and be sure you have plenty of matching plant material in case replacements are needed.

Stuff the entire frame with sphagnum moss which must be thoroughly wet when you start. Pack the moss snugly into the frame and tie in any areas that seem insecure.

When the frame is packed and loose ends of moss are trimmed off, add the cuttings. Chances for success are better if you choose a plant that roots readily, like ivy or creeping fig. To hasten root formation, dip the ends of the stem cuttings in a rooting hormone recommended for the specific plant selected. This information is available on the product label.

After preparing the cuttings, use a dibble or pencil to make holes in the moss. Insert the cuttings; it is wise to use two or three in each hole. Evenly space them around the entire frame.

It is critical to mist every cutting regularly during the first two weeks. If you have a propagation mist bed, the success rate will be higher. If you are misting by hand, you may need to do it as often as every daylight hour for the first week, gradually reducing until the cuttings have rooted. Remember when we talk about misting over, it is just that—misting. Do not put the topiary in the shower or blast it with a hose until all the plants are well established. A harsh stream of water will wash away the cuttings. Make sure the topiary is not overly saturated. This causes stem rot and other diseases.

Maintenance

Pruned and trained-up styles that feature potted plants should be maintained in the same manner as regular house plants. Water as needed and establish a normal feeding and grooming schedule.

On the other hand, stuffed figures should be misted over daily for the first two weeks. After that, a regular watering schedule should be followed. The moss should never dry out completely. Areas such as hands, wings, and tails will dry first.

Take your topiary to the shower occasionally or give it a good soaking outdoors, weather permitting. Take care not to let the bottom of the topiary become saturated. This can be avoided by placing it on a well-drained base. A liquid fertilizer should be used on a regular program according to the plant's requirements. Feed more often during the growing season and less often when plants are not as active.

If your topiary is the one-plant-stuffed style, water the planted area as needed. You may have to stick your finger into the root zone to test for moisture. The moss around it should be moist but not soggy, so that vining plants will root readily into the entire figure.

Topiary plants are susceptible to the same insects and diseases found on normal garden and house plants. Treat as for any house plant. Always be extremely cautious when using chemicals indoors. Simple procedures such as an alcohol wipe or a soapy water bath and rinse will often do a good job if the insects are discovered early. Remember that under the best cultural conditions, insects and diseases will be less likely to appear.

Pinning, pruning, and grooming on a regular basis are a must. Keep your topiary pinned close to the frame and prune long runners. Do not wait until the topiary is overgrown and the shape has disappeared. It will take a long time to regain the proper appearance if not pruned regularly. Always keep an eye out for exuberant, excessive growth-spurts such as occur in spring. Good cultural practices will keep your topiary looking attractive and bring you months, possibly years, of enjoyment.

Take well-established, stuffed topiary to the shower occasionally for a thorough watering.

A sunny bathroom is an ideal position for a stuffed topiary.

Carole Guyton with one of the finely detailed mini-topiaries from Topiary Inc., Tampa, Florida.

Mini-Stuffed Topiaries

Mini-topiaries are often done in the one-plant-stuffed style. Topiary Inc., of Tampa, Florida, has created a whole line of mini-topiaries including rabbits, bears, turtles, and much more. Carole Guyton, co-owner of Topiary Inc., plants these 5- to 8-inch creatures by stuffing the head, tail, legs, and other extremities first with moistened sphagnum moss. Water is added to the moss, which is placed in a large plastic bag and allowed to absorb the water until it is moist and flexible but not dripping. The moss is held into the frame by wrapping it with lightweight clear fish line, 8 to 10 pound test. Always ensure that the moss is tightly packed into the frame. At the end of the legs or at the tip of the ears, a little of the moss is allowed to hang over the edge. By folding the excess over the frame and wrapping it into place, the areas where the frame shows are hidden.

After the extremities are stuffed, Carole treats the body much like a tiny hanging

Half-stuffed rabbit.

Making the well to take the creeping fig plant.

Pinning down the creeping fig.

Trimming the ears.

Completed rabbit.

MINI STUFFED, ONE PLANT TOPIARY BY CAROLE GUYTON OF TOPIARY INC.

basket. Moss is packed to line the area and create a pocket which is filled with soilless, all-purpose potting mix. One young plant or a few rooted cuttings are planted into this pocket. The top of the soil and root area are covered with more moss. As with the Longwood one-plant-stuffed method, the topiary is acting as a container for the plant.

Before pinning down the plant stems to the body, groom the sphagnum stuffing by clipping off any excess or loose moss. The plant is then secured to the topiary by pinning the runners to the body. If the pins are too long to be used in some areas, small lengths of flexible wire can be bent over and used instead.

The fun part, according to Carole, is that everyone adds their own special touch to a topiary. This is true of mini as well as large examples. Bending one ear here or adding a little extra moss there to the cheeks for a puffier face can give personality to each topiary.

Carole Guyton created this mini-swan, with creeping fig, which will eventually cover the whole bird.

69

Ivy Bells

Ivy bells are nothing more than hanging baskets with graceful runners. Begin by lining a wire hanging basket with wet sphagnum moss, live or dried but never milled. Be sure the sphagnum is pressed tightly into the frame. Continue lining until reaching the rim of the basket. Always add a coating of wet moss tucked around the rim to add a cushion of protection for the runners that will hang over the edge.

Fill the center of the basket with a well-drained potting soil. Plant three to six ivies into the center. Water regularly, but make sure the water runs through the soil and does not puddle at the surface. Testing the moss at the bottom for dryness is a good method of determining the watering schedule, but testing the soil surface regularly is also important.

Trailing ivy is the best choice for ivy bells. Do not use a cultivar that branches readily or your basket will have a bushy, rounded shape rather than the desired bell form. The shape comes from pruning techniques and growth habit. No topiary frame is required. Allow the ivy to grow down until it reaches the approximate length of the bell desired. At this point, cut off all ivy runners. This will encourage breaks near the pruned ends and force the runners to flair at the bottom, creating the ultimate bell shape.

There are many good trailing ivy cultivars, including *Hedera helix* 'Chicago', 'Pittsburgh', 'Pittsburgh Variegated', and 'Fantasia'. Or try 'Lalla Rookh', a curly ivy with an unusual leaf shape, for a slightly different look.

Maintenance is minimal. Some trimming may be necessary, especially when the ivy is actively growing. In addition, annual renewal pruning will keep the bell in good shape all year round.

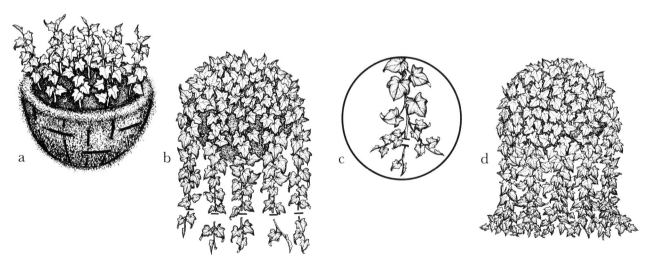

How to make an ivy bell.
a) Plant several rooted ivy cuttings into a moss-lined wire basket.
b) When the ivy runners reach the desired length, cut them off and allow them to break at that point. Prune off each runner at the same length.
c) (spot) Cut the runner.
d) The ivy will send off new shoots at the pruning point and create the skirted flair for the bell shape.

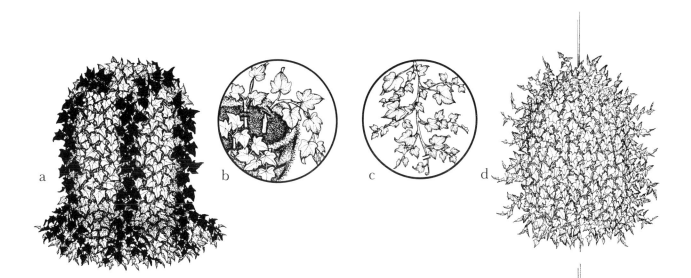

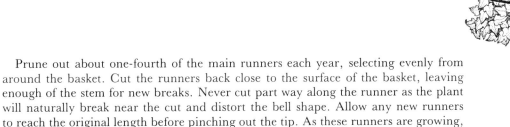

How to maintain an ivy bell.
a) To maintain the bell in good condition, prune out one quarter of the stems each year.
b) (spot) Select the older woody stems and prune level with the basket rim leaving two or three nodes for new breaks.
c) (spot) Some ivies will branch without pruning, others will branch along the stem when pinched.
d) A readily self-branching ivy will be too bushy to create a bell shape.
e) Out-of-shape ivy bells can be pulled into shape by tying at the waist.

Prune out about one-fourth of the main runners each year, selecting evenly from around the basket. Cut the runners back close to the surface of the basket, leaving enough of the stem for new breaks. Never cut part way along the runner as the plant will naturally break near the cut and distort the bell shape. Allow any new runners to reach the original length before pinching out the tip. As these runners are growing, you may need to tuck them in among the mature stems to help keep the outline of the bell shape.

The rule for selecting the runners to be pruned out each year is to cut the oldest or woodiest stems. The newer stems will be green and pliable. If this pruning is done regularly, it will keep the runners forming the bell young and in perfect shape. It will certainly increase the longevity of the bell.

If the bell loses its shape, take green string or fishing line and tie it around the bell's "waist" and pull it back into shape. This is a quick but temporary solution.

As the ivy grows, spray water over the foliage regularly to encourage the cascading habit. The weight of the water pulls the runners down. During summer months, spraying with water discourages the insect population. In the winter, ensure that there is plenty of air circulation so the foliage will dry between sprays.

Remove dead leaves regularly to promote air circulation through the plant and to discourage insects and diseases. A vigorous shaking usually does the trick.

Another method used to create a bell is by grafting an ivy cutting onto *Schefflera* or x *Fatshedera* as described for making an ivy standard. *Hedera helix* 'Pin Oak' has been used successfully in this way.(See page 108.)

Ivy bells decorated at Walt Disney World Resort® in Florida.

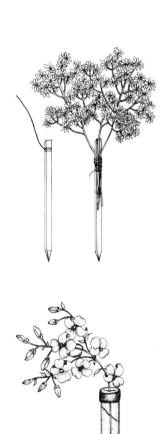

Decorate your bell for holidays or parties. White ribbon makes a perfect addition for a wedding celebration. Other appropriate decorations are balls, bows, flowers, and clusters of berries. These may be draped from the top of the bell or suspended from the center as a clapper. Fruits and pine cones are appropriate at Christmas. The fruit of an osage orange is often used at Longwood as a clapper. Its bright green color is attractive with a dark green bell. Another trick is to suspend an Oasis® ball (floral foam) as a clapper filled with contrasting cut greens or tightly stuffed with flower blooms.

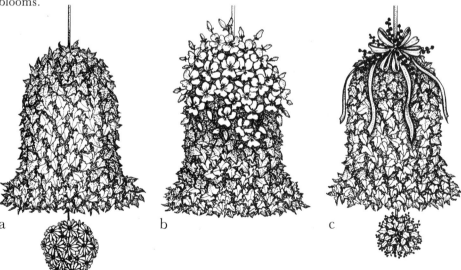

a) Fresh flowers in water picks cover the top of the bell.
b) A floral foam clapper covered with flowers.
c) Ribbons, berries, and other cut greens.
Left: Dried material can be attached to a wooden pick and then inserted. Flowers or any perishable material can be placed in a water pick.

Two-tone ball at Walt Disney World Resort® in Florida. The plant material is *Alternanthera* 'Rosea Nana' and 'White.'

Topiary Balls

There are at least four different techniques used at Longwood to make topiary balls: Pre-Made Ball, Two Halves, and two styles of hanging baskets. The balls range in size from very small, tightly-pruned, 8-inch spheres to very large and loosely flowing fuchsias displayed every summer in the conservatory. The method chosen depends on the size of the finished ball, on the size of the plants, and, most importantly, on the type of plant material. All three types can be displayed by hanging from chain or from wire hangers. They can also be mounted on a metal stem or rod coming up from a base.

Begonia used to create this ball at Longwood.

Another begonia ball hanging above the hibiscus at Longwood.

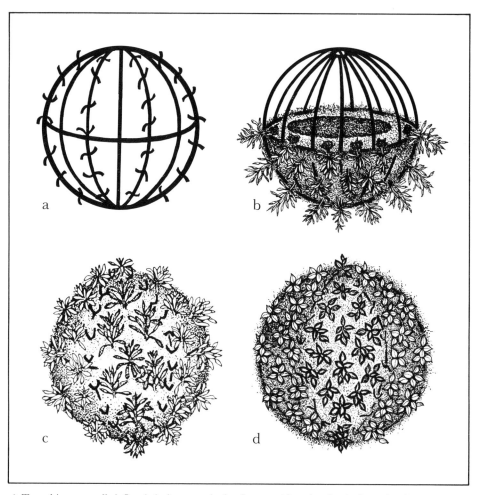

a) To achieve a well-defined design, mark the frame with twist-ties before planting.

b) Pre-formed: build like any other stuffed topiary.

c) Developing designs on the ball, use two or more cultivars of the same plant.

d) After the ball is planted, leave the markers. Although they will be hidden by the plant foliage, they can be located and used as a pruning guide.

Pre-Made Ball

The simplest way used to make a topiary ball is to buy a pre-made ball or sphere-shaped frame. Assembly would be the same as for building a stuffed-type topiary. Start with a layer of sphagnum moss at the bottom of the ball and then add plants around the perimeter of the moss. Repeat this layering method, alternating moss and plants, and add soil to the center cavity of the ball as you build. Remember to pack the moss as tightly as possible and space the plants evenly around the sphere, pinning down the plant runners as they grow. After the plants have grown and the ball is covered, maintain by trimming and pinching. Try to keep the ball closely trimmed or the sphere may become lopsided and lose the desired shape.

The list of suitable plant material for this type of topiary is endless. Try vines, compact bushy flowering annuals, and even cacti. At Walt Disney World Resort® in Orlando, Florida, I have seen elaborate decorative designs achieved by careful planting and pruning. Gardeners there choose wax begonias or alternanthera. Using two or more cultivars of the same plant, they achieve a terrific blend of colors neatly defined one from the other.

Such a disciplined design should be marked out before planting. As these decorative balls grow, their maintenance needs special attention. Pinning and pruning are important. Each different color or variety of plant needs strict management to keep the distinction perfect.

Two Halves.

The method most often used to make a ball begins with two wire hanging baskets. Start with a good layer of wet sphagnum moss in the bottom of each basket. Add plants evenly around the perimeter of the moss, allowing the plants to protrude through the wire frame. Continue layering moss and plants. As you plant each layer, it may be helpful to alternate the plant row location. This will help you space evenly so that coverage is adequate in all areas.

When the two halves are completed, water both thoroughly. This will settle the soil and moss. More soil can be added if necessary. Finally, the two halves must be joined together. (Ideally, you should wait a few weeks until soil and plants are settled and secure.) Add a layer of moss to cover the soil and to ensure a tight fit when the two parts are joined. After adding the sphagnum, tie it in by using string or fishing line back and forth over the flat inner surface.

Alternatively, cover the top of the basket to be turned upside down with a heavy sheet of cardboard or thin plywood. When the two halves are together, carefully remove the cardboard and securely connect the bottom and top together in several locations. As the plants begin to grow, pin them over the seam of the ball to hide it.

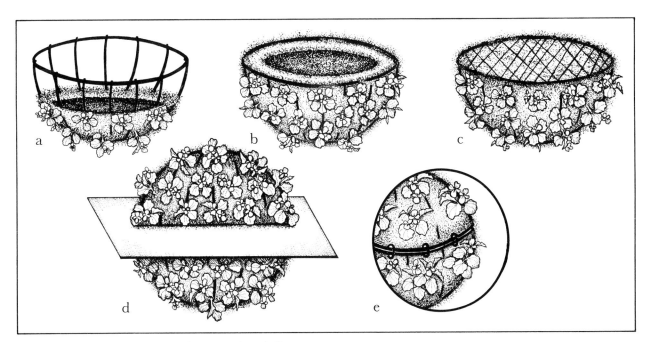

a) & b) Use two wire hanging baskets to make a ball.
c) To aid in turning one half onto the other, cover the soil with a layer of wet moss and tie in with string or fish line.
d) Or, turn one half onto the other by using a thin board or heavy cardboard to hold in the soil, moss, and plants when the halves are in position. Remove cardboard before securing.
e) Secure with wire clips.

An example of one wire basket ball using *Solanum pseudocapsicum* 'Variegatum' as the plant material. The perforated white pot is clearly visible.

One Wire Basket

A third method used at Longwood constructs the ball using only one wire basket. The basket is lined with moss enclosing the soilless mix. Planting is done as for previous balls. An empty, perforated plastic pot is then positioned on top of the soil in the center of the basket. The completed ball is achieved by building the moss in layers around the pot. The ball is watered by filling the perforated pot, allowing the water to filter evenly into the entire form. This lessens the danger of washing away the constructed wall built above the basket frame.

Central Pot

Planting a vine into the central pot (filled with soil) and allowing it to grow down over a completely sphagnum-filled form is another way to make a ball. As it grows, pin the runners down over the moss ball. If the plant produces lateral branches, it will soon envelope the ball and actually hold the whole thing together.

Plants with upright woody stems that naturally droop into a ball shape do not work well when pinned to a moss surface. Generally the woody stems do not root into the moss because they are brittle and break easily. Fuchsias and ivy geraniums are typical examples. If they are planted in the center of a wire basket, however, they will naturally form a ball. Skilled pruning encourages the desired shape.

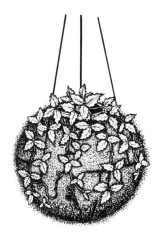

Plant a vining plant into the pot and allow the plant to trail over the moss and cover the form.

Variegated Jerusalem-cherry balls almost ready for display indoors.

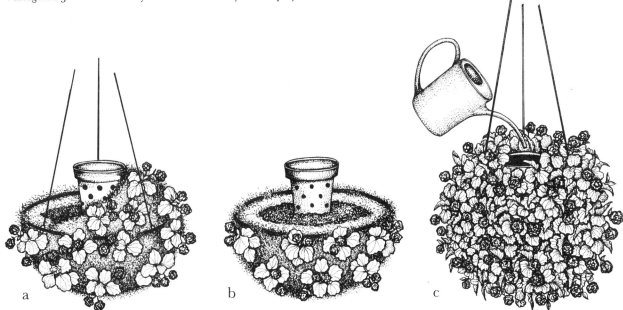

a) Add an empty plastic pot with holes to the center of the hanging basket.
b) Continue to build around the pot.
c) The pot acts as a reservoir and distributes water evenly through the ball.

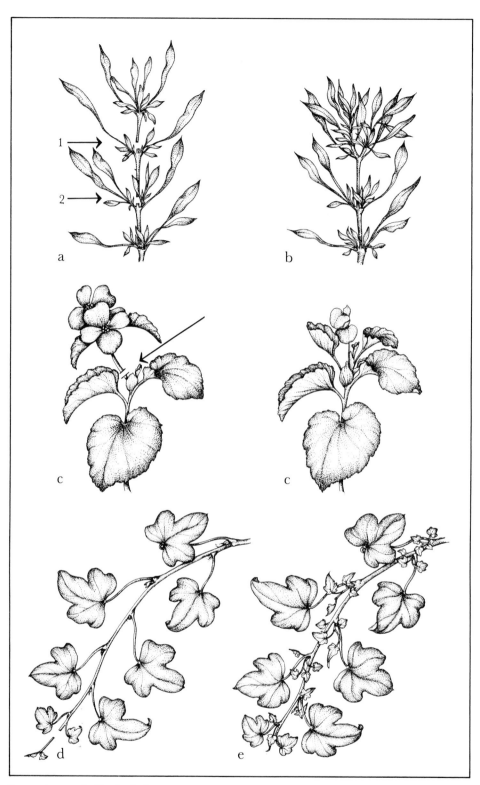

Some plants suitable for balls.

a) Alternanthera - pinching at location (1) will cause the ball to become very large and quickly lose shape. Pinch close (2) to maintain tight form.

b) Alternanthera, like many other plants, will break just below the pinch.

c) Begonia - always pinch begonias at a formed break. They do not break as readily as many other plants.

d) Ivy - pinch out the tip.

e) Ivy - tip pinching will encourage many lateral breaks on many cultivars.

Basket Variations

Rather than joining the two halves of a ball, consider suspending them separately, one above the other. To do this, leave an empty pot in the center of the bottom half for fresh flowers or a decorative potted plant, ideally something which contrasts with the ball. If you place a pot in both baskets, you will be able to rotate the top and bottom, and exchanging the two occasionally will keep them uniform. To grow them, stuff and plant as previously described (on page 75), but do not use any soil. Place empty pots in the center of each moss-filled basket and cover the area around the pot with tightly packed moss. Some tying may be needed to hold each pot in place. After securing, turn each basket upside down and set the empty pot over an inverted pot that is slightly larger than the first. This will allow the plants to get the light required. Water by spraying regularly. Every few days allow water to penetrate through the ball.

Clarification needs to be made at this point regarding pruning or pinching to maintain shape. For most vining plants like ivy, pinching out the terminal tip when the plant has reached the desired length will encourage new shoots. Many vines will break at each set of leaves and in turn grow and cover rapidly. These new runners can then be pinned to the surface and again tip pinched once the desired length has grown. After the plants have completely covered the form, regular pruning will keep them under control and the topiary neat and compact.

However, when using upright plants like wax begonia and alternanthera, pinching methods are a little different. Always pinch above a set of leaves. Remember that the location of the pinch is important because with upright plants, most breaks will only come just below the pinch. To maintain shape, pinch often and pinch back leaving only one or two sets of leaves. (One caution - do not pinch away all nodes so that there are none left to initiate new growth.) After the topiary has filled in, the pruning still requires attention. Always consider the type of plant used before beginning any pinching or pruning.

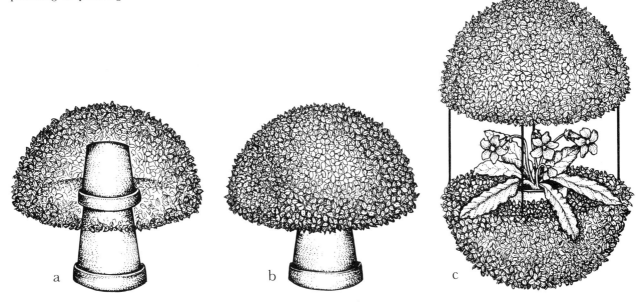

a) Completed half basket positioned on second pot. (Note center pot.)
b) Second basket growing well.
c) The two baskets suspended by wire. A plant is added for decoration.

The magnificent elephant was created for the 1987 festival at Longwood. This is an excellent example of a large-scale, stuffed topiary. The plant material used was the ivy 'Telecurl'.

The same elephant positioned outside the Atlanta Botanic Garden, Georgia.

3. Large-Scale Stuffed Topiaries

A topiary that is too large for one person to pick up, tuck under his arm, and move around falls into the category of large-scale topiary. There is practically no limit to the size or subject of topiary, just individual restrictions of space and movement.

You do not have to have a conservatory to house a large topiary. It is quite possible to keep it on the patio or in the garden and only bring it into the house for special occasions. A 6-foot rabbit dressed in butler's tails can add an unusual decorative touch to a Saturday night dinner party.

News clippings from all over the United States describe home gardeners and their topiary, everything from one special specimen to entire herds of animals and shapes. A lady in Maine has a stuffed topiary whale as a garden focal point. The whale is elevated on a steel pipe with a garden hose hidden in the body so that it can spout water just like the real thing, thus enabling the whale to water himself with a turn of the tap. Both formal and whimsical topiary can be found in every flower show across the country. Many public gardens have devoted a permanent corner of a greenhouse to creating animals and shapes from living plants. Shopping malls and large office buildings have discovered how topiary can create a pleasant atmosphere. Stuffed topiary has become an important part of interiorscape programs everywhere. Small businesses in Philadelphia, Baltimore, Atlanta, San Diego, and Portland, Oregon, have invested in living topiaries to attract and please their customers.

Most large-scale topiaries are custom designed and, when positioned in the display location, demand certain physical requirements from the frame, perhaps a head turned to the right or left, one arm raised to hold a sign, or a figure running or sitting.

Size is an important factor, and planning is needed to make sure the topiary fits the chosen spot. Decisions have to be made on the proper size and scale for the frame, the number of plants needed, and how to keep large animals from becoming too heavy to move when stuffed and planted.

At Longwood each large-scale topiary starts with a sketch that includes the final location and the positioning necessary to suggest the character's desired action. With the Longwood Carousel the pose of all the animals gave an appearance of uniform motion. Our large elephant was to spray water, so we positioned his trunk upward; and because he was to stand on a small incline, his back legs were built 8 inches shorter than the front legs.

On the plans, we also note what plants are to be used, including different ones to accent features on larger topiaries. Two ivy cultivars were used on the 1986 penguins: dark green ivy for the main body or dark plumage, with white variegated ivy for the belly and to define the penguin's tuxedo. Glenda the Good Witch wore a white gown of curly white ivy decorated with scallops of dark ivy, but her arms were made of creeping fig to define the boundaries of the dress sleeves. To maintain the facial features of the frame, it was tightly covered with sheet moss. Her hair was made of yet another ivy.

Sometimes a single plant is all that is needed to give a bird a bushy crest or colorful tail. We gave the Cowardly Lion a royal robe of flowering chrysanthemums and a robust mane by using the spider plant (*Chlorophytum comosum* 'Variegatum'). Brightly colored foliage plants can be used to add spots or stripes to an otherwise plain green surface.

Large-size topiary requires a work space large enough to stuff, plant, and grow the specimen. This is not a project that can be done Saturday afternoon on the kitchen table. A space must be set aside that may be used for several days and is large enough to hold the supplies needed.

Reindeer and other large animals standing outside in the fall sunshine at Longwood Gardens.

While planning, consider how to maintain the topiary. Can it be watered and fertilized in all future locations or readily moved if needed? Will repairs be possible in the final location? Will treating insects and diseases be possible?

As you are planning and building, keep detailed records. Write down the number and size of the plants used, the hours spent on building, and the maintenance needed. Longwood records all the details of how many plants, how much time, how much sphagnum moss and soil, and even how many pounds of fern pins. This record-keeping will be helpful for future topiary planning and in case you need to rebuild a figure.

Always collect the necessary supplies and prepare the work area before you begin the project. The ingredients for large-scale stuffed topiary building are frames, moss, filler, plants, fish line, fern pins, and gloves.

Frame

The frame is the skeleton and sole support for the plant sculpture, and it must be in good condition. Check all the welds, making sure there are no sharp edges. Frames should be rust-protected, since most large topiaries will be used for a considerable length of time. Preparation of the frame before planting is essential, otherwise time will be wasted later doing repairs and replants.

Don't bother to start with unsuitable frames that will need to be repaired soon after planting. Remember that frames that are not strong and in good condition could be unsafe and result in an accident or injury.

Glenda the Good Witch: her dress is ivy 'Calico' trimmed with ivy 'Garland'. Glenda's arms are creeping fig, her hair ivy 'Shamrock.'

Moss

Sphagnum moss is a bog plant which is harvested for horticultural use. For topiaries, use the natural fibrous form. Do not buy milled sphagnum moss or milled peat moss as these products are processed and have a powdery consistency not suitable for topiary work.

Good moss should be free of sticks and other debris. Moss that has been stored for longer than a year disintegrates rapidly after the topiary has been stuffed. This is particularly bad for large topiaries which are generally made to last for years.

Some topiary builders use live sphagnum moss on small topiaries to good effect. However, live sphagnum is not readily available in large quantities and would be difficult to pack tightly, which makes it unsuitable for large creations.

For large jobs, start soaking dry moss the day before you plan to use it to ensure that it has absorbed as much water as possible. An inexpensive child's swimming pool is suitable. Position the pool where you will be working, since moving it afterwards is almost impossible.

Soak only as much moss as you will use within two or three days. Never allow it to stand in water more than three days, especially if the weather is sunny and warm as it may give off an unpleasant odor. Stagnant moss can, however, be drained and rinsed, then reused. The odor eventually dissipates and does not harm the plants.

Recently the Florida Department of Agriculture and Consumer Service, Division of Plant Industry, has reported a disease hazard for people handling large quantities of plants and plant-growing media, particularly sphagnum moss. The disease is called sporotrichosis and is caused by the fungus *Sporothrix schenkii*. Infection is usually contracted in exposed skin areas that have a previous injury breaking the skin. The report instructs gardeners to avoid exposure to hands, arms, legs, and feet. Wear waterproof gloves for proper protection. **This information should not cause alarm; it is simply an effort to advise gardeners to practice caution and avoid an unpleasant situation.** Although not a widespread epidemic, the fungus could cause serious health problems if left unchecked.

For more information, refer to:
Plant Pathology Circular No. 286, August 1986
Florida Department of Agriculture and Consumer Service
Division of Plant Industry
P.O. Box 1269
Gainesville, FL 32602

Planting Media and Fillers

A planting medium as lightweight as possible is a requirement for large-scale topiary to ensure easy mobility. Longwood uses a commercial, soilless mix. The topiaries are usually built for temporary displays lasting from six to eight months. The medium inside does not have a major effect on the growth of the plants, since even topiaries that remain on display for extended periods receive most of their nutrients from the fertilizer that is applied during routine watering. Most plants used on Longwood's topiaries grow well even when planted only into sphagnum moss.

When a topiary is planned for long-term display, the mix inside should be a lightweight, soilless mix with a loose texture, so that the plants can readily root into the medium. Some commercial potting mixes contain small amounts of fertilizer, which is not harmful to most topiary plants.

In addition to regular surface watering, an occasional drenching is beneficial. Watering by repeatedly spraying over the entire surface encourages plants to develop

A large penguin, stuffed and planted with contrasting ivies.

massive root systems concentrated near the surface rather than deeper into the topiary body.

There are several soilless mixes available in garden supply shops and from wholesale horticultural supply companies. Depending on the ingredients, the weight usually ranges from five to twenty pounds per cubic foot (see source list).

The Longwood blend contains milled Canadian sphagnum peat moss, horticultural vermiculite, coarse horticultural perlite, granite sand, processed bark ash, and composted pine bark. Our choice is based on the overall needs of Longwood Gardens, not on just the topiary's. It is a good coarse mix that has excellent absorption designed for long-term crops. You may want to use a mix that weighs less, such as one without sand. Another common ingredient is ground polystyrene, a very lightweight additive used by many growers in mixes designed for hanging baskets.

It is important to use a sterilized medium. The soilless mix used in stuffed topiary is enclosed in a constantly moist envelope of sphagnum, creating a perfect environment for soil-borne organisms that could affect the health of the topiary.

When topiaries are very large, such as life-size elephants and 40-foot dragons, we add styrofoam packing peanuts as a filler to the body cavity. The frame openings do not allow the peanuts to be added in the original bag, and it can be messy to pour them in loose. Funneling the bits of styrofoam into smaller plastic bags placed inside the frame is the easiest and most efficient method. The smaller bags are readily adjusted and can be moved about as you are building the topiary. Many of

The Piano and Violin players: both penguins were installed in the Music Room at Longwood for the 1986 Christmas Display.

Longwood's large topiaries are made outdoors, and the plastic bags prevent loose bits of styrofoam from blowing away. This also makes a neater job when dismantling the topiaries.

We have also occasionally used rigid styrofoam as filler, the styrofoam blocks being added while assembling the frame. However, stiff filler is very difficult to adjust and arrange while building, especially after the topiary is half built. Although Longwood's single attempt to use an aerosol insulation foam as a filler failed, with more experimentation this could become a practical alternative. In our case the foam would not stick to the inner pipe skeleton of the topiary frame. This type of filler would create a permanent fill that could be used repeatedly with minor maintenance.

Plants

Good plant selection is the reason Longwood has been so successful with topiary. Although plants are discussed in Part Four: Elements of Topiary, a few remarks are in order here.

Determine the number of plants needed. Research growth habit and rate to make a good choice. We recommend five newly rooted cuttings per square foot for plants such as ivies, which will cover the desired area in around three months of optimum growing season. Not all plants are as easy to predict as ivy. Each species will be needed in different quantities to cover the same area in a given amount of growing time. Also, much depends on what size plant you start with and how well it is rooted. Growth habit is important, too. For plants that simply expand from a central crown and do

The Lion shows an excellent choice of plant material; his body is creeping fig and his mane spider plant.

Hardly recognizable, the Pianist Penguin sitting outside at Longwood.

Back view of Glenda showing the contrasting plant material.

Fully groomed, the Penguin Waiter with props positioned waits to serve the guests.

not trail over the frame and moss, as many as ten plants per square foot may be needed.

Calculate how many plants will be needed per square foot, then estimate the square footage of the entire topiary and multiply. This is not precise, but it provides a working figure. Add 5 to 10% extra.

Fishing Line

Many gardeners use thread or string for building small topiary, but this is not suitable for larger specimens. A much stronger binding is needed. Heavy string or rope would be bulky and visible. Fishing line is a perfect support in large-scale topiary and is almost invisible when grown in. It holds everything together, keeps the stuffing snugly in place, and is an important part in building large stuffed forms.

Openings must be left in the wire frame for stuffing with moss and planting. When you have finished stuffing and planting a section, close the openings by adding a wide

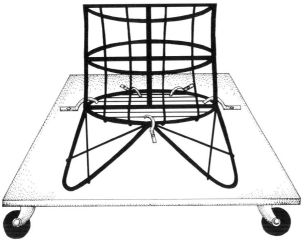

When anchoring the frame to a platform, use clamps that are bolted on one side only. Position these bolts so that they can be removed if needed after the topiary is stuffed and planted.

netting of fish line. This holds the newly planted areas firmly and allows the plants to develop their own holding system.

A wax-coated string is available that is stronger than regular string, but it has the same drawbacks as single-strand fishing line, namely, it is slippery, hard to tie, stretches, and may cut your fingers.

Although fishing line is frequently coated with polyester or nylon, it is still single ply. Multi-ply premium braided Dacron line is suitable and is rated from twelve to one - hundred - thirty pounds test. Most topiary work does not require a high test. Dacron does not stretch and is much easier to work with in wet conditions. It is easy to weave and tie into knots when your hands are wet or you are wearing gloves. It is available in sporting goods stores carrying fishing tackle.

Fern Pins

Fern pins are available from all floral supply companies in different lengths and sold by weight in boxes ranging from eight to twenty five-pounds. The size we use most often is 1 ¾ inch. Sometimes a shorter pin can be very handy when working with small topiaries or thin appendages like monkey tails. Generally, we buy the longer pins and snip them into smaller sizes with wire cutters, as needed.

The pins are very useful during the building process and for maintenance, so buy plenty of them. They are also invaluable when maintaining the detailed outline definition of the frame.

The steel pins rust rapidly, so keep the unused supply dry. However, in time, the rust helps to hold the used pins and their subjects firmly in place. Eventually they disintegrate, but by then the topiary is well-established.

Never add dismantled topiary debris to compost. The steel pins disintegrate rapidly, but there are always some slightly rusted but still sharp pins in the topiary, leaving a potentially hazardous condition for anyone handling compost. Gardeners dismantling topiary should be clearly cautioned about the fern pins.

Wheels

When possible, put large topiaries on wheels before you begin to build. A plywood platform with freely moving casters works very well. Be careful to ensure that this platform can be removed once the finished topiary is moved to its site.

If you are building a topiary that will weigh several hundred pounds, the ability to move and rotate the topiary makes the job progress much quicker. I find having all of my supplies stationary while moving the frame is the best method. On a few occasions, I have left the topiary stationary and put all the supplies on wheels.

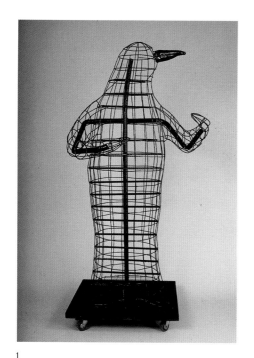

1

2

3

4

5

THE PENGUIN VIOLINIST

1. Frame for the penguin secured to a platform on wheels.

2. The first layer of plants, moss, and soilless mix.

3. The first styrofoam packing peanuts in bags are now added.

4. More moss, soilless mix, and plants are added around the packing.

5. Two people working together ensure even building of the filler, moss, soilless mix, and plants. It also takes less time to build.

6

7

8

9

6. Nearly completed body.

7. The arms are now planted but none of the plant material has been pinned down yet.

8. Detail showing arm planting.

9. The completed penguin, pinned and groomed and ready for display.

Step-by-Step

Each topiary subject may have slightly different features that require special techniques, but generally the following step-by-step directions for building a 7-foot penguin will demonstrate how the large topiaries at Longwood are constructed.

To begin with, the frame (if not new) has been repaired and painted, is on wheels, and is ready to be filled. This penguin did not require much preliminary tying, but many frames, such as a 10-foot-tall elephant, will. The underside of any topiary should be tied with fishing line before the plants and moss are started. Areas where gravity works against the stuffing will need to be strung and tied. The elephant's belly is a prime example; under his chin and the bottom side of his trunk also need the extra webbing. However, do not overdo the fishing line, as it can interfere with planting.

Topiary building is not dissimilar to basic house construction. Start with a good foundation and work your way up. The foundation is the tightly packed layer of wet sphagnum moss. As you build, adding plants, soil, and filler, the moss should be constantly worked and manipulated to become evenly and tightly packed.

Packing that is even ensures consistent moisture throughout the topiary. Places that are loosely packed will dry faster and require more water, and, in extreme cases, exposure of the root area and continual drying will injure the plants, increasing maintenance and repairs. I have often related packing and shaping to kneading bread, always working out hidden air pockets and developing the perfect consistency.

"Topiary Erosion" is a phrase originating with our increased volume of large stuffed topiary. Loosely packed outer shells of moss often develop eruptions in the surface created by regular watering. If there is a weak spot in the moss, a regular path will develop and, before long, much of the inside filler will begin to wash out through the hole. Evenly packed moss will help to disperse the water uniformly.

A beginning layer or foundation of 3 to 5 inches of moss is ideal. The first layer of plants can be added at this stage. The top of the root ball should be positioned just below a thin covering of moss. If the roots or surface of the root ball are left exposed, the plant will dry out rapidly. At the same time, it is important not to plant too deeply. Outdoor ivy topiaries are the exception; they do better in freezing winter conditions if the root ball is planted at least 2 inches below the surface. Refer to the original plan for the number and spacing of plants so that the finished topiary will look evenly planted and well balanced.

The outer surface of the moss and plants should be continued upward, adhering to the shape and outline of the frame. Pack the moss tightly downward and outward against the frame, creating a pocket or bowl on the inside that will be successively filled and packed as the topiary progresses upwards.

Fill the center of the bowl with the lightweight, soilless mix and styrofoam packing peanuts as the topiary takes shape. It is faster to arrange the bags of filler in a bed of soilless mix slightly above the area of stuffing and building. As the outer skin of moss and plants progresses, continue to fill in around the styrofoam peanut bags with mix, packing and tamping to prevent topiary erosion.

The moss depth should be backed by enough planting medium to ensure plenty of growth space to support the root system for the life of the topiary. Try, when possible, to have a soil buffer zone about 2 inches deep between moss and styrofoam. Maintain an even depth of moss for the entire topiary.

Pouring the soilless mix into the form sounds easy, but it can be difficult to distribute into all the cracks and crevices between the bags of filler. Take particular care to fill these areas. Use a tamper to eliminate any hidden air pockets. Our topiary team has created funnels and shoots to get filler into every space.

The soilless mix filler should be watered as the topiary is being built. The waterings help to compact the soil and fill in unwanted air pockets. Another reason for watering

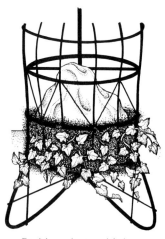

Carefully position each root ball in the bed of moss ensuring that the entire root area is covered and not exposed and allowed to dry out.

Position plants with long runners near areas like feet, arms, and wings. These areas can be covered by tying the long runners on the frame.

as you plant is that it is almost impossible to saturate the inside fillers once the topiary has been completed.

The Penguin

It is much easier to construct large topiaries in teams. Two people were needed to build Longwood's penguin evenly and simultaneously on both sides. With the elephant, we started with four people - one person on each leg - and finished with six to eight people. Packing both sides at the same time keeps the fillers at proper depths.

Building a large topiary by oneself requires lots of turning, shifting, and balancing to keep a tight, even structure. Regardless of how many hands are working on a character, it is essential to step back and walk around the character periodically to be sure everything is in harmony.

Planting patterns should be closely followed and continually checked against the original plans. The white front of the penguin was outlined on the frame with long, brightly colored twist-ties. Variegated ivies were planted inside the twist-tie boundaries and the remaining area was planted in green ivy.

Continue building until the main body is completed. Legs, arms, and other appendages can usually be left until last. The penguin's feet were covered by planting long runners into the main body at the point where the feet begin to protrude. The plant runners were tied along the outline of the frame. As the ''feet plants'' grew, they were tied and pruned to maintain the fine detailing required.

The wings were stuffed and planted like the body. The wings were not large enough to use any filler and were completely packed with sphagnum moss. Plants were added at the same time as the moss. The fishing line was wrapped and tied around the outer surface of the frame, moss, and plants to help hold everything together. Never wrap the fishing line over the plant stems. This could snap the stem or restrict the plant growth if the binding is too tight. Wrap the line under the stems and then pin the runners over to help secure and hide the mechanics.

Plants should not be placed into the moss just above any frame wires. As you are packing and building, these plants could be pushed downward against the frame wire and their tender stems broken. Position the plants just under the wires.

After the frame is planted, the topiary will look rather shaggy. Take time to groom and pin the character to perfection. Trim and tuck in bits of moss that protrude. Use dabs of moss to cover exposed frame. Pin carefully to maintain the fine detailing of the frame shape and the pattern of different plants.

Pinning is an art and should get special attention. Start either at the bottom or top of the newly made topiary and continuously work in one direction. I always start at the bottom and pin the runners in a downward direction. Try to space the runners evenly, and the final appearance will reflect consistent building and grooming. If you work in one direction and pin evenly, it will be much easier to plug a plant or two into obvious gaps. Later, as the plants begin to grow, maintenance pinning will be less critical.

Always start pinning the individual runner near the area where the plant comes out of the moss surface and continue pinning towards the tip of the plant. Be sure the entire runner is flat against the surface. Later pruning and clipping could prove deadly if loops of stems are left sticking up above the surface. It is very easy to cut a main stem, leaving a large gap once the runners coming from the stem have died.

If the runners are long enough to meet the next layer of plants, pinch out the tips and encourage new shoots. After the topiary has filled in nicely, keep it clipped and

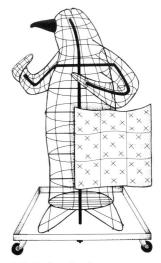

Mark the planting pattern on a sheet of squared paper first. Then put in the plants.

Elegant props for the Reindeer guests.

A self-watering elephant.

pruned to maintain shape. Neglected growth can be clipped and pinned back into shape, but some of the details will be lost if woody stems develop without training. All of these instructions are for plants that are vining and trail over the surface of the topiary. Other plants can be groomed and shaped according to their individual growth habits or to the needs of the topiary.

Be meticulous about finishing touches. Careful grooming does show; every plant must be properly pinned to the moss. Always cover and hide the mechanics of the topiary. Remove any yellowing or dead leaves. Plug in extra plants if a noticeable gap occurs. If you are adding special props and extras, be sure they fit the character and add to the story you are telling. Don't make your audience wonder what you are trying to portray. Eyes give many topiaries a special personality and can be ordered from a taxidermist supply company. We take great care to choose the most suitable eyes for each character. Fun eyes with 1½-inch eyelashes were added to our green, 16-foot giraffe!

Dresses, saddles, hats, gloves, and jewels have all been successfully used at Longwood. We have decorated our topiaries with miniature lights and added special effects like spouting water and music to complete the story. Each is meticulously planned and carried out to the smallest detail. Finishing off a topiary with sloppy props can be be a disaster.

Maintenance and Restoration

Regular maintenance needs to be carried out monthly on large topiary. After the plants have completely covered the form, prune off unwanted runners. Remove yellowing and dead leaves to maintain appearance and to avoid conditions that harbor insects and diseases. Groom just as though it were your pet horse or dog.

After a topiary has been growing for six months or more it will probably need some restoration. Begin by vigorously hand brushing the entire topiary to remove any dead leaves and other debris. This process permits close visual inspection. If areas need more cover, plug in additional plants. Be sure they are exactly the same as the original planting.

Kudu head with magnificent horns.

If holes develop from "topiary erosion" or decaying moss, now is the perfect time to repair. Pack wet moss tightly into the holes, working it behind the root area of the topiary skin. Large areas can be refilled from one location by gradually working the moss in every direction. After the hole is nearly filled, extra plants can be added to cover repairs.

Painting the toucan beak, Palm House, 1987.

Tusks, Beaks, Horns - What Harvey Does!

Starting with Longwood's first group of topiaries in 1984, we found there were some spots that needed "something." Sometimes plants just didn't work or certain areas couldn't be planted properly. The first problem was how to make bird's feet. We eventually discovered glazing compound was the answer. Harvey Allaband, a craftsman working in the paint department, developed a technique that, so far, has proved excellent for topiary features that cannot be effectively represented by plants.

Harvey starts by filling the shaped appendage of the frame with styrofoam (often insulation scraps). If the volume is small, the frame may not need filling. Styrofoam

Harvey Allaband shaping the teeth of the dragon.

Harvey Allaband smoothing the dragon's tongue with wet hands.

minimizes weight and takes up space otherwise occupied by glazing compound, hastening drying.

The styrofoam-filled antler, beak, or other shape is then covered with latex glazing putty. Any brand will do as long as it is latex. This is the same compound used for home window repair and it is used straight from the can. After the initial shaping with wet hands and water to moisten the shape and smooth it out, the texturing is done with fingers and sometimes a putty knife.

The putty is allowed to dry without being disturbed. A week is optimum, but overnight will do. It will not harden completely for a long time, perhaps months. We usually let it dry at least twenty-four hours, then paint it using regular indoor latex flat paint.

Do not use an oil base putty compound as the oil sweats. Always ensure that the sculptured feature is completely covered with putty to prevent water from getting inside. We water the topiary thoroughly the morning before the putty is applied and, if possible, not again until the paint is dry. It is best to make putty features before planting the topiary.

To create a row of fin-like plates standing along the back of an ivy-covered stegosaurus, Emanuel Samanick, of the Julius Roehrs Company, used vinyl concrete available at hardware stores. He covered the framed outline of each fin with a fine meshed wire and then mixed the vinyl concrete with water until it was the right consistency to be applied with a putty knife. Then he dipped clean soft pieces of cloth, cut into squares slightly larger than the fin, into the mix and covered the fin with the squares, overlapping the extra cloth over the frame edge. After the mixture had a little time to set, he went over it with a small wet paint brush smoothing out the wrinkles and bumps. After it was dry, waterproof paint was used to paint the fins.

Close-up of dragon's tongue.

4. Standards

Many different plants are grown as standards at Longwood Gardens, but they all have one thing in common: a single stem trained up with a head of foliage and/or flowers. Standards can be used where permanent planting is not practical. Not only location but size and height of the standard is subject to personal choice and various design considerations.

At Longwood, the mention of standards brings to mind John Testorf, the gardener who has been fondly accused of trying to make standards of almost every plant in the garden. He has been responsible for wonderful standards of fuchsias, zonal geraniums, lantanas, and coleuses. But standing straight and tall among these relatively common topiary trees might be standards of ivy geraniums, plumbagos, variegated Jerusalem -cherries, bougainvilleas, and allamandas.

Most gardeners use standards in pairs, which should be started simultaneously and grown and cultivated side by side. However, if identical twins are necessary, start three. The extra specimen is insurance. It might take years to grow a ''mate'' for a widowed standard, and chances are it will never match perfectly.

Trained-Up Standard (the most common technique)

A standard of this type is grown from one healthy rooted cutting. When the rooted cutting is potted for the first time, it is kept in a state of vigorous growth in a warm location. As the plant grows, it is staked to keep the stem straight and help support the new growth. The leaves on the main leader are left on during this stage, as the plant needs as much foliage as possible for optimum growth. Side shoots developing along the main stem should be removed if they are not intended to be part of the developing head.

When the plant has reached the desired height, the tip of the terminal shoot should be pinched out. This will encourage side growth and branches will develop at the top of the main stem. Strip all foliage below the new head at this stage.

In the early stages of head development, side branches should be developed and pinched back to two or three breaks, as this will produce a compact and full-headed standard. Later, after the head is well established, selective pruning should eliminate weak and spindly stems and achieve an open head necessary for good air circulation.

Fuchsias, coleuses, and chrysanthemums are important crops for standards at Longwood Gardens.

Fuchsias

Tip cuttings (4- to 5-inch terminal end cuttings) are taken from mid-October until the first of November from hanging-basket-type fuchsias for standards with pendulous heads. The cuttings are placed under mist on a greenhouse bench with bottom heat (75° F.). They root in two to three weeks. Soon after, the new plants are potted into 3-inch clay pots. As each new plant is potted, a bamboo stake is added to train the central leader. This is usually in mid-November. The optimum conditions are temperatures of 60° F. at night and 70° F. during the day with high natural light.

As soon as the fuchsia begins to grow, attention is directed to developing the main stem or central leader. By January the young standard will be shifted to a 5-inch clay pot. In April or May, it will be ready for repotting again into an 8-inch pot; the stake remains with the plant. Longwood always uses clay pots, and as the plant grows, a

A well-grown poinsettia standard.

Top Left: A newly rooted fuchsia cutting has been potted and staked for training as a standard. Left: As the new standard grows, attention should be given to developing a straight stem by staking and tying.

properly sized stake is important. This is the critical stage for stem development, and the stem should be tied securely. Because the stem creates the topiary tree effect, twists and turns should not be allowed to develop by careless tying practices. Waiting too long to tie the stem allows the soft new stem to fall over, and a permanent bend results when it is secured back to the stake. The stake must be anchored firmly in the soil and be strong enough to support the plant. A young standard that leans for any prolonged time may develop a woody trunk that can never be straightened.

Young fuchsia standard.

A fuchsia standard. The growing techniques are explained on the following pages.

Right: When the young stem has reached the desired height, pinch out the tip.

After five to six months of growth, the new standard should be almost 5 feet tall. The very tip of the stem can then be pinched out to encourage side branches.

To develop the head, branching should be allowed on the top 6 to 8 inches of the stem. When the newly developed shoots begin to grow with three sets of leaves on each shoot, the tips should be pinched out again, leaving two sets of leaves. Regular and prompt pinching will encourage more breaks and create a fuller head. To promote upper growth, the original foliage should be left along the trunk; it will naturally drop off with time. New shoots developing below the designated 6- to 8-inch head area should be removed.

During the first year, the standard should be kept in an 8-inch pot. If it is planted in an over-sized pot, the roots stay wet and root rot may occur. To keep the standard from becoming top-heavy as the head is growing, the 8-inch pot holding the plant should be sunk into a 12-inch pot and the larger pot filled with terragreen or sand. Both pots should have the same surface level so that watering needs can be monitored properly. Terragreen or sand acts as an insulator by helping to protect the roots from overheating during the hot summer months.

By the spring of the second year the root system should be well developed and the standard ready for a 10-inch pot with a permanent support rod. Clay, wood, or fiberglass tubs can be used with a sturdy rod. A painted, stainless steel rod that is well anchored or bolted directly through the bottom of the pot is ideal; it will last indefinitely and can be re-used. Bamboo and wood eventually rot or break.

Throughout the entire development stage, the plant should be kept in a vegetative

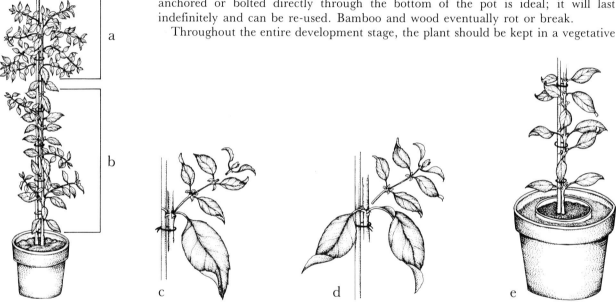

a) For head development, allow branching of the top 6 to 8 inches.
b) Leave the original foliage on the lower stem but remove the lateral shoots.
c) When the new shoots have 3 or 4 sets of leaves, pinch back to 2 sets to encourage branching.
d) Remove the entire shoot of unwanted lateral breaks.
e) Double potting.

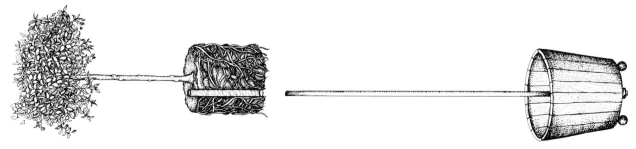

To stake and repot an established standard, lay new pot and rod on its side and slip the standard onto the rod by using the old stake hole. After the stem is secured, turn upright.

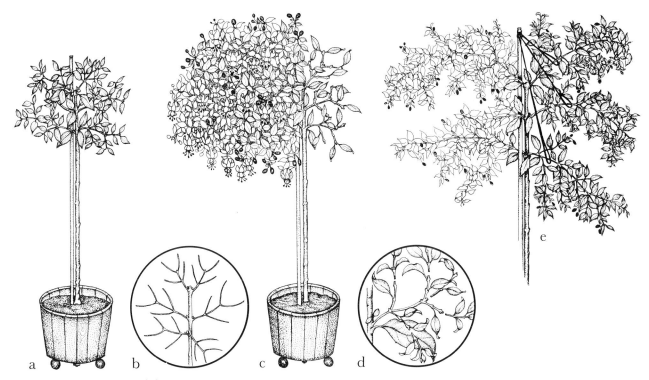

a) Fuchsia standard in training.
b) (Spot) Proper branching pattern of new head.
c) Pruning back a mature fuchsia standard.
d) (Spot) Detail of (c).
e) Tying - loop string around the stem and tie onto the stake.

state and flowering should be discouraged. Flower buds should be removed continually. Proper watering, fertilizing, and warm temperatures are all-important.

To establish the main branching pattern, pinching should be done three or four times. After the main branches have developed, the plant should be allowed to grow during the remaining summer. When the fuchsia is one year old (October), the head structure will be well defined. It can now be pruned back to one or two bud eyes (leaf nodes) on the most current lateral shoots. Shorter days, no flower production, and slow growth will indicate the resting period. Temperature should be maintained at 48° F. nights and 55° F. days. Water should be applied sparingly, but the plant is not dormant. Fertilizer should be withheld but full light provided.

As growth begins again and reaches three sets of leaves, pinching should be started once more. The first pinch will probably be in December, and pinching will continue until the end of March, when pinching should be stopped and the plant allowed to flower.

To support the new branches, the head should be tied or cradled with green string. Tie from the top of the stake, carefully looping the string around each branch so that the growth of the stem is not girdled.

Each October, the cycle of pruning back should be repeated and the plant allowed to rest. Most fuchsia standards last five years. New plants are started each year for constant rotation. Each plant should be labelled and dated, with records kept for future reference. Comparing treatments and weather conditions over a period of time helps define the optimum conditions and practices for developing the best standards.

Each year, fertilizing should begin in January, slowly increasing from once every two weeks to once a week and finally to twice a week by April. In May after blooming begins, fertilization should be increased to three times per week. As a general rule, Longwood uses liquid fertilizer at one third the recommended rate three times per week during the flowering season. Liquid fertilizer rated 20-20-20 or any well-balanced blend recommended for tropical plants is suitable.

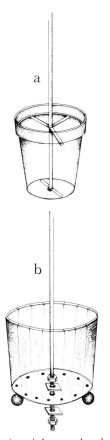

a) A stainless-steel stake anchored into a pot.
b) Bolting method for stainless-steel stakes.

101

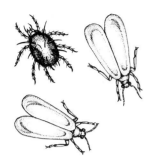

Whitefly and spider mites.

Single ball coleus standard.

Two-ball coleus standard.

Whiteflies and spider mites are the most common pests. Both can be found on the underside of the leaf. Whiteflies are tiny white insects which will fly around when the plant is brushed or disturbed.

Spider mites are not as easily detected. They are tiny red spider-like insects which, during warm periods (70° F. and above) are found on the underside of the leaf. Webbing indicates heavy infestation.

There are several cultural techniques that should be practiced to prevent or reduce most insect and disease problems.

1. Keep plants and pots clear of dead debris. This is where most problems breed.
2. Good air circulation is important.
3. Keep plants properly watered and fertilized to reduce stress. Do not overwater.
4. If growing fuchsias outside, place them in partial shade. Full sun will burn and stress the plants.
5. Reduce spider mites by spraying cool water once or twice a day over the foliage during hot and dry periods.
6. Use insect sticky traps (without pesticides). These not only reduce local insect populations but also offer good monitoring tools.
7. If using chemical controls, always follow directions completely. Be sure the pesticide label recommendation includes fuchsia.

The fresh green and red coleus standards (Pineapple Beauty) add light and color to the Christmas displays at Longwood.

Early stages of a coleus standard.

Three-ball coleus standard not yet fully developed.

A fully developed coleus standard on display.

Coleus Standards

A rich and vast selection of colors and leaf shapes characterizes coleus. Knowing what to select for standards can sometimes be difficult.

Longwood uses two varieties of *Coleus x hybridus* for standard topiaries. 'Pineapple Beauty' (probably the fastest growing) with yellow and deep red-purple leaves and dark stems is good for late summer to early fall display. Foliage and stem color become deeper and darker during the shorter days of fall.

At Christmas, the fresh green and white foliage of *Coleus x hybridus* 'Green Jade' is used. With scalloped margins and slightly curved leaves, it makes a dramatic accent for the holiday display. 'Green Jade' is slow growing, rarely reaching 'Pineapple Beauty' height.

The coleus cultivar should be selected and cuttings taken at the beginning of November, following the propagation procedure described for fuchsias. The first potting will be about three to four weeks after propagation, as coleus are fast rooting. Stakes about 8 inches long should be added to keep each stem upright and secure. After three months, the new plants will be ready for 5-inch pots and longer stakes. The final containers will be 10-inch pots.

As each plant grows, the terminal should be tied up the stake. If flowering occurs, it must be pinched out and the next highest or healthiest side shoot trained up to be the leader. Flowering occurs with some cultivars more commonly than others so it can happen more than once on the same plant.

Longwood's coleus standards are often grown to have more than one ball. 'Pineapple Beauty', a fast grower, can reach 5 feet with three balls in nine months. Standards are grown in a warm greenhouse (60° F. nights and 70° F. days) all winter. They are fertilized twice every week with one-third strength of a well-balanced fertilizer, 20-20-20. To mix a small amount at home, one teaspoon of fertilizer can be used with one gallon of water and applied twice per week. If other formulations are

Three-ball coleus standard.

103

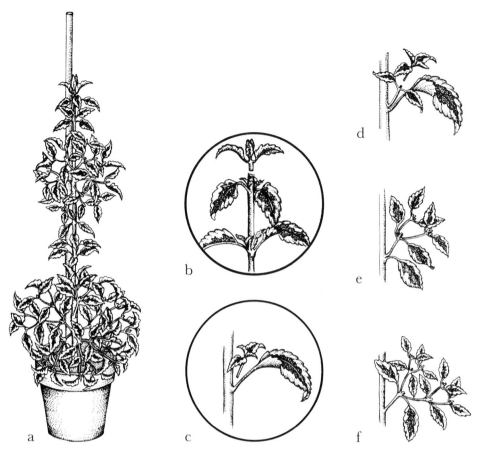

a) To develop a ball at the bottom, leave 6 shoots on the lower 6 to 8 inches of the stem.
b) Pinch out tip of leader when desired height has been reached.
c) As each ball develops, the foliage and unwanted lateral shoots can be removed.
d) First pinch.
e) Second pinch.
f) Third pinch.

used always follow instructions on the label.

If the first ball is to be at the bottom of the topiary, six side shoots should be left on the lower 6 to 8 inches of the stem. The central leader must continue to be trained up but the foliage along the central trunk should be left until it drops naturally or until the standard is well developed.

The terminal tip can be pinched out when the desired height is reached. If two or more balls are to be developed, they should be centered at 2-foot intervals along the main stem. When making pairs or multiples of standards, equal measuring and marking of the stems with a plastic twist-tie will ensure uniform shape and height. The twist-tie should be removed when the ball area has been established.

To develop attractive, dense balls, each set of six side shoots should be pinched back to one set of leaves (or breaks). All new shoots should be pinched out until the ball is almost the desired size and ready for display. After the shoots for the balls have been chosen, all other side shoots should be removed. At this point, the standard will have begun to take shape, so that pinching and pruning will be much easier to understand.

Pinching to one node is not a hard-and-fast rule. Occasionally, two or more breaks can be left to obtain the proper shape or to fill holes. Some selective pruning cuts and removal of stems may be necessary to correct or maintain the shape. The goal is to have each ball uniform and all standards matched.

Coleus are fast growing, and by the end of the first year they will have developed some woody stems. After display, the balls can be cut back and allowed to grow out again. Dieback often occurs at this point. As it is difficult to refill damaged areas,

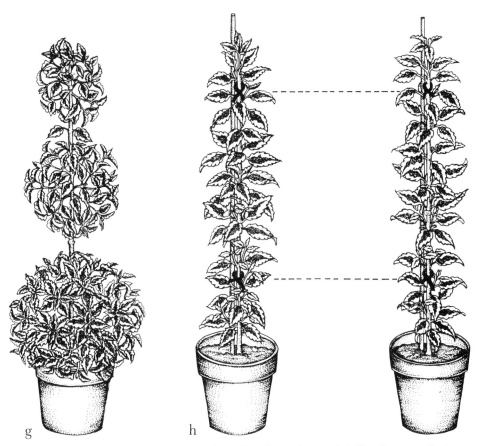

g) Three balls on a young standard. With continual pruning, each ball will eventually be equal in size.

h) When making pairs, mark with twist-ties the location of the balls so that the topiaries match perfectly. Measure and space the balls evenly along the stem (2-foot spacing).

Longwood starts new coleus standards each year. Since this crop is so fast (started in November and ready in July), a new crop can be produced annually.

The soil mix used for coleus is a general, well-drained medium, one-third soil, one-third peat, and one-third vermiculite, or any commercial mix suggested for general use.

Coleus standards are virtually insect-free. If the plants become infected, follow the cultural practices outlined for fuchsia standards.

Chrysanthemum Standards

Another trained-up standard produced at Longwood is the chrysanthemum standard. We grow thirty four chrysanthemum standards each year, eighteen 'Golden Crystal' and sixteen 'Snow Crystal'. When selecting a chrysanthemum for a topiary tree, avoid what the trade calls a "standard" type (a single-stemmed plant with one large flower often referred to as a football chrysanthemum) and choose a spray-type instead. We use plants with small- to medium-size flowers, daisy or pompon types. Almost any greenhouse chrysanthemum (not hardy garden chrysanthemums) will do for a tree form if the flower is not too large. Larger flowers will pull down and break the stem.

Many chrysanthemum catalogs list their plants according to "weeks" or response time, in other words, how long it will take to bloom after the onset of short days (less than fourteen hours of daylight). The response time will range from seven to eleven weeks.

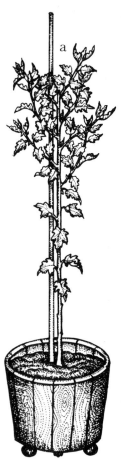

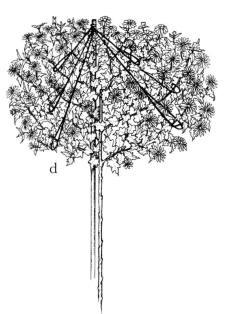

d) Tie each of the 7 original stems to prevent breakage.

An adult ivy standard in Liddon Pennock's garden, Meadowbrook Farm. Note the flowers.

a) Pinch terminal tip at 30 inches. Leave 7 lateral shoots to develop a head. Remove all shoots below head.

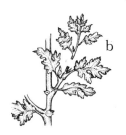

b) Pinch lateral stems leaving 2 or 3 nodes.

c) Each pinch will produce 2 or 3 new shoots.

At Longwood, newly rooted cuttings arrive the first week of February, are planted in 6-inch clay pots, and grown in a warm greenhouse, 70° F. day, 60° F. night. To prevent premature flowering, the dark period each night is interrupted with artificial light. The lights come on for three hours, decreasing fifteen minutes per night each week until May 1. After the beginning of May, with naturally longer days, the plant will not produce flower buds.

As each cutting is potted, it is tied to a bamboo stake. The growing stem should be kept tied to the stake to ensure strong, straight growth. As the plant grows up, side shoots should be removed but not the leaves of the main trunk. The terminal stem should be pinched at 30 inches and seven or more lateral breaks left near the top to develop a head. Again, each standard should be pinched at the same height of 30 inches for uniformity. A finished standard about 50 inches high is recommended.

The standards should be potted for the final time in 10-inch tubs the third week of May. The standard will have been pinched at 30 inches and have some side breaks. For this final potting Longwood uses stainless steel stakes bolted to the bottom of the tubs (see page 101). Because the roots are well developed, it may be necessary to drill a hole through the root ball about ½ inch away from the stem to position the stake.

Pinching is scheduled every two weeks, leaving two nodes. Later, only one break should be left if the head size needs control.

Before the last pinch on September 1, pinching should occur every week for better shape and size control. At the time of the last pinch, each of the seven stems in the head should be tied to the center support stake since the branches will have become quite large and heavy with flowers. Moving the finished topiary could cause heavy, unsecured stems to break. Also, standards will begin to droop from the prolific bloom.

After the last pinch, and with 2 or 3 inches of new growth or two leaf nodes, Longwood gardeners treat the plant with a growth retardant, B-Nine, at a rate of 25% as a foliar spray. Good coverage is needed on all the terminal buds. This treatment should be repeated after two weeks. Some cultivars need a higher percentage of B-

Chrysanthemum standards on display in the Acacia Passage at Longwood.

Nine. Trial and error will result in the right combination.

Basic cultural recommendations for pot mums apply to chrysanthemums grown as standards. Watering and fertilizing should be closely monitored. Ideally, water is needed when the soil surface begins to dry slightly. Soil should not be allowed to become too dry. After standards have been potted into the final tubs, every third watering should include fertilizer at one-half the recommended strength (20-20-20 liquid feed) throughout the entire growing season.

This summer crop is grown in natural temperatures most of the growing season. The ideal night temperature is 55° F. and supplementary heating may be required to maintain that. When the plant is in the finishing stages after the last pinch and days are getting shorter again, buds will form. Most cultivars will flower seven to eleven weeks after the onset of short days.

Greenhouse-type chrysanthemums are readily available from mail order growers. Most catalogs have excellent information covering everything from cultural needs and growing tips to how to prevent and control insects and diseases (see source list).

Ivy

Ivy comes in two forms, juvenile and adult. Juvenile ivy has a vining habit and does not produce the woody or upright stems required for standards. It never flowers and is easily propagated. Several cultivars have varying leaf shapes, either slightly or deeply lobed. Most groundcover, hanging basket, and topiary ivy is juvenile.

Adult ivy is upright in habit, has stiff stems, and is shrub-like, making it ideal for self-supporting standards. Frequently the adult form can be found at the top of a vertical patch of well-established ivy growing up a wall. The plant's characteristics change as the ivy reaches the top. Adult forms flower and fruit in late summer or early fall and have unlobed foliage with a coarser texture than the juvenile forms.

a

b

Examples of ivy 'Gold Heart'.
a) Juvenile ivy. b) Adult ivy.

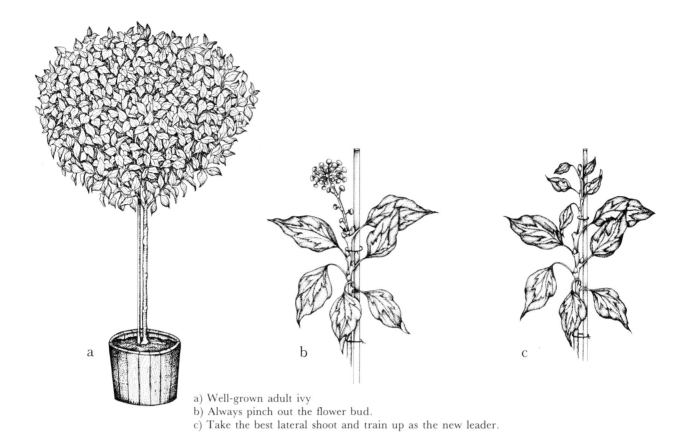

a) Well-grown adult ivy
b) Always pinch out the flower bud.
c) Take the best lateral shoot and train up as the new leader.

To develop an adult ivy standard, cuttings should be taken from adult specimens generally found at the top of a vertical patch. Propagating adult ivy is difficult and best done in late summer to early fall.

Roots will appear in three to five weeks in a warm greenhouse (75° F. night), with bottom heat (75° F.) in the propagation bench. Cuttings should be treated with a rooting hormone for soft, woody cuttings and placed under mist. If mist is not available, spray over. The cuttings should be stuck into a well-drained rooting soil (Longwood mix: one-third peat, one-third perlite, one-third charcoal). Most propagation media will work. Longwood has had success with pure vermiculite or vermiculite and perlite, as well as with good potting mixes that drain readily. Cuttings should be placed in the shade for the first two to three weeks and humidity provided by spraying several times per day with clear water. Adult ivy may take much longer than juvenile ivy to root, but it can be done.

Adult ivy can be grown as a standard by using the general trained-up style described earlier. It is important to keep the rooted ivies in a warm location and fertilize regularly (once every two weeks) to keep the plants actively growing and to discourage flowering. The main leader will develop a straight stem if the plant does not flower. When the desired height is reached, pinch out the terminal tip and allow the head to develop. If flowering does occur, remove the flowers and select the next best shoot to train up and take over as the main stem. Always stake standards during training.

Adult ivy standards can be used as permanent plantings in protected sites. They need protection from harsh winter winds, and areas that experience rapid temperature changes in early spring are not suitable. Developing a standard takes time so taking risks could be costly.

There are many other broad-leaved evergreens and many hardy plants that make wonderful outdoor standards. Choose plants that are hardy in your area. Consider the plant's normal growth habits. Will it develop a straight stem readily? Will it tolerate continuous pinching and pruning?

Supplies needed for grafting.

Prepare understock by removing terminal tip. Make several T-cuts.

Grafted Standards

Another Longwood method for developing a standard is by grafting two different plants to form one. The grafting technique is called T-budding. The understock (host plant) and scion (top material) are usually closely related, always from the same plant family. The scion is grafted onto a variety that will produce a straight strong stem with vigorous growth.

The poinsettia standard is an important example of this method. A cultivar with floriferous, pendulous growth is grafted onto a cultivar that grows 5 to 6 feet tall and develops a large, thick stem that can support the massive head boasting as many as one hundred blooms.

Grafted ivy standards displayed at Longwood are usually cultivars of *Hedera helix* (juvenile stage) grafted onto × *Fatshedera lizei* or *Schefflera arboricola*. Although different genera, these plants both belong to the aralia family and are graft compatible.

In general, supplies needed for grafting include a sharp pocket or budding knife, raffia (a natural material for wrapping) or rubber budding strips, and plastic bags. Before any procedure is started, a clean work area is necessary.

Most standards should be grafted when the plants are growing strongly (early June). The understock should be under three years old, with a not-too-woody stem.

The scion plants and understock should be well watered and only plants in optimum health should be used before starting the budding process in a cool, shaded area. Budding material from the current year's growth, with a stem size large enough to work with comfortably, should be used. The buds or T-incision must not dry during the procedure.

Practice is needed in preparing buds and making the incisions before attempting the first standard. Longwood's gardeners suggest practicing with maple saplings, using a sharp knife and making one clean cut for each incision. Do not go back over cuts or scrape the bark.

Prepare the understock and the T-cut before taking the bud from the donor plant. The understock should be straight, sturdy, and fairly young. Do not try to use a stem that is hard and woody or a plant whose bark must be pried from the woody tissue beneath. Usually these conditions will not encourage a good union between the host plant and the grafted bud. Choose the height desired, and bud around the top 8 inches of the stem. Graft six or seven buds around each stem. A few may not survive, but the others should develop into a full head.

To make the T-cut in the host plant or understock, start with the vertical cut by pressing in and drawing down to the length desired, approximately ½ to 1 inch. Now make the horizontal cut at the top of the vertical cut about one third the way around the stem. Each cut should be made through the bark to the woody inner tissue. If you give the knife a slight twist as the horizontal cut is made, the flaps of the bark will open. The size of the T-cut should be no larger than is needed to receive the bud shield comprised of the bud and attached patch of bark.

The buds needed for this procedure are found in the leaf axils along the stem of the plant chosen for the standard's head. Take the selected bud, along with a section of the stem about ⅜-inch long, keeping the petiole in place. The petiole or leaf stem will be helpful as a handle to insert the bud into the prepared cut. Now take about one-third off the back side of this portion of stem, leaving the dormant bud centrally located on the scion material. Cut from the bottom up. If you should slip, the bud will not be ruined. A downward cut risks breaking or damaging the bud. When cutting upward, if the bark should tear upward, leave the tail in place until the bud has been inserted into the cut. Then cut the tail off evenly with the cross cut of the understock.

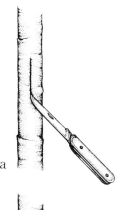

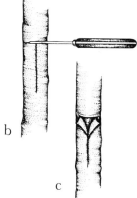

a) Vertical cut about ½-to 1-inch long.
b) Horizontal cut ⅓ of the way around the stem.
c) A twist with a knife will open the bark.

109

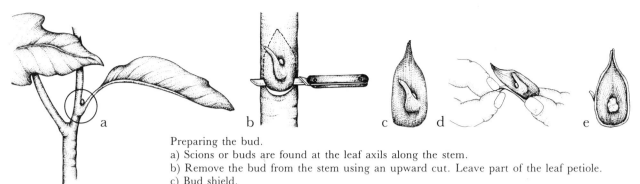

Preparing the bud.
a) Scions or buds are found at the leaf axils along the stem.
b) Remove the bud from the stem using an upward cut. Leave part of the leaf petiole.
c) Bud shield.
d) Separate bud from bark.
e) Back view of bud shield.

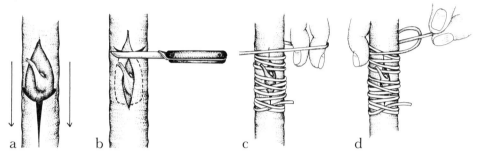

Marking the union.
a) Insert the bud shield into T-cut.
b) Cut the top of the bud shield to fit perfectly into the horizontal cut.
c) Wrap from the bottom up with raffia or grafting rubber.
d) Finishing tie.

Poinsettia standard.

Separate the bud and bark layer from the woody tissue by slipping the knife to the side with a twist. This is called "bark slipping." If you pull forward or pry with the knife, there is a risk of separating the bud from the small scale of wood (bud trace) directly behind the bud. This may remove the growing tip from the bark layer and will terminate any new growth.

Now insert the bud shield into the prepared T-cut and gently push it downward until the horizontal cut of both are even. If a flap remains on the shield, cut it off to match perfectly with the horizontal cut of the understock.

Wrap the newly grafted buds with grafting rubber or raffia. It is important to wrap snugly but not too tightly or girdling may occur. Start wrapping below the bud and wrap upwards. Cover the entire incision but do not wrap over the bud, since growth may be restricted or the bud crushed. To finish off and tie, wrap the rubber or raffia around the stem and two fingers, then pull the tail through the loop made around your fingers.

Cover the grafted buds with a plastic bag and close the bag below the new buds. This creates a microclimate with high humidity. When water begins to collect in the bag, puncture the plastic and allow the excess water to escape. Keep the bag on for three to five weeks, allowing gradual acclimatization to the air by the end of this period. The covered plants should be kept in a shaded area to avoid heat building up in the plastic bag.

Within several weeks, as soon as it is apparent that the buds have taken, remove the grafting rubber or raffia. The foliage that remains on the understock should be removed after the buds have started to grow. Do not remove these leaves too soon. It may also be necessary to remove new growth from the understock during the early stages of the standard.

Pruning is very important as the head starts to develop. Prune new shoots to encourage lateral buds to grow. The general rule is to prune each shoot leaving two breaks (two sets of leaves). Always look at the entire shape and prune to develop a symmetrical head.

Poinsettia standards on display.

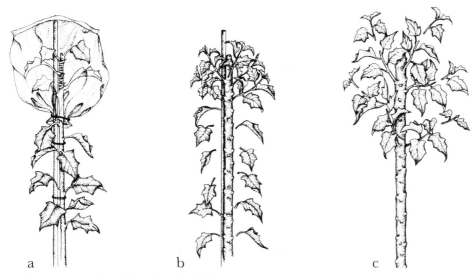

a) Cover new grafts with a clear plastic bag.
b) After new grafts are well-established, remove any growth below from the understock.
c) To develop a head, pinch each new stem to two sets of leaves.

Poinsettia

A full year of growth is invested in the poinsettia *(Euphorbia pulcherrima)* understock before it is grafted. Cuttings of the understock are taken in early May. The longest growing season possible is needed to get the poinsettias tall enough for grafting. Again, the height of any standard depends on individual preference. Remember, however, to keep the head in proportion.

The root stock used at Longwood is the Eckespoint C-1®, selected for its straight upright growth with minimal side branching. For a small-scale operation, visit a local retail greenhouse in December to obtain one or two stock plants.

The potting soil should be slightly acid (pH 6-6.5) and similar to that recommended previously for standards. Start the new rootstock plants in 5-inch pots and later move them into 8-inch pots. Staking early is a precaution but not absolutely necessary. This type of poinsettia will grow quickly and have very few or no side shoots. (We do stake at the time of final potting with a well-anchored metal stake, long enough to reach into the top growth.)

Plants will flower naturally in January. The color bracts and the flowers should be removed, and the plants will rest if you reduce water and eliminate fertilizer. The soil should be kept barely moist but never completely dry. Resume watering and fertilizing in the spring as the plants begin to sprout. They will sprout at the top; retain this foliage and graft below these sprouts. This new growth sustains plants until after the grafted buds begin to grow and produce sufficient foliage. Once this occurs, remove all understock shoots and suckers.

The budding is done about June 1, and six to eight buds around the stem of each plant will make the best head. When the new grafted buds have grown and have three or more sets of leaves, pinch back to the second set. Give only one pinch the first season. Flowers may occur this first year.

In January cut the flowers and colored bracts off and let the standard rest for three to four months. Recommended temperatures are 70° F. days and 60° F. nights.

In early April, cut the stems back to two sets of leaves. As new growth starts, pinch again and begin to thin out or remove weaker stems. There will be a total of three pinches in the growing season but do not pinch after September 20 to ensure flowers for Christmas. Each year repeat this January rest period and the pinching program starting in April.

Younger plants may not need as much thinning as older plants. Thinning and the removal of dead wood will produce bigger flowers on the remaining stems. Heavily thinning older plants will not hurt them. Each year as the standard gets bigger, you will become more comfortable about removing so much growth. Every September 1, Longwood's collection of nearly two dozen specimens, some over ten years old, are pinched and thinned. I always fear we have removed too much, but by December the standards are huge and covered with white, pink, or red floral bracts.

In the fall, provide additional support by tying the top growth to the metal stake using long pieces of string. This lessens the chances of breaking branches, especially while moving the standard into the display site.

To have flowers for Christmas, poinsettias need to have an uninterrupted natural dark period. When it is dark outdoors, the poinsettia should be in absolute darkness; this is often difficult at home. Keep your plant in a spare room where artificial light will not be used. Follow the natural light period until the end of October. The dark period must not be interrupted, not even with a flashlight. If you do not have a spare room, use a closet and move the plant into this dark chamber every evening. Covering the plant with horticultural black cloth is a possibility, but caution must be used to

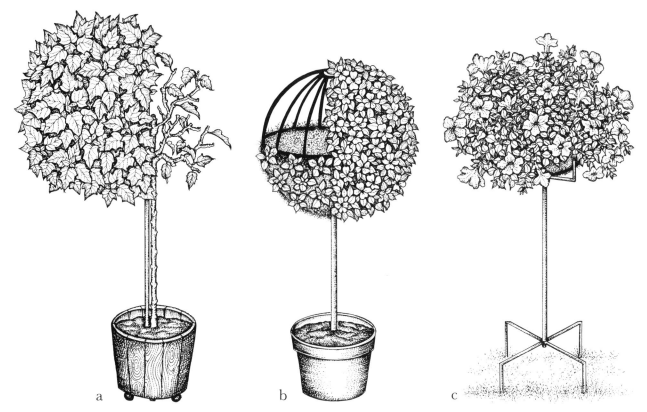

a) Each year prune back the poinsettia standard.
b) Sphagnum moss-stuffed ball attached to an artificial stem.
c) Hanging basket on a metal stand. Prongs are to anchor into the ground.

prevent breakage caused by draping directly onto the plant. Using an old sheet will not work because all light must be eliminated. The standard top must be totally enclosed, and the cloth must be secured at the bottom as well.

Much time and effort is needed to successfully produce a poinsettia standard, but the rewards at holiday time are worth the effort. The satisfaction derived from a spectacular holiday specimen will not be equalled by any other standard.

Shortcuts and Other Techniques

There are shortcuts and special techniques for producing standards. One possibility is to make a topiary standard using a sphagnum-stuffed ball attached to an artificial stem. The head could be made using the method described on page 76.

The top could also be an empty ball frame welded or bolted to a rod at the chosen height. Be sure to rustproof the metal frame parts to ensure the longest life for the standard. The ball must be securely attached to a sturdy metal trunk. This metal stem must be anchored to the pot. A good method is to use a threaded rod that can be bolted through the bottom of the pot using a small metal plate to help secure and stabilize the topiary. Be sure to fill the pot with sand or cement to counterbalance the top weight.

Think of all the opportunities for combining plants and colors in such a standard. Try an artistic layout of different colors or combine different plant species to obtain sculptured textures.

Ivy balls attached to artificial stems along the flower drive at Longwood.

Mandevilla being woven around the frame by students at Longwood.

In full bloom and on display.

The newly planted and trained mandevilla, now moved outside and coming into bloom.

Plant a vining plant such as ivy or bougainvillea into the pot and train it up and around the same frame. One or more main runners should be tied up the stem. When the plant or plants reach the top, pinch and allow enough breaks to tie one or two new runners to each rib of the frame. As the standard matures, you could allow the foliage to cover the entire head, or you could meticulously prune to keep the vines restricted to the pattern of the frame. This would give the topiary an open and airy appearance.

The Potted Plant in Atlanta, Georgia, makes ivy standards using three runners of juvenile ivy trained up an artificial stem to a ball or umbrella-type frame. The three runners are braided up and around the stem and, as they develop, the metal stake disappears. The foliage is removed from all the lower stems and the vines become woody in a short time. This technique produces standards with lush, full heads from ivy cultivars grown on their own roots. It is quick, easy, and fun.

Commercially, there are only a few growers producing any type of standards in volume. One nursery growing thirty-five thousand standards per year is Allen C. Haskell, Horticulturist, in New Bedford, Massachusetts. Among more than twenty genera he uses for topiary, the most popular are *Eugenia, Myrtus, Rosmarinus, Serissa,* and *Leptospermum scoparium.* The smallest Haskell topiary at present is a 12-inch fuchsia 'Isis'. The largest range from 6- to 8-foot myrtles.

A magnificent hydrangea standard.

Ivy standard with a spiral stem.

a

b

a) Mandevilla trained up the frame.
b) Ivies trained on an umbrella- type frame. Three runners are braided around a stem.

Miniature standards grown by Carole Guyton of Topiary Inc.

Variegated Jerusalem-cherry standards at Longwood.

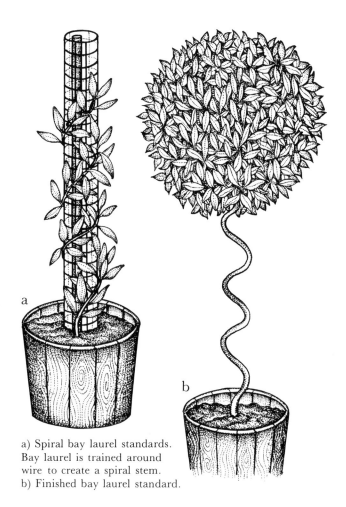

a) Spiral bay laurel standards. Bay laurel is trained around wire to create a spiral stem.
b) Finished bay laurel standard.

Presently, Haskell is developing a new idea for standards. He is creating 5- to 6-foot laurels *(Laurus nobilis)* as spiraled stem standards. The support structure is a piece of PVC pipe, ¾- to 1-inch diameter, placed in a column of wire about 2½ to 3 inches wide. The pipe supports the column of plastic-coated, 1-inch-square wire. As the main stem of the plant grows, it is trained and tied around and up the column. Each tie is spaced according to the counted squares of the wire, and when each standard is finished, the spirals will be uniformly shaped.

After the laurel spiral reaches 5 feet, it is allowed to develop a head. Once the stem has become woody and substantially developed, the framing will be removed, allowing the topiary to be freestanding.

Allen Haskell's secret with topiary standards and, in fact, with all his nursery stock is that each plant gets exactly what it needs. Every cultivar has a special soil mix, using natural materials, prepared at the nursery. Each has its own watering, pruning, and training schedule.

Plants currently grown as Standards at Longwood Gardens

Scientific Name	Common Name
Abutilon hybridum	Flowering-maple
Abutilon pictum 'Aureo-maculatum'	Flowering-maple
Acacia longifolia var. floribunda	Sydney golden wattle
Allamanda cathartica 'Hendersonii'	Allamanda
Bougainvillea glabra 'Penang'	Bougainvillea
Brugmansia suaveolens	Yellow angel's-trumpet
Buddleia alternifolia	Fountain buddleia
Camellia sasanqua 'Yuletide'	Sasanqua camellia
Chrysanthemum x *morifolium*	Chrysanthemum
Chrysanthemum frutescens	Marguerite
x *Citrofortunella microcarpa*	Calamondin
Citrus x *nobilis* 'Temple'	Temple orange
Citrus x *paradisi* 'Marsh'	Grapefruit
Citrus reticulata 'Dancy'	Mandarin orange
Citrus reticulata 'Fairchild'	Mandarin orange
Clerodendrum trichotomum	Harlequin glorybower
Coleus x *hyridus* 'Pineapple Beauty'	Coleus
Cytisus x *spachianus*	Sweet broom
Erica canaliculata	Christmas-heather
* *Euphorbia pulcherrima*	Poinsettia
Evolvulus glomeratus	Blue daze
Fortunella margarita	Oval kumquat
Fuchsia x *hybrida*	Fuchsia
* *Hedera helix*	Ivy
Hydrangea macrophylla	Big leaf hydrangea
Iboza riparia	Iboza
Jasminum mesnyi	Yellow jasmine
Lantana camara	Lantana
Laurus nobilis	Laurel
Malus 'Snowcloud'	Flowering crabapple
Myrtus communis	Myrtle
Nerium oleander 'Sister Agnes'	Oleander
Pachystachys lutea	Golden-candles
Pelargonium x *hortorum* 'Eashum Pink'	Zonal geranium
Pelargonium peltatum 'Rycroft Surprise'	Ivy geranium
Plumbago auriculata	Cape leadwort
Rosa	Hybrid tea rose
Salvia leucantha	Mexican bush sage
Solanum pseudocapsicum 'Variegatum'	Variegated Jerusalem-cherry
Tibouchina urvilleana	Glory bush
Ugni molinae	Chilean guava
Verbena x *hyrida*	Garden verbena
Westringia rosmariniformis	Victorian-rosemary

* Grafted

Variegated ivy wreath which has been grown up from the pot to cover the frame.

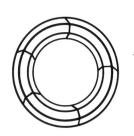

 5. The Wreath

From the earliest times, plant fanciers have been shaping plants and plant products to make wreaths. Wreaths have been used for many purposes, from decorating famous and infamous heads to celebrating happy occasions and commemorating death. Wreath makers have used everything from herbs and vegetables to flowers and thorns to create all sorts of rings. Today, wreaths remain very popular.

Stuffed and Planted Wreath

As with tabletop topiaries, a wire frame, home made or manufactured, holds very moist sphagnum moss into which rooted cuttings are evenly tucked. The secret for securing the moss and plants is to wrap a corded fishing line around the frame and filler. Care must be taken not to restrict the stems of the plants. A good rule is always to wrap the line against the moss and frame but under the plant stems. As the mossed areas are wrapped, the planted root balls will be secured to the wreath. If the cording is wrapped too tightly against stems, they could be broken or their growth restricted.

The wreath will be molded into the desired shape in the process of planting, packing, and tying the moss onto the frame. The amount and consistency of the moss will determine the final thickness of the wreath. It is important to build and shape the wreath evenly.

If a vining plant is selected, pin down the runners. The vine stems should be kept against the sphagnum moss so that it can root into the surface along the stem. All the plants should be pinned in one direction around the circle. This will prevent tangling the longer runners, and the wreath will be more evenly covered.

With stuffed and newly planted material, spraying with water several times for the

118

Living ivy wreath using the stuffed method.

Living wreath of cryptanthus exhibited at the Philadelphia Flower Show.

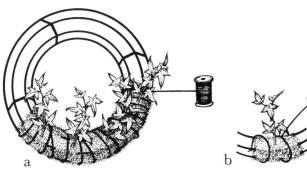

a) Tuck rooted plants into wet moss in the frame and wrap with fish line to hold it all together.
b) Do not wrap the fish line over the stem.

c) Pin the runners down, working in one direction.
d) Close-up - pin runners snugly against the moss.

first few days and even for the first two weeks helps to establish the plants. Watering can be reduced later. Never let the moss dry out completely. If this does occur, soak immediately by totally submerging it in tepid water for several minutes. It may even have to be left for a few hours or overnight. Some plants will not tolerate a total submersion, in which case the underside of the wreath should be laid in water until it has soaked in all it can hold.

The wreath is decorated with fresh herbs.

Fresh flowers and greens make a colorful wreath.

Unrooted - Stuffed and Stuck

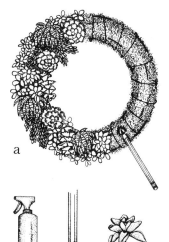

Many plants that can be used for a living wreath do not need to be rooted before planting in the sphagnum moss. Of course, any plant will need to be kept warm (75° F. in most cases) until the roots have formed, and misting over with water several times a day will help the rooting process. A plant that is easy to propagate should be used.

The frame should be filled with firmly packed, wet sphagnum moss and holes poked in the moss with a dibble or pencil to accommodate the cuttings. If possible, the cuttings should be dipped into a recommended strength rooting hormone before being stuck directly into the moss-filled frame. Any loose cuttings can be secured by using fern pins to anchor them into place. Some plants suitable for this method are: ivies, herbs, wintercreeper euonymus, earth-stars (*Cryptanthus*), succulents, cacti, cotula, and ferns.

Trained-Up

The "trained-up" topiary technique discussed previously can also be used to make a wreath. A commercial or home-made frame of wire or natural materials such as grape vine or birch twigs is ideal. The frame should be anchored in the pot with a central supporting stem. When the frame base is positioned at the bottom of the pot, the soil will hold it firmly.

A vining plant is planted in the center near the support stem. A plant with a single runner can be wrapped around the frame in a forward direction or, if the plant is less pliable, tied onto the frame with green or brown string that will not show.

To cover the support on an ivy wreath, use a plant with two to four runners and wrap them around the frame in a spiralling fashion. As the plant matures and the stems become woody, the frames will be completely hidden.

If the plant has more than one runner when it has reached the wreath, they should be separated into opposite directions. As they grow, continue to tie them until they meet. When the topiary is well covered, pinch off the tips of the plant runners. This usually causes most plants to break new growth along the runner, and the wreath will gain in thickness. Using more than one plant in the pot is a form of insurance. If one

a) Moss-filled wreath with unrooted cuttings.
b) Spray, pencil, and unrooted cutting.
c) Unrooted cuttings anchored with fern pins.

a) Basic wreath frame with stem and base anchor for trained-up wreath.
b) Train the potted vine up and around the frame.
c) Secure the vines by loosely tying with string.

plant should die, there is still another to continue around the circle and fill in the wreath.

Meticulous pinching and pruning keep the wreath in shape. Pay particular attention to the inner circle to maintain a neat outline.

A frame of natural material can be attractive in its own right if covered with a small and slow-growing plant. A vigorous plant should be regularly pruned, sometimes by removing new runners, so as not to hide the frame completely.

Wreath shapes can be circular, multi-circular, egg-shaped, or even geometric. A heart-shaped grapevine wreath, covered with the heart-shaped ivy *Hedera helix* 'Deltoidia', is a favorite at Longwood.

Oasis® Wreath

Garden centers often stock Oasis® wreaths, either in a plastic frame or on a plastic base, or wreaths of just Oasis® (see page 128.) Oasis® has tremendous water-holding capacity.

To make a wreath of Oasis®, soak it until it is saturated. Make cuttings of whatever material you choose and stick them into the wreath. Arrange these sprigs closely together to fill the wreath. Try fresh herbs, ivy, boxwood, holly, or any evergreen. Many will root so that the wreath can be kept fresh and alive for an extended period of time. Water regularly as for a fresh floral arrangement. If the material has rooted into Oasis®, water regularly and soak it every few weeks in a very dilute liquid fertilizer. Try decorating it with fresh flowers, fruit, berries, ribbons, strings of beads, and holiday ornaments.

Another common wreath is a fresh flower arrangement. Fill the Oasis® with cut flowers and greens. It makes an ideal centerpiece for the party table or around the base of a punch bowl, as a candle ring or even a hanging decoration.

The fresh herbal wreath will keep a long time, and bits of herbs can be used for cooking while you still enjoy the decoration. It makes an excellent gift for a dinner hostess!

A heart-shaped frame covered with *Hedera helix* 'Deltoidea'.

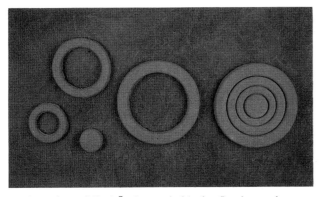

Various sizes of Oasis® rings suitable for floral wreaths.

A floral-foam wreath filled with unrooted herb cuttings.

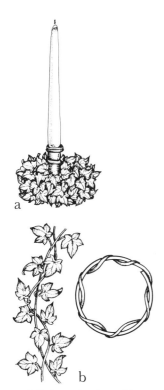

a) Mini-candle ring of ivy.
b)The vines are braided together without a wire frame. The ring size should be proportional to candle height.

Floral wreath with candle by Sharon Fisher of Longwood.

Wire Wreath, Kissing Balls, and May Garland

The vine-wrapped wire wreath is made with a piece of 9-gauge wire or a wire coat-hanger shaped into a circle. Cut long runners of ivy or other vining evergreens and soak them in lukewarm water for several hours or overnight. After removing the runners from the water and allowing them to dry, dip them in Johnson's clear floor wax to preserve the foliage. (Longwood, after trying many different solutions, has found that clear floor wax is the best.) Other floor waxes work but you will need to experiment. Wrap the vine around the wire while it is still wet and flexible. Allow the wreath to dry. It may be preferable to dip the entire wreath after it has been made, if it will fit into the dipping tub and if all foliage will be completely covered with wax. It will last three to six weeks. This method can be used for other shapes such as garlands, kissing balls, candle rings, and even table garlands. Try mini-wreaths as napkin rings or as a distinctive band for a straw garden hat.

Another twist to this idea comes from John Enterline, Director of Operations at Conestoga House, Lancaster, PA. After soaking ivy in water for at least two to three

Ivy kissing ball.

a

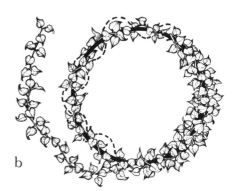

b

a) Use more than one vine for a fuller wreath.
b) Wrap or braid around the wire frame.

Right: A base of dried artemisia decorated with dried material in contrasting colors - made by Caprilands Herb Farm, Coventry, Connecticut.
Left: Another Caprilands wreath.

hours and allowing it to dry completely, he sprays the whole wreath with gold paint - a modern interpretation of Victorian gilded ivy. Alternatively, a cluster of gold leaves, as an accent point among the greens, could be used instead.

Dried

Dried flower wreaths are usually made from flowers specifically grown for drying, such as strawflowers *(Helichrysum bracteatum)*, globe amaranth *(Gomphrenia globosa)*, cockscomb *(Celosia cristata)*, and thistle. After the flowers have been harvested and allowed to dry naturally, they are ready to add to a wreath. A base that works well is the pre-made straw ring. This comes in several sizes. The flowers are hot-glued on to cover all the visible surface.

Dried fruit wreaths are made the same way but the fruit is dried differently. Cut

Dried flowers hot-glued to a straw base.

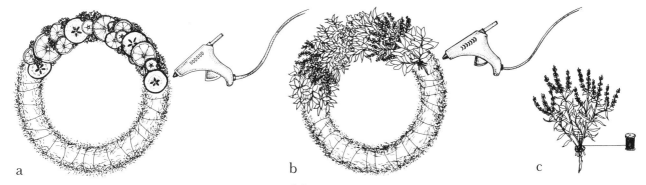

a) Dried cross-sections of fruit hot-glued to straw wreath base.
b) Hot-glue dried herbs to a straw wreath base
c) Tie a bunch of fresh herbs to a stick and hot-glue the stick to the wreath base.

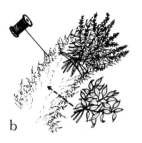

a) Tie dried herbs to an artemisia wreath base.
b) Positioning the herbs onto the base.

the fruit in cross-section slices and place the pieces on a screen in an oven at a very low temperature to dry. Usually the lowest temperature setting is best, and in a gas oven the heat from the pilot light will do the job. This process could take from one to three days. Food dryers used for preserving food also work well, but always follow the manufacturer's directions. During drying, turn the fruit slices occasionally. Some suitable fruits for drying are oranges, pineapples, apples, lemons, limes, bananas, pears, and raisins. Dried flowers and nuts in shells can be added for decoration to fruit wreaths.

Both types of wreaths should be sprayed with plastic to help preserve the materials and discourage insects. There are two major methods for making herb wreaths, one using materials already dried, the other using fresh materials that are allowed to dry on the wreath. Pre-dried herbs can be hot-glued to a natural base like straw or artemisia, or bunches of herbs can be tied or wired to a frame. Colors and scents can be combined according to personal preference, and each wreath can be designed with a specific need in mind. Many skilled herbalists simply wire clusters and sprigs of herbs together and shape the wreath in the process. It takes practice to achieve a perfectly symmetrical wreath.

Fresh herbs, too, can be shaped into wreaths using the methods just described. Some modification may be needed for hot-gluing fresh materials. One method is to tie fresh herbs to a woody twig, which can then be glued to a natural base. Otherwise, simply tie the fresh herbs to the base without glue. All fresh wreaths made to dry must hang in a natural position with good air circulation.

Cut Greens

At Longwood each December, highly skilled wreath makers set aside their regular horticultural duties and go into mass production of cut evergreen wreaths. About two hundred are made annually. For several years all the wreath bases were handmade of evergreens from the grounds. Now almost all the bases are bought and finished at Longwood to save time and money and to conserve plant material. It has been estimated that one pick-up truck load of greens is needed for fifteen to twenty wreaths!

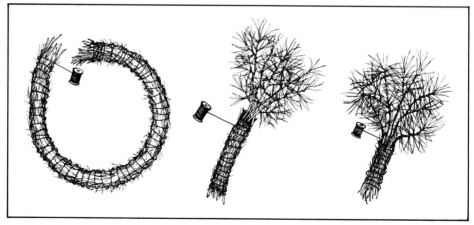

A handmade wreath base made from stems of evergreens tightly wrapped and shaped into a circle.

124

For those who would like to start from scratch and create the entire wreath, make the base from stems of greens tightly wrapped and shaped into a circle. Use 9-gauge wire and bind into a circle until you have reached the desired size then fasten the ends together with florist wire (about 20- to 22-gauge.) Leave the spool of florist wire attached to the wreath base until the wreath is completed. Suitable plant materials for the wreath base are arborvitae, hemlock, yew, straw, hay, or twigs. For the homeowner, using prunings of the least desirable evergreens would probably be best, saving the choicest ones for the top decoration or face of the wreath. Before you start making the wreath, consider its location. If it is to hang on the front door, make it to scale, and if a storm door will be covering it, consider the thickness. The base may need to be thin to accommodate plump decorations and ornaments.

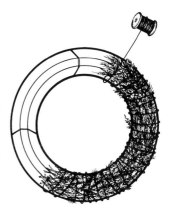

Leave the wire attached to the spool.

Take a handful of tightly bunched base material and begin wrapping it to the frame with the florist wire, keeping to the original shape of the heavy wire outline. The greens will look as though they are covered with a net of wire. Continue around the wire until the base is completed. Control the thickness of the wreath by the size of the bunches being added to the wire.

With the 20- to 22-gauge florist wire still attached to the base, start adding the top or final greens. Lay three or four pieces about 8 inches long (if too long they droop) on top of the base and fasten the stems to the wreath base. With the attached wire, continue this method, overlapping the first bunch and always going in the same direction. The top bunches should always overlap the previous addition by one-half to two-thirds. Wire only the stem ends to the base. The top greens should be free and natural in appearance. When you reach the spot where you started, lift the first bunch and lay the final bunch under it and against the base, wrapping the ends securely. Tie off the wire on the back side of the wreath.

For a two-sided wreath, repeat the above steps for the back. Try to line up the stem ends with the completed side. (Wrap the ends with the florist wire, taking care to lift and wrap the wire under the greens on the completed side.) Both sides should remain loose and free. Two people working together can each do one side at the same time.

Leaving the wire attached to the spool for the entire procedure makes the finished product much neater and more secure. There will not be several wire ends sticking

a) Lay the greens onto the base and tie on the stem ends with wire.
b) Overlap the previous bunch with the next. Overlap the final bunch with the first.
c) Tie off the wire in the back. Leave a loop for hanging the finished wreath.
d) For a double-faced wreath, repeat the process on the other side.

A 10-inch Christmas wreath, with ivy growing up from the pot.

Cut green wreath decorating the Horticultural Building at Longwood.

out all around the wreath. Considerable time will be saved as there is no need to re-attach the wire with each step.

Suitable top greens are spruce, holly, pine, or any other evergreen with colors ranging from bright blues to dark forest greens. Try combining different colors and textures. By wrapping wire tightly around arborvitae stems, the greens will stand up and give a fluffy appearance. Hemlock is the only plant material Longwood's experts do not recommend. Hemlock will lose needles within two or three days if the temperature is above freezing. Holly drops leaves rapidly indoors but is fine outdoors. Do a little testing before finalizing the wreath material.

There are products on the market to help preserve wreaths made of freshly cut greens. At Longwood, wax, shellac, floral spray, and hair spray have been tried. Nothing has prolonged the life of a wreath more than a few days and most treatments change the natural appearance. Longwood does not treat any cut green wreaths.

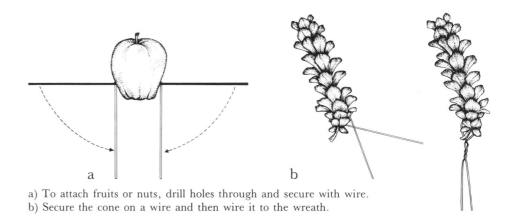

a) To attach fruits or nuts, drill holes through and secure with wire.
b) Secure the cone on a wire and then wire it to the wreath.

Ivy wreaths exhibited at the Philadelphia Flower Show.

Ideas for trimming are endless. Decorations can range from colonial-style fruit to shiny Christmas ornaments. At Longwood, wreaths are decorated with fresh fruit and nuts. (Attach by drilling holes through each and wiring securely.) Cones of white pine cut into cross sections look like little stars or wooden flowers. Waxed fruit has been tried but it looks artificial; the fruit is usually replaced as needed. Try decorating with berries or conifer cones. There are many ornamental plants that have beautiful fruits available during the winter months, such as winterberry *(Ilex verticillata)* and dogwood. Seed pods are plentiful during the colder months. Dried flowers and herbs are perfect for decorating.

Homemade wreaths are always special. Each can be shaped and decorated to perfectly suit your needs. Remember that wreaths can be for any occasion and for any time of the year.

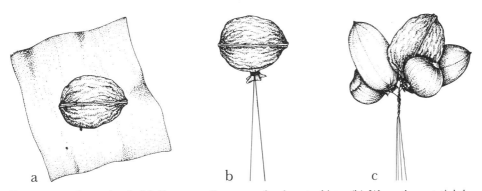

For nuts an alternative is (a) Cut a small square of nylon stocking, (b) Wrap the nut tightly and secure with a thin wire, (c) Nuts can be bunched together and added to the wreath.

6. Specialty Topiaries

Topiaries and Flowers

Historically, florists and floral arrangements have influenced portable pre-formed topiaries. The Victorians created arrangements for funerals and other occasions by shaping chicken wire, filling it with wet moss, and adding cut flowers. Although such floral topiaries have been more fashionable at some times than others over the past one -hundred years, they have never disappeared completely.

Traditionally, florists have used the term "topiary" for the floral bouquet arranged on top of a stem. Many people would think of this as a floral standard, consisting of one or two spheres mounted on a stem of natural branches, wooden dowels, plastic, or steel. This design is now very popular and has been created in many styles, from a very formal sphere to loose-flowing and almost abstract shapes.

Topiary in many forms has become part of the floral arts world. Topiary figures have been used as containers for floral arrangements and sometimes topiary creatures have been made entirely of flowers and cut greens. Flowers and topiary together are important elements of design.

Basic supplies and tools needed for floral topiary are:

Wire	Wire-cutters
Floral stem tape (such as Oasis® tape)	Pruners
Floral foam	Scissors
Chicken wire	Floral adhesives
Sharp knife	Floral spray

Floral Foam

Over the past thirty years, Oasis® (floral foam) has given every floral designer the answer to the biggest problem - keeping flowers in place. Flowers can be kept fresh and beautiful for days by using a foam block that holds fifty times its own weight in water.

Oasis® is available in regular or instant brick-sized shapes. Instant Oasis® absorbs water quickly and is saturated in one minute; the regular form is slower. Soak the brick in a bucket until it sinks to the bottom or under slowly running water until it is saturated and ready to use. It can be left in water until needed. Once wet, never let Oasis® dry out, as it is difficult to re-wet completely.

It is easier to cut or shape Oasis® while it is dry, and there is less chance of breakage. Use a sharp knife and wear a dust mask if working with large quantities to avoid breathing in the fine foam particles.

To secure Oasis® to a container do not use wire or string which will cut through wet foam; florist's tape is the answer. To coax maximum life from flowers, soak Oasis® in water treated with floral preservatives. Never stick a flower into an old hole in the foam since air pockets form and the flower may not receive water.

Oasis® is available in different densities to suit the strengths of various flower stems. Choose flowers for topiary with good quality, sturdy stems. In many cases the entire shape of the topiary depends on this. Choose a good all-purpose Oasis® .

Sahara® has been created for dried flower and foliage arrangements and is much stiffer. Both Oasis® and Sahara® are trade names that have become generic within the industry, but several other brands are available. This book does not intend to indicate that one brand is superior to another.

Flowers

When choosing flowers, consider the color, texture, form, size, and, most importantly, quality. The flowers should be fresh; old flowers do not last. Fresh flowers with sturdy long stems are ideal.

Pick flowers that are long lasting, with blooms that hold up an average of four to five days once cut. Flower size is important. It should be compatible with the size of the frame, i.e., small blooms for small characters and so forth. Depending on the topiary planned, the flower form should complement the shape. If you are making a small creature on a wire frame, choose a flat simple bloom that will cover but not disguise the shape. Rounded or three-dimensional blooms can be used on larger shapes but be sure the topiary is suitable. Also, flowers with fuller shapes can be combined with flat blooms to give depth and accent to a figure. Texture is important, so do not mix very fine and very coarse flowers together but, rather, use a gradual blend of fine with medium texture or medium with coarse.

Colors should interpret the topiary but also blend with or match the color schemes of the room. In the home where the normal light is dim, use light colors. If the display will be spot lighted, use bright colors. Consider the size of the room. Cool colors such as greens, blues, and purples tend to disappear in large rooms; hot colors like pinks, reds, and oranges would be best in these circumstances. Color can be an important accent. Bright blue bachelor's-buttons down the front of a dress created with white chrysanthemums were stunning on Longwood's swinging girl. Yellow yarrow flowers made excellent hair, both in texture and color.

Fresh flowers used for topiary arrangements must be "hardened off" to ensure the longest possible bloom life. Remove all foliage from the stem and make a fresh angle cut at the bottom of the stem with a sharp knife. Place the stems in 6 to 8 inches of water treated with a floral preservative twenty-four hours before using. As each flower is used, re-cut the stem, on an angle, to the length needed.

Floral Standards

Start the frame by attaching a stem to a sturdy base, then anchor it securely by filling the container with concrete to within 1 inch of the rim. The stem could be a wooden dowel, metal rod, or something natural such as white birch branches and can be formed by twisting or braiding two or more stems together.

Decide on the correct height of the topiary for the size of the display room. A dinner table centerpiece should rise only slightly above eye level so that you will be able to see your guests across the table. A side table or pedestal topiary should be one-third of the distance between tabletop and ceiling. If used for weddings, it should fit the scale of the church yet not obstruct any view. When used on either side of an entrance, it should be in scale with the door.

Pre-made, commercially available Oasis®—filled cages can be attached to the top of the stem. Cages are easily made by attaching two cross-pieces such as popsicle sticks to the top of the stem, setting a cube of floral foam on top of the braced area, and covering it with chicken wire. The chicken wire cage keeps the Oasis® from splitting apart during construction. Soak the Oasis® first, as it is very awkward to wet once the frame is constructed.

The foam cube should not be too small or it will come apart when you add flowers. If it is too large, the flower arrangement will become top heavy and fall over. The size

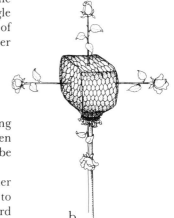

a) Push the styrofoam top onto the stem. Use the first four flowers as markers to set the line. They should be evenly spaced, vertically and horizontally.

b) A chicken wire cage fixed around the Oasis® will prevent it from disintegrating when flowers are pushed into it.

Another fresh flower standard. The spiral stand is anchored to a base decorated with greenery.

Charming example of a standard with fresh greenery and flowers decorating the head. The antique plant pot completes the arrangement.

Large leaves being pinned to an Oasis® base. The finished decoration will hide the base completely.

Head detail from the completed standard opposite.

130

Fresh flowers and greenery are used to decorate this delightful standard. The rustic stem and clay pot are an excellent combination.

of the final arrangement can be adjusted by the stem length of the flowers. When the frame is constructed, start the arrangement by putting in four flowers or stems of greens to set the perimeters of the arrangement. The four markers should be evenly spaced, vertically and horizontally. Always fill in the greens first, mindful of the pre-set boundaries, covering all the Oasis® and other mechanics. Then add the flowers, keeping the arrangement well balanced and natural looking. The arrangement should appear pleasing from all sides. These "floral topiaries" may take on any shape, from very formal, tight balls to loose, open arrangements.

Using more than one sphere is also possible. Again, add Oasis® to the proper location and secure by cross braces and chicken wire. The spheres should be equally spaced along the stem and can be any size (from 4 inches to 6 feet!) as long as they are in proportion to the setting.

Stems can be made of anything that will do the job. They can be perfectly straight or spiralling but should not be so distinctive as to take attention away from the rest of the topiary. Wild flowers can be complemented by twigs and vines that are informal and relaxed. A modern design may need a metal swirling stem that is painted to match the flowers or theme. Often you can accent a mundane metal rod with vines and greens. A wooden stem can be covered with mosses, grasses, and other materials by gluing or by tying with raffia.

The base area can be treated in as many ways as the stem. Use something compatible with the topiary style. Modern designs are attractive, with black pebbles filling the recessed area and covering the cement, or a more rustic covering of mosses or lichens. Even the container can be covered or placed in a slightly larger, decorative pot.

Developing an arrangement of flowers at the base will cover the mechanics, soften the topiary, and carry through the theme. If this is your choice, leave a deeper recess in the base to add floral foam. Anchor the foam with Oasis® tape.

At the Cottage Garden in Atlanta, Georgia, topiaries made entirely of vegetables have accented outdoor barbecue parties. Fresh kale, carrots, red beans, garlic, mushrooms, onions, squash, and ears of corn were used. The vegetables were wired to a moss-covered styrofoam ball attached to a wooden dowel. The stem was wrapped with green corn husks, with greens and more vegetables at the base. These casual vegetable towers were adapted from the same classic style used for formal occasions.

In January 1989, over two hundred floral designers volunteered to help prepare for America's biggest party — the Presidential Inaugural in Washington, D.C. Apart from the fresh flower decorations, topiary arrangements from 4 to 12 feet tall were included. About eighteen-thousand red roses were used to make more than four dozen 48-inch spheres that lavishly decorated the Kennedy Center. The spheres rested on top of 8-foot columns draped with fabric. Crowning each arrangement was a 3-foot golden eagle.

Dried Topiary

The frame structure for a dried topiary is the same as for a standard. Use the Sahara® floral foam (for dried flowers). You may need to wire the dried flowers onto a wooden stick to give them a sturdy stem, or tape the blooms onto small twigs or stems. Try to bunch dried filler flowers together on a stick. This will make fewer holes in the stiff foam and reduce chances of breaking.

It is harder to achieve the rounded shape of a sphere from dried flowers. Again, set the boundaries and work to keep the rounded shape. Use filler flowers to cover the mechanics.

Styrofoam balls attached to the top of the stem can be used for dried designs. Push the ball directly onto the stem, but fasten something to the stem to keep the ball from sliding down. Push the stake all the way through the ball only if more than one ball is used for the topiary. Flowers and other dried materials can be applied with hot glue.

When using hot-glue guns:

1. Buy one with a kick stand to hold the gun in an upright position.
2. Never lay a hot gun on its side, otherwise the casing fills with glue.
3. Clear glue dries clear.
4. Heat up time is five to ten minutes.
5. It's ready to use when the glue makes cobwebs.
6. Hot glue burns fingers!

Decide what flowers will go where before you begin to glue. Always apply the glue to the styrofoam and then add the flowers. This will reduce the risk of burning your fingers. If gluing flowers onto a topiary with several spheres, work from the top down so that dripping does not damage the completed work. For potpourri, use a spray adhesive on the styrofoam and then roll the latter in the potpourri.

Once the dry topiary is done, apply a protective spray formulated for dried materials. This will preserve the flowers and help hold everything together.

Dried arrangements on a stem do not have to be strictly spherical; styrofoam can be purchased in other shapes or cut up with a sharp knife. Carve out a giant tulip, daisy, or star – the design is up to you.

An endless assortment of material is available for dried crafts. A popular creation is a cinnamon stick tree made by layering pieces of cinnamon on a styrofoam cone like shingles on a roof. These dried topiaries are long lasting and can be easily rejuvenated with a few new flowers and decorations.

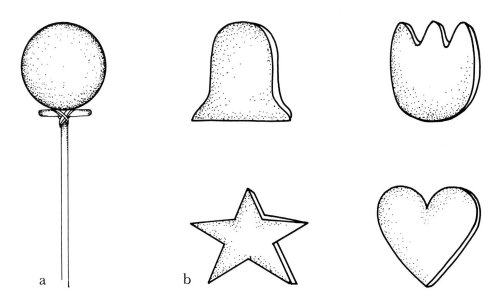

a) Attach a stop onto the stem to keep the topiary in place.
b) Suggestions for other shapes for dried topiary standards.

Lycopodium (sheared).

Dried celosia.

Lycopodium (sheared).

Three charming examples of dried standards using various plant materials and differently styled containers.

Cut floral foam into pieces and stuff into frame. Trim off protruding edges by running a thin wire over the frame's outline.

Mushroom wire frames stuffed with Oasis® and decorated with fresh flowers.

Wire-Frame Floral Topiaries

Secure the foam in the frame with Oasis® tape or plastic-coated twist-ties.

The same topiary frame that is used for living vine-covered figures can be filled with Oasis® and covered with fresh flowers. For a first project, choose a frame that has simple lines. A character with tiny legs and arms will be particularly difficult to fill with flowers and still retain the shape. Cut dry Oasis® into pieces that can be stuffed into the frame snugly. Start with the thinnest areas first. Do not worry about corners or edges of floral foam sticking out. After the frame is filled, trim off the excess by pulling a flexible wire (18- to 22-gauge) over the frame outline and shaving off any extra Oasis® . Small cracks between the Oasis® chunks, if not too large, will be covered by the flowers.

The best way to secure Oasis® to the frame is with Oasis® tape or plastic-coated twist-ties. Uncoated wire or string will cut through the foam after it is wet and heavy.

Once the frame is stuffed and secured, soak it in water. Allow the Oasis® to absorb as much water as possible. Follow previous directions for preparing flowers and Oasis® to get the most out of this short-term creation.

The delightful girl on the swing is suspended in the rose arbor at Longwood. This Oasis®
filled frame topiary is decorated with fresh flowers – chrysanthemum, yarrow, rose buds,
and strawflowers. Her arms, legs, and face are covered with sheet moss.

Three stages in shaping the Oasis® for the base of the floral fish.

The Oasis® is now horizontal and the fresh flowers are being added to the fish form.

Start adding flowers to the thinnest part of the figure first. The healthiest blooms with short stems should be used in areas where there is the least amount of Oasis®. Make fresh cuts on each stem as you use them, and when pushing them into the thin areas avoid jamming the stems through the other side of the foam. The foam will vary in thickness and the stem length should vary accordingly. The flower must have a constant supply of water, so make sure the Oasis® is saturated and the stem makes good contact.

The flowers should fit closely to the frame unless they are highlights, accents, or decorations. The entire shape will disappear if the flowers are too large or the texture is too coarse. Covering the skinny areas first will set the proportions of the topiary, and the rest of the design should fall into place. Start with flowers and foliage that are the dominant materials, then add the accent and trim flowers.

Spray finished floral topiary with an anti-desiccant. There is also a spray available to help prevent petals from shattering.

Check the floral topiaries every day for water and treat them like any other fresh floral arrangement. If the design allows, it would be easiest to set the Oasis® bottom into a tray of water to absorb the maximum amount. Topiaries that do not have an accessible base should be taken to an area where they can drip, and water should be gently added to the Oasis®. Try to avoid getting the flower petals wet. Once Oasis® becomes dry, it is difficult to re-wet. Old Oasis® should never be re-used for topiary pieces because it never has the same water-holding capacity, and there is the risk of air pockets in old holes.

Floral Topiary Without a Frame

These are usually small topiaries made from a single block of Oasis®. Extra pieces can be added by using reinforcing dowels to hold the foam parts together. The weight of wet Oasis® will restrict the size of a free-form Oasis® topiary.

Create the dry foam shape with a sharp knife. Wear a dust mask when cutting large quantities of dry foam. The shape should be proportionately reduced so that after the flowers and greens are added the finished size will be correct.

Soak the shape as suggested above for the Oasis®—filled frame. When it is saturated, add the flowers and foliage. The basic body shape is usually designed with flowers and greens, but appendages can be created by more stylized use of plant materials. Bird wings could be formed by adding plumes of grass or feather-like foliage.

General care is the same as for Oasis® in a frame. Since there is no supporting wire frame, this style is more fragile. The topiary should be planned so that the weight is supported by the main body.

Feathery greenery completes the tail and fins.

A fish bowl, glass marbles, spikey leaves, and the floral fish. Plants used: statice, yarrow, globe amaranth, arborvitae.

The Boxwood Tree

Among traditional decorations created each year by florists across the country are boxwood Christmas trees. To build one, stand a block of Oasis® upright in a shallow container not much wider than the block. Secure the foam with two long pieces of Oasis® tape fastened to the container and over the block. The top corners can be shaved down to help in the shaping, but it is not absolutely necessary to do this. Cut a small pie-shaped wedge from the bottom of the Oasis® as an opening for adding water after the tree is finished.

Use pieces of boxwood (or other evergreens) to set the tree lines: one vertical stem for the top of the tree and four (one on each side) as a guideline at the bottom. Visualize a line from top to bottom for your outline.

Fill in with greens from the bottom and work towards the top. The base-line greens should slant slightly downward to cover the container. The tree should look full but not stuffed! As you are building upward, keep the lines of the tree in mind. Some trimming may be needed when complete.

Several variations are possible in shape and size. Combine different greens for interest and decorate with natural berries, seeds, nuts, bows, ribbons, or tiny ornaments. Keep the tree watered and it should last through the holiday season.

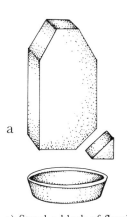

a) Stand a block of floral foam upright in a shallow container and secure with tape. Shave top corners to give shape. Cut small, wedge-shaped corner from bottom.

From left to right: The Oasis® in container with the first outline of boxwood positioned. The shape is now completely covered by box. The last stage shows the finished tree with all the decoration: red bows, cinnamon sticks, and gold balls.

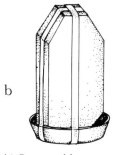

b) Secure with tape to the container.

Ivy umbrella for a grand yearly event: The Garden Party at Longwood Gardens. Ivy *Hedera helix* 'Shamrock'.

Topiary as Containers

An ivy-covered basket that holds a blooming plant is probably the most familiar topiary container. A space is left open when building the topiary by adding an empty pot and building around the reserved area, or by incorporating this space into the wire frame. Baskets in all shapes and styles are now available. Pier 39, in San Francisco, often exhibits a giant ivy basket the size of a small bathtub filled with an array of colorful annuals. Ivy watering buckets hold blooming plants, branches of flowering shrubs, or large floral arrangements. In Atlanta, a 5-foot ivy champagne glass often filled with hundreds of tiny balloons for special occasions stands in a private garden. This topiary has also served as the pedestal for some grand floral exhibitions.

Longwood has two swans about 30 inches long with openings in their backs. Clay pots are recessed to their rims in these openings. A watertight container is placed in the pot, then foam is added to hold the floral arrangement in the topiary.

With container topiaries, keep the Oasis® high so flowers branch around the entire topiary and the arrangement can be viewed from all sides. The flowers should be kept in scale and not overpower the container.

Other special container topiaries include sitting monkeys holding candlesticks. A small swan with a fountain is perfect for a buffet centerpiece that could incorporate flowers, fruits, or vegetables.

Small tabletop topiary animals can be further decorated by pushing a few fresh flowers into the moss filler. Water tubes hidden in the foliage will increase the life of fresh blooms. An ivy kangaroo with a small wedge of floral foam tucked into the pouch could accommodate a few fresh flowers.

Floral Umbrella

Longwood has developed its own version of the ever-popular floral umbrella designed to hold an 8-inch hanging pot of ivy with long runners at the top. Each runner is tied down one rib of the umbrella. After the ribs are covered with live runners, long ivy streamers are cut from greenhouse stockpots and attached to the main stem of the frame with green twist-ties. The final decorations are fresh blooms glued onto the umbrella. The flowers and cut ivies are temporary but can be added when needed. The topiary umbrella can remain covered with living ivy, which is easy to maintain

Living ivy-covered swan with cut flowers added for decoration.

A rose, boxwood, and apple standard displayed among the rosebeds in the Rose House at Longwood.

since it is in a pot. If space is limited, remove the vining plant, store the frame, and maintain it as a hanging basket until the umbrella is needed again.

You can use the frame of an old, discarded umbrella by removing the fabric and positioning the ribs open. The umbrella is then secured into a container and a vining specimen is planted and trained up to cover the frame. It will take several months to get a good plant cover.

Flowers

Scentific Name	Common Name
Achillea	Yarrow
Allium sphaerocephalum	Drumstick allium
Ageratum houstonianum	Ageratum
Anaphalis spp.	Everlasting
Aster novi-belgii	Michaelmas daisy
Carthamus tinctorius	Safflower
Celosia cristata	Cockscomb, Celosia
Centaurea cyanus	Bachelor's-button
Chrysanthemum x morifolium	Chrysanthemum
Cynara scolymus	Globe artichoke
Eryngium alpinum	Eryngium
Helichrysum bracteatum	Strawflower
Limonium latifolium	Sea-lavender
Limonium sinuatum	Statice
Nigella damascena	Love-in-a-mist
Rudbeckia hirta	Black-eyed Susan
Scabiosa caucasica	Scabiosa
Solidago spp.	Goldenrod
Trachelium caeruleum	Trachelium
Trachymene coerulea	Blue laceflower

Foliage

Scientific Name	Common Name
Ammi majus	Whitelace flower
Banksia spp.	Banksia
Buxus sempervirens	Boxwood
Codiaeum variegatum	Croton
Eucalyptus cinerea	Silver dollar eucalyptus
Foeniculum vulgare 'Purpureum'	Bronze fennel
Galax urceolata	Galax
Hedera helix	Ivy
Lycopodium spp.	Clubmoss

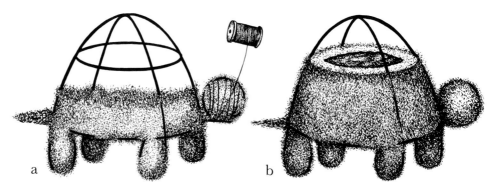

a) Stuff the frame with wet sphagnum moss and secure with fish line.

b) The body area can be filled with soilless potting mix.

Moss Topiary

Often in garden shops you will see wire frame topiaries stuffed with sphagnum moss without living plants. These topiaries are left unplanted so that gardeners can choose the plant coverings. Occasionally, the moss-filled figures are used just as they are without any green plants, or with nothing more than a bow for decoration. Combinations of half-planted and half-moss topiaries can be very effective.

At Carter's Grove in Colonial Williamsburg, Virginia, moss topiaries have been used as part of the holiday decor. One theme focused on fox hunting. A small, ivy-clad horse stood on the hearth among poinsettias, and moss-filled fox heads hung from the brick wall, each decorated with red plaid bows.

Moss-filled topiaries can be displayed and then stored away just as they are, awaiting the next occasion. Caring for these is similar to caring for a dried flower arrangement, and the plantless creations can be used on the finest furniture without danger of water damage.

To make a moss topiary, moisten sphagnum until thoroughly soaked and stuff the entire frame, packing it tightly. Secure the moss by wrapping with a clear, lightweight monofilament fish line. The finished topiary need not be watered.

If the topiary is to be planted, the body area can be filled with a soilless potting mix at the time of stuffing. When you are ready to plant, soak the entire topiary in warm water until it is saturated. Make a hole in the body and insert the roots of the plant into the soil filling. After it is planted, the topiary should be cared for like any stuffed figure.

Sphagnum-filled frames can be covered with sheet moss then wrapped with clear fishing line or invisible thread. If wrapped snugly, the sheet moss will form a skin-like covering. Cover the small areas first, such as limbs on animal figures, then continue on to the larger areas. It may be necessary to go back and fill in small spots with bits of the sheet moss to cover the frame completely.

The sheet-moss-covered topiary can be planted just as you would plant the sphagnum-filled variety. Maintenance is also the same.

Sheet moss comes both in natural sheets and with artificial backing. For planted topiaries, use the natural sheets. The artificial backing is usually a loosely woven material, but for best results don't use it if water will be needed to penetrate through to the roots.

Attractive effects can be created by planting special areas on moss-filled and covered topiaries. A good example is Barbara Gallup's lion orchestra. The lions were

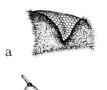

a) Sheet moss with artificial backing.
b) Cover hollow frame with chicken wire and hot-glue sheet moss onto wire.

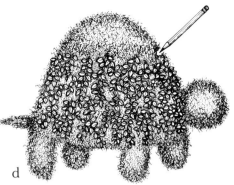

c) Cover the filled topiary with sheet moss and wrap with clear fish line.

d) Turtle frame covered in sphagnum moss with creeping fig for eventual cover.

e) To plant, make a hole in the form and insert the root area of the plant into the soil or wet moss.

completely covered with sheet moss and only the manes were planted with a vigorous green and gold ivy, 'Gold Child'.

There are several other materials that could be used to fill a frame, such as styrofoam or newspaper. Hollow frames can be covered with poultry wire or aviary netting and then enclosed in sheet moss. For hollow topiaries, it is best to use sheet moss with an artificial backing.

Longwood's monkeys from the 1987 Safari display were all made of sheet moss. A 36-inch monkey took about five hours to make. Our method was to hot-glue sheet moss directly onto the empty frame. The glue was applied to the frame and nylon-backed sheet moss was then stretched over it. Small pieces of moss were used, since the glue dried fast. The moss had to be stretched and fitted so that the shape of the monkey was not lost. Some areas, especially the long, skinny tails, were tedious and time-consuming to do.

Since the hot glue seeped through the moss, wooden spoons had to be used to press the moss down onto the frame. Our monkeys probably could have been constructed more quickly had the largest openings in the frame been covered with wire first, thus creating more surface area for gluing the moss. It was important to keep the moss pulled tightly over the frame so that the animal shape was not lost.

To keep dry moss green, spray it occasionally with a solution of green and yellow food coloring, or use commercial floral sprays. Sheet moss can also be purchased live in some areas. To use the live moss, keep the topiary moist; care and maintenance are the same as for any other living plant topiary.

Try more than one type of moss for topiary projects. One that has been very successful at Longwood is Spanish-moss *(Tillandsia usneoides)*. We have used it living and dried. The living moss is more flexible and less dusty. It is suitable for hair, mustaches, dragons' whiskers, and even an entire 6-foot-tall elephant.

On small areas, such as for dragons' whiskers, the long strands of moss are wrapped onto the frame and shaped with "invisible" thread. Larger characters made of Spanish-moss require more effort. The elephant started with a basic steel frame covered with chicken wire a little area at a time. Each cell in the wire was then plugged with a handful of moss from the inside. The moss was poked through, leaving about one-third on the back side to hold it in place. The moss was fluffed on the outside to cover the wire and to look uniform. This project required a huge amount of Spanish-moss, and finding a source was difficult.

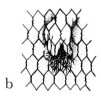

a) Cover the metal frame with chicken wire.
b) Plug each cell of the wire with Spanish-moss. Plug from the inside and fluff from the outer surface.

Easter rabbits covered in sphagnum moss.

The Tarantula is decorated with dried sweetgum seed pods, and dried flowers.

Mia Hardcastle of Topiary Inc. designed and made this moss-stuffed chimpanzee for Jane Goodall.

Turkey made of dried material in 1984 for display at Longwood Gardens.

A realistic-looking little owl decorated entirely with dried plant material.

Dried Topiaries

Dried flowers, fruit, pine cones, and nuts have often been used for craft projects displayed at Longwood, including topiaries. Most of the materials come from the garden.

There are some very practical reasons why dried topiaries could be the best choices for specific situations. Once completed, they require minimal maintenance. Not only are they good for areas where topiaries cannot be watered, but they work in spots without sunlight. Moreover, dried flowers are an important method for adding color to topiary. Dried topiary can be built using regular topiary frames or frames modified to accommodate dried materials. Intricate designs using individual dried flower petals may require special frame designs.

To add dried flowers to a regular topiary, it is necessary to modify the frame and add a base to which the flowers can be glued. Grapevine, for example, can be gathered while it is still flexible, woven in and around the wire frame, and allowed to dry a few days. Longwood's Garden of Oz in 1986 included a hot-air balloon and Toto's basket which were both wire frames woven with grapevine without any other decoration.

A frame to be decorated should include enough grapevine so that the dried materials can be hot-glued evenly around. If the frame has large openings or if a very dense covering is needed, it may be necessary to add a material, such as burlap or plastic screening, to the frame to hold the dried flowers. Test your choice to ensure the glue will stick, then cover completely with dried materials so that the mechanics do not show.

Longwood's original grapevine turkey was covered with dried cockscomb, statice, sedum, and similar flowers, and the tail was accented with great plumes of miscanthus and other grasses. This led to many other dried topiaries, including replicas of hot-air balloons. The frames were made to order and designed much like regular wire hanging baskets, but in the shapes of inflated hot-air balloons. Each frame was about 18 inches by 20 inches. The metal frame wires were wrapped with florist tape of different colors chosen to complement the flowers. To reduce the openings, the frames were covered with chicken wire. Yarrow, goldenrod, sedum, strawflowers, and different colors of statice were then hot-glued to each other and to the frames. Small, woven reed baskets were suspended from the balloons using brightly colored ribbons.

Remember, dried topiaries require less maintenance, keep for years, and are easy to repair. When not on display, dried topiary can be protected from dust by covering and storing it in a dry place until the next appropriate display.

Cork Trees

Creating Longwood's Garden of Oz provided many opportunities to explore different types of topiary, including four exciting cork apple trees with eyes that glowed in the dark. For frames we used fiberglass tree trunks left over from a past display. The cork was added to the trees with hot glue.

Cork is commercially available and is collected from cork oak, *Quercus suber,* native to the Mediterranean region. The exobark is harvested every five to seven years from these trees. Our cork pieces were dry and hard, so cutting and shaping each piece to achieve a proper fit required several wood-working tools, small saws, and a vice. It was critical to apply and glue each piece evenly up and down the trunk to create as natural an appearance as possible. Straps made by cutting old inner tubes into strips were tied tightly around the tree to hold the glued pieces on. Each trunk took about twenty-four hours to dry.

a) Reduce the openings of the frame by adding a covering such as chicken wire. Hot-glue the flowers to the covering.

b) The frame wires can be wrapped with floral tape to help cover the topiary mechanics.

c) Weave grapevine around the frame and hot-glue the dried flowers to the vine.

144

Finishing touches for the cork trees in the Enchanted Forest, part of the Wonderful Garden of Oz.

The completed cork tree.

After the trees were covered with cork, faces of papier-mâché were added and painted to blend perfectly. Small holes were drilled into the faces and tiny red lights added for the eyes. The cork-tree faces were decorated with shelf mushrooms and lichens. During installation, apples and branches with leaves were added. The leaves quickly withered but hung to the stems and gave just the right feeling to this enchanted forest.

The Flying Butterflies

In 1987, Longwood made three giant butterflies covered with thousands of individual dried flower petals and other dried materials. Their wings were made of filon, a coated fiberglass used as a greenhouse covering. An assortment of weights, electric motors, and pneumatic valves created the illusion that the giant creatures were actually flying.

The frames alone were terrific inventions, but that was only the beginning. We used an endless list of flowers, seeds, leaves, and spices to create authentically colored South African butterflies proportionately true to scale. All the covering materials were natural, and many were available from the gardens.

a

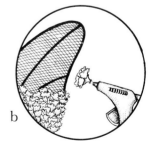

b

a) The frame has a tight mesh covering.
b) Individual floral petals can be hot-glued directly to the topiary frame.

145

Close-up of a 1984 butterfly. The dried materials are tea leaves and dried flower petals.

Butterflies decorated with a variety of assorted dried flowers, tea leaves, coffee beans, and dried herbs and spices. Longwood Gardens, 1984.

Most of the flowers were dried in silica gel, but a few were done in a microwave oven to save time (check your microwave instructions carefully before attempting this drying method). The flowers dried in gel were the best. Most of the butterfly wings were covered completely by hot-gluing individual flower petals to the pre-designed pattern traced on the filon. On areas including heads, bodies, and some wings where herbs and seeds were used, white glue worked best.

A frame made of 2-inch aluminium hinged strips inside a flexible clothes dryer hose turned into a moving caterpillar. Air pistons moved the frame in a track creating an inch-worm slink for the giant caterpillar. As one portion of the body went up, it forced another part to go down. Needless to say, this caused many squeals and giggles from young visitors. The caterpillar was covered with dried basil leaves, with *Stifftia chrysantha* tufts on his back.

From start to finish, the butterfly project took over four-hundred hours to complete.

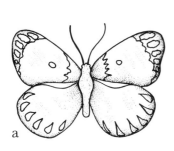
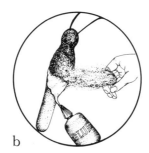
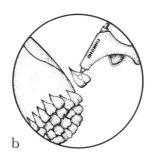

a   b   b   c

Dried materials for butterflies:

a) Before adding the covering, the design was traced onto the wings.
b) Some areas and some materials such as herbs and seeds adhere best with white glue.
c) A finished butterfly.

basil leaves	delphinium petals	poppy seeds
bugleweed leaves	evodia seeds	rose petals
carnation petals	jet bead seeds	sesame seeds
celery seeds	marigold petals	smoketree flower clusters
chrysanthemum petals	Mexican sunflower petals	sunflower petals
coffee beans	parsley leaves	tea leaves
coneflower petals	peppercorns	zinnia petals

The Weather-Maker Dragon decorated with natural plant material and given a spray of iridescent paint.

Weather-Maker Dragon

A 15-foot-long dragon known as the Weather-Maker Dragon, made of dried items, was developed at Longwood in 1988. Southern magnolia leaves preserved with glycerin were used as scales on the upper side of the body, and corn husks dyed green were used for the belly.

The belly was covered first. The rows of magnolia leaves on the body had to overlap to make the scales appear natural. Preserved ferns were added randomly for accent, and the wings were billowy puffs of dried pampas grass plumes.

The dragon's finishing touches were blue whiskers, horns, and toenails painted metallic silver; the extended serpent-type tongue was fierce bluish-purple. A final spray with bluish-green iridescent paint completed the animal.

All of these coverings were added to a frame designed and built at Longwood. The first step was to transpose a 1-inch equals 3-foot scale drawing onto a large, gridded sheet of cardboard at full size. The basic topiary wires were then cut and shaped to match perfectly. The third dimension was achieved by adding circles and loops using the same construction methods that our outside contractors use to custom-build frames. After these components were welded together, we had to find a material that could hold glued leaves securely.

Copper fly screen was the final choice. Its fine mesh would hold the glue and it would bend and mold around the frame. (Plastic materials were rejected because they would burn or melt from the hot glue application.) Part of the frame was made from ⅛-inch stainless-steel rods welded together, since copper screen would solder and adhere to it well.

The dragon was made in pieces then fastened together during installation using 8-inch cable clamps. The final character hung from heavy, 30-pound test fishing line.

a

Christmas display at the conservatory entrance at Longwood.

a) A topiary made by adding stems of evergreens to shapes made of styrofoam.
b) They were often decorated with real lemons.

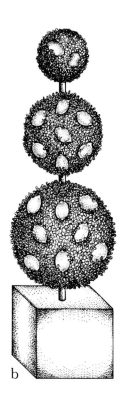

b

Cut Green Topiaries

Over the last twenty or thirty years, Longwood's staff has created several styles of topiary made of cut greens. Some designs created in 1960 are still being constructed each December. Most are built using the same basic technique, although a few have had to be modified to achieve special effects.

Early topiaries were three-tiered standards using spheres 16 inches, 12 inches, and 6 inches on top. The forms were made of styrofoam and ½-inch pipe. Each ball was stuffed solidly with boxwood cuttings, and the pole was covered with cork bark and anchored to a wooden base. Later, they were decorated with real lemons, or red bows. Lights were never used.

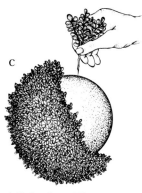

c

c) Poke the stiff stems directly into the form, covering it completely.

During the late sixties, a huge sphere hung in the Exhibition Hall, 10 feet wide and filled mostly with spruce. The frame was constructed of pipe and turkey wire. There were also "Kissing Balls" made of American holly displayed in the Peirce du Pont House Conservatory. 12-inch styrofoam balls were stuffed with holly, trimmed with mistletoe and red ribbon, and hung in threes. The completed balls were 2 feet wide.

During the early '70s, six shapes were created from boxwood. These topiaries had four tiers: a 4-foot-square by 20-inch-high base covered with sheets of refrigerator styrofoam, a 2-foot ball, a 3-foot cone with a flat top, and a 15-inch pointed cone on top. The stems were covered with cork bark.

Today, we use only two cut green topiaries. There are no bases, and the topiaries are anchored into large, old, decorative crock pots filled with jumbo terragreen. The stems are fastened to a circle of wood that fits into the giant flower pots and holds the topiary up straight. They are decorated with ornaments and colors to match the Christmas theme.

Reindeer

To make a cut green topiary reindeer, take yew branches with flexible stems about as thick as a thumb and averaging about 2 feet long and weave them through the wire of the frame in the body area first. Always work in one direction, front to back, so the needles lie in one direction and appear fur-like. Be sure to weave the greens through the frame tightly to create a full effect, especially since the body interior is hollow.

For the thin legs, antlers, and tail, the greens are held to the outside of the frame and wrapped with green florist wire, 20-22 gauge. There must be plenty of wrapping to mold the greens to the frame so as not to lose the desired shape. Usually only areas like the ears need trimming after completion; select the best greens for these.

The completed reindeer can be decorated with strings of white lights, about two hundred per small animal, and then mounted on a wooden base. If the display site is outdoors, the sod is removed temporarily, and the base is anchored to the ground with a large U-shaped rod. Outdoors, the greens should remain fresh for up to six weeks without any special treatment.

a

b

a) Other designs such as this standard can be covered with cut greens.
b) This style is nicely accented with small lights.

a

b

c

Reindeer.
a) On thin areas wrap the greens on with florist wire.
b) A close-up view of weaving. The needles lie in one direction for a fur-like appearance.
c) Weave the branches through the wire.

The completed group of cut green reindeers with their lights on ready for the Christmas display at Longwood.

The reindeer head being covered with cut greens.

Tying in the greens onto the antlers.

Cut greens decorated with lights and balls for Christmas 1971 at Longwood.

7. Good Ideas from Others

Callaway Columns

Callaway Gardens in Pine Mountain, Georgia, and Longwood Gardens joined forces in 1988 to present the first topiary conference held in the United States. Debbie Rogers, Production Manager at Callaway Gardens, showed participants how to make Callaway Columns, which range from 4 to 8 feet tall and have boundless possibilities for planting, such as with poinsettias, chrysanthemums, verbenas, petunias, impatiens, or grape-ivies.

The columns were developed when it was found that vertical designs worked well in many areas at Callaway's Sibley Center. As commercially available columns were never quite right, a custom-made armature was designed.

The basic column is made of PVC thin-wall pipe. Regular PVC will do, but drilling the holes is easier in the thin-wall pipe, especially if you are drilling several holes. The Callaway columns are usually made of 8-inch pipe.

After an 8-foot section of pipe is cut, mark the length with four straight lines, equally spaced around the pipe. Start on one line and mark down ½ inch for the first 2-inch planting hole. Each hole after the first should be on 4-inch centers along the entire line. The second line should have the first hole 2 inches down, the third line 3 inches down, and on the fourth it should start somewhere between the other three holes. Each line should have holes every 4 inches on center, and the holes should be staggered around the pole. By alternating the holes, you can space the plants so that the entire PVC column is covered, creating a tower of blooming plants. Mark all the locations before drilling any holes to prevent uncorrectable errors. An 8-foot tall, 8-inch diameter column will have approximately fifty holes.

Use a heavy duty drill to make the holes. Make a pilot hole with a small bit, then use a 2-inch hole saw bit.

Approximately 30 inches up from the bottom, or at about knee height, drill two holes directly across from each other but not in any row with the other holes. These holes are for a handle to lift and transport the column when it is completed. A pipe can be pushed through the middle, and two people can use it for carrying. The holes should be located just below fingertip height, so the movers need only lift the heavy columns a few inches. Without the pipe handles, there is no place to hold the column after it is planted.

The column also needs a heavy base to hold it upright. Set the column in a shallow metal pan about 3 or 4 inches deep and fill the pan with a fairly wet concrete mix. Be sure to drop some concrete down the center of the column. A few scraps of wire around and in the pipe at the base area will help the concrete adhere to the column and will reinforce the base.

Spray-paint the entire empty column and base with flat black paint after the concrete has dried completely. This will help to camouflage the structure should there be any gaps in the foliage and flowers.

Experimentation with soil mixes and different moisture levels has revealed that a very wet slurry of commercial soilless mix is best. The mix must be wet enough to fill the column completely without leaving air pockets but not so wet that it runs out of the holes. If the mix is not wet before it is poured into the pipe, it is very difficult to saturate afterward. After the column is filled with planting mix, it should be allowed to sit overnight and settle completely. Additional mix may have to be added the next day.

Planting should start from the bottom and proceed upwards. (Do not plant in the handle holes.) Cell plugs or plants with a root ball smaller than the 2-inch holes are best. Finish by planting two or three into the top of the pipe.

A selection of decorative columns from Callaway Gardens.

Opposite page:
a) An 8-inch thin-wall PVC pipe with four rows of holes drilled on 4-inch centers.
b) Drill two holes specifically to use for carrying handles.
c) A heavy base filled with concrete.

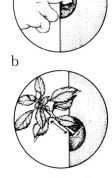

a) Add two or three plants to the top.
b) Place young plants into each hole.

Watering is not needed for the first few days, but it is important to spray over the plants to help them adjust to transplanting. After three or four days, water thoroughly at the top, allowing the water to percolate through the column. Also water up and down each line of plants, making sure some water gets into the holes. This is particularly important for plants at the middle level. The lower plants do not dry out as fast as the top plants which benefit most from the waterings. Watch the middle carefully. Check by occasionally poking a finger into the holes to test the soil. Do this randomly around the column and soon you will learn the spots that dry first. Also, be sure that water doesn't collect at the base, or the lowest plants will soon suffer from ''wet feet.'' More holes should be drilled near the bottom if necessary.

Spreading plants such as cascading chrysanthemums and garden-nasturtiums (*Tropaeolum majus*) are ideal for the columns. Many plants will need regular pinching to encourage them to fill out and maintain a uniform shape on the column.

Callaway has developed giant ''wind chimes'' made of these columns to be used in the Sibley Center. They are from 6 to 12 feet long and are suspended from a wooden base. The methods for construction and planting are the same as for free-standing columns.

Top: Poinsettia flowers, red and cream, make
this a festive-looking column.
Above: Golden chrysanthemum columns
outside at Callaway Gardens.
Left: Flowering column in the greenhouse at
Callaway Gardens.

This two-ball ivy standard is typical of Ivy Guild topiary work.

This lobster was created by The Ivy Guild.

Woven Topiaries - Ivy Guild Method

The largest commercial ivy grower in the country, The Ivy Guild, produces thousands of instant topiaries every month by training container-grown vines over frames. (This "woven" topiary technique is covered in detail on page 156.) Ivies developed enough to cover the entire frame are used. In only a few days the leaves will assume a natural-looking orientation and the topiary will be ready for sale.

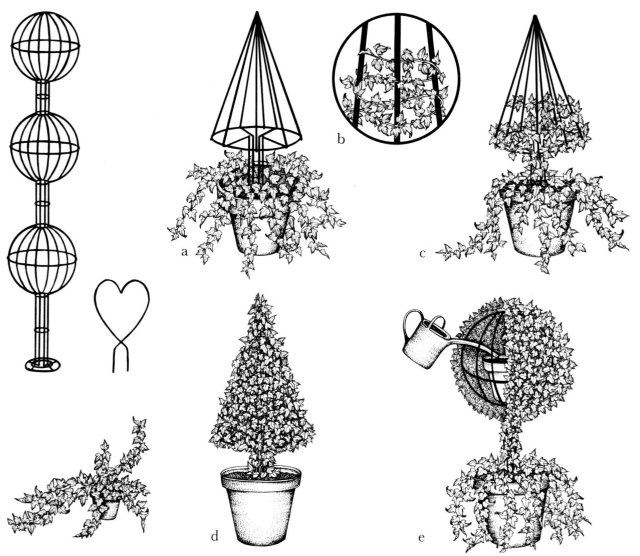

Above: Ivy plant and frames for woven topiary.

a) The frame is set into a pot which is then planted with an ivy with several long runners.
b) Close-up of weaving.
c) Weave the runners up and around the frame.
d) A finished tree.
e) If the topiary is tall, another pot of ivy is located inside the frame. Remember to water each pot of ivy.

One style is a small, tree-shaped frame (20 inches high) planted into a pot full of ivies. Long runners are woven up the frame wires of the trunk and continued around the entire tree to create a Christmas tree shape. For larger frames, an additional pot of ivy is inserted into the body of the tree to cover the top of the frame.

Another interesting form is the standard-type topiary ranging in height from 22 inches to 9 feet. The small 22-inch frame is inserted and anchored into a 6-inch pot of ivy with runners woven up the stem. The ball splits in two and envelops another 6-inch pot of ivy that in turn is woven around the ball head. The Ivy Guild calls a 3-foot 8-inch standard with one sphere at the top "Mama." "Papa," 6 feet high, has two spheres, one at the top and one midway up the stem. The spheres are 18 inches across and have 12-inch pots of ivy inside. The "Mirabelle" is smaller, with two spheres 12 inches across with a 10-inch pot in the top ball. The ball at the bottom has ivy from the base carefully wrapped around the frame but with an open outline of ivy. The top sphere is allowed to fill in solidly with vines and foliage.

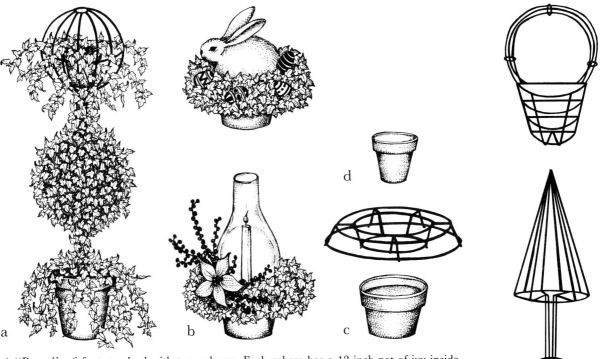

a) "Papa," a 6-foot standard with two spheres. Each sphere has a 12-inch pot of ivy inside.
b) Two examples of ivy wreaths used for centerpiece decoration.
c) Ivies are planted in a pot and woven around and attached to the wreath frame.
d) A small pot in the center creates an area to be filled with a candle or other adornments.

Above: Two frames suitable for woven topiaries.

The Ivy Guild produces a range of topiary baskets different in size but all in the same style. A filled pot of ivy is dropped into a basket outline. Part of the runners are woven down around the bowl area, hiding the pot completely. A few of the longest runners are neatly woven up and around the handle of the basket. When these topiaries are finished, all one sees is an ivy basket—no frames, no pot. Half baskets done with this method can be hung on the wall.

An elegant "Ivy Centerpiece" is made of a four-wire wreath frame around a 6-inch pot. Ivies are planted around the pot with an empty 3-inch pot inserted in the center. The ivy runners are "woven" around the frame. The 3-inch pot can be filled with a blooming plant, fresh flowers, or a candle.

The Ivy Guild also makes large custom topiaries using this woven style, having created everything from traditional cone shapes ("The Versailles") to an over-sized tuna in a tuxedo. Only the pots need to be watered, so these topiaries can be displayed in areas where stuffed topiaries could not be watered readily. The light ivy vines do not need as strong a frame as stuffed topiary, and the finished piece can be moved more easily. Also, should a plant start to die, it can quickly be replaced by another pot with long runners.

A disadvantage, however, is poor definition of character. The weaving style is more effective on frames that do not have thin appendages or detailed shapes such as fingers, toes, and ears. With only a few pots of vines, subtle mixing of plant materials is difficult. Stuffed topiary gives unlimited ranges of plants and plant combinations with fine detailing of features. But under the right circumstances, the Ivy Guild method can be wonderfully effective.

Connie's grass-sculptured pig and an empty frame.

A pair of rabbits with an egg.

Grass Sculptures

Invented by Connie Swensson of Media, Pennsylvania, grass sculptures are unique topiary creations using chicken wire frames and a covering of dried grass.

Connie had been working with Philippine grass for some time, which is stiff and lends itself nicely to self-structural sculpting. She then discovered a wonderful, golden-colored, matted grass known as stilt grass, *(Microsteguim vimineum)* while walking near her home. The stilt grass, however, was fragile by comparison and needed a frame of crimped chicken wire to control its form. The grass skin was then held in place by an invisible acrylic thread. The resulting sculptures received widespread attention when they were used to decorate the Blue Room for Christmas at The White House.

Stilt grass is native to Southeast Asia and has naturalized in the United States, where it is considered an invasive weed. It is an annual, fine-textured, soft-green grass with an airy appearance. It blooms in late summer, but the flowers are inconspicuous. Seeds germinate in early spring, sending out long single stems that quickly cover other vegetation. After the stem reaches an average height of 18 inches, side branches develop and send down roots ("stilts") through neighboring vegetation. The grass continues to spread, forming massive colonies.

Microsteguim can be found in moist, shady areas along streams and lakes, edges of woody areas, and roadsides, thriving in areas which have been disturbed by man. Locate this plant during the summer, but harvest it after the first frost when it turns light tan. Store it in open grocery bags. Other supplies you will need to make a grass topiary include chicken wire, needle-nose pliers, size-50 acrylic thread (called Invisible Thread and available at sewing supply stores), and a pair of gloves. Choose a flexible chicken wire that will be easy to shape.

Find a picture of an animal or bird you would like to make. Decide on a pose, starting with a simple yet life-like posture. Easy shapes are turtles, pigs, and small geese.

Size can vary, but beginners should start with an 18-inch square of chicken wire. Shape the wire into a cylinder to start the skeleton and fold the edges of the wire into the center. Secure them along the underside to form a seam. Shape the head and tail first, then mold out other appendages such as legs, arms, or long necks. Some snipping of the wire may be required to achieve the properly shaped appendages.

To transform the basic outline into shape, use pliers to crimp the hexagonal openings of the netting. Start at one end and work towards the other. Constantly use your hands as well as the pliers to shape the creature.

Before covering the wire, clean the grass by rolling it between your hands. Remove flower heads and crumbly leaf bits, but don't overwork the grass or be too meticulous. Just passing it a few times through your hands should make it flexible.

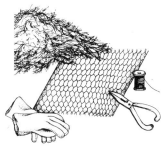

Supplies needed for a grass sculpture: dry grass, chicken wire, wire cutters, gloves, and invisible thread.

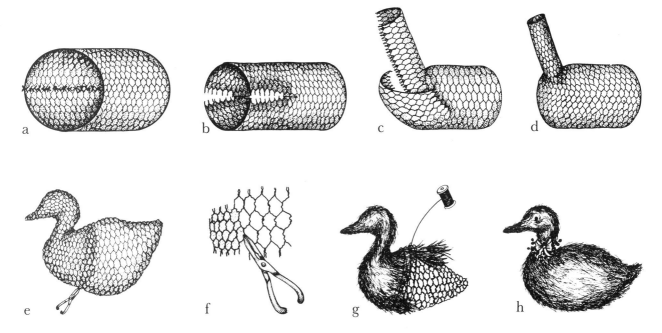

a) Shape the 18-inch square of chicken wire into a cylinder. Join ends together along underside.
b) Some figures may need snipping to achieve proper shape.
c) & d) Shape the head and tail first (only head section shown).
e) Crimp the openings of the netting.
f) Close-up of e).
g) Wrap grass onto the armature with invisible thread.
h) Finished grass sculpture.

Another of Connie's charming grass sculptures.

Take a handful of grass and hold it in a bunch against the frame. Begin to wrap the grass onto the frame using the acrylic thread. There is no need to loop or knot the invisible thread; just wind it until it catches. Start with the head and wrap it snugly. As you wrap more and more grass from head to tail, continue to mold with your hands and work your creature into the desired form. Concentrate on the sculpture more than on the grass and thread. If the thread should break, just start wrapping again. Use plenty of thread and wrap in alternating directions to avoid a build-up of thread in one area.

For the head and legs, take a handful of grass and bend it over and around the appendage. Wrap tightly to form the desired characteristics. Several layers of grass may be needed to cover the wire completely. No wire should show through, but don't worry if the grass isn't perfect.

When your new grass sculpture is complete, spray on a coat of diluted wax to preserve it and to keep the grass from shedding. Use one part clear liquid wax (any brand) with one part water.

As time goes by, the sculpture can be re-grassed, trimmed, and even washed. The hollow sculpture will dry quickly after a gentle bath and look fresh. This topiary needs no special care and it will provide decoration and give pleasure for years.

Part III
Application

1. Festival Topiaries

2. Topiaries for Children

3. Interiorscaping, Outdoor and Turn-About Topiaries

1. Festival Topiaries

Elaborate topiaries using a variety of techniques have been featured at Longwood Gardens for a number of years. These "festival topiaries" have served as centerpieces for themed celebrations which have attracted thousands of visitors. A discussion of some of the more unusual topiaries should prove useful for creating your own show-stoppers.

Building a Carousel

The first Longwood Carousel, built over and around a conservatory pool, was the idea of staff gardener Mary Mizdail Allinson. The wooden structure was a simple design: a circular plywood cap to cover the eight-sided pool, poles for the sides, and a wooden roof to match the base. This was topped by a metal frame suspended from the roof of the conservatory, planted with a vining and curling ivy, *Hedera helix* 'Manda Crested'. Wide ribbon streamers of soft pink hung down to match the color scheme of the entire display.

The scalloped trim of the roof was built to hide the pots of the cascading chrysanthemums, watering systems, and electrical wires. The final 2-foot-high facade was trimmed with three shades of pink. Plexiglass mirrors, also cut in rounded scallops, enhanced this nostalgic merry-go-round.

A hidden 12-inch shelf around the top of the frame held eight pots of cascading chrysanthemums and, later, long-trailing variegated yellow-archangel (*Lamiastrum galeobdolon* 'Variegatum') that draped over the roof at each pole, softening much of the wooden structure. Sixteen pots of ivy with vines 6-feet long trailed up long chains and connected on the suspended metal top to the wooden carousel. The top hung from the greenhouse roof on an electrical pulley system allowing it to be raised and lowered for watering and routine grooming. The top was planted with thirty-two long-trailing ivies, sixteen following the chains down to meet the ivies climbing upward and sixteen covering the framework and reaching the top. The very top was accented with a giant pink bow with streamers spilling down between each trail of lustrous green 'Manda Crested' ivy.

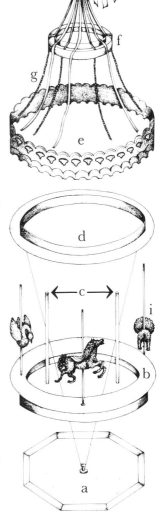

The Carousel construction: Top right
a) The octagonal pool.
b) A circular plywood cap designed to cover the octagonal pool.
c) Two of the eight poles joining the base (b) to the roof (d).
d) The wooden roof of the carousel.
e) The scalloped trim (see detail) added to roof.
f) The metal frame suspended from the roof of the conservatory.
g) Metal chains link the roof (d) of the carousel to the top metal frame (f).
h) Decoration, pink ribbons, and top bow.
i) Animals positioned on poles.

j) Thirty-two trailing ivies planted around the metal frame at the top (f).
k) Sixteen trailing ivies planted in the 12-inch shelf around the roof of the carousel. Eight pots of chrysanthemums planted at the top of each pole.
l) Plexiglass mirror decoration on the scalloped edge (e).

Frame designs by Gerry Simboli for the swan and ostrich. They were produced by Topiary Inc., Tampa, Florida.

Ideas and pictures of real carousel figures were sent to the frame-makers, Topiary Inc., in Tampa, Florida. They developed drawings of horses, goats, lions, camels, and deer incorporating a feeling of excitement and motion. Many improvements in construction were made based on experiences from the previous year. Legs were distinct from the body, structural support was improved, and detailing was refined.

Planning for the plants started nine months before display. Four animals were done in creeping fig and four in ivy, and two of the ivy-covered animals were planted with variegated cultivars to add variety. The final selections were as follows:

Goat	*Hedera helix* 'Calico'	Two horses	*Ficus pumila*
Reindeer	*Hedera helix* 'Ivalace'	Camel	*Ficus pumila*
One horse	*Hedera helix* 'Telecurl'	Lion	*Ficus pumila*
One horse	*Hedera helix* 'Eva'		

The four horses and the lion were trimmed in cascading white chrysanthemums, a new idea for stuffed topiary. Tests and trials indicated it would work. The chrysanthemums were grown and trained in pots and added to the planted animals as tails and manes immediately before display. The topiaries were grown with empty plastic pots reserving the space for these later additions. The empty pots were then removed and the chrysanthemums implanted.

A temporary structure had to be built to support the pole-mounted figures for planting in upright positions (see illustration). The Carousel required uniformity, so the gardeners followed a standard procedure. Two people planted each animal simultaneously from both sides. Building from the bottom up, they maintained a uniform thickness of moss and added a lightweight soilless mix to the body cavity. When each figure was completed, the team pinned down all the plant runners, starting from the bottom and working upwards, pinning so all the runners were secured in a downward direction. This systematic approach helped to create the uniform finish required. It took one hundred and twenty-five hours to stuff and plant the eight animals. The cascading chrysanthemums accenting the horses and the lion were

Two more Carousel animals showing the temporary structure built to support the pole-mounted figures.

The 1985 Carousel in all its glory.

Assembling the 1985 Carousel.

The horse with saddle and rein for the 1987 Carousel.

Lion for the 1987 Carousel. Body: *Hedera helix* 'Eva'; mane: *Liriope.*

started during the early summer, grown in pots, trained, pruned, and groomed all season using cultural techniques similar to those for bonsai chrysanthemums. Wire and regimented pruning were used to shape tails and manes. Saddles woven of jute and raffia were designed for each animal. Carousel music made the topiary display complete. In all, more than forty people, including carpenters, electricians, plumbers, painters, students, and gardeners, worked on the display, and there was no dress rehearsal!

Two years later for a ''Winter Carnival'' theme, the topiary carousel made a repeat appearance. A new coat of paint, two new characters, and some fancier saddles and trimmings gave the display a new look. The cascading chrysanthemum tails and manes became more formal than before; the tails were held high and, like the manes, were kept short and compact. The method of training the mums on wire was modified slightly to achieve the controlled finish.

The plant for the horse's tail is trained along a wire to help with shaping.

165

A new 'A' frame, this time on wheels, was designed to simplify planting the 1987 Carousel animals.

Two new characters, a swan and an ostrich, replaced the camel and the reindeer to give variety. The swan was covered with a distinctly white variegated ivy, *Hedera helix* 'Little Diamond'. The diamond-shaped leaves, each with a downward-pointing center lobe, created a feather-like texture. A pink saddle and headpiece decorated with pearl-white beads and sequins completed the effect.

The ostrich body was covered with an ivy called 'Leo Swicegood', which has small, dark green, lance-shaped leaves. In contrast, *Euonymus fortunei* 'Minima' was used on the long skinny legs. The flat habit of the variegated wintercreeper euonymus, *Euonymus fortunei* 'Gracilis', was ideal for the remaining unfeathered areas. The tail of cascading chrysanthemums was grown on a flexible wire structure and later shaped and trimmed when added to the bird. This allowed the tail to be manipulated so that only the bloom side could be seen. Extra-sturdy stainless-steel rods were added to keep the tail horizontal without sagging.

The saddles used previously were replaced with shiny blue, purple, pink, and green fabric dressings all highly decorated with sequins, beads, feathers, and gold and silver trim. Feather headpieces completed the dressing.

New "A" frame racks on wheels, designed by Longwood's carpenters, made it easy to move and maintain the topiaries. Each frame was designed to hold two animals. The characters were mounted to rotate inside the frame, making it much easier to work on a figure. The gardeners could now set up supplies and tools in a centralized work area and move the characters there.

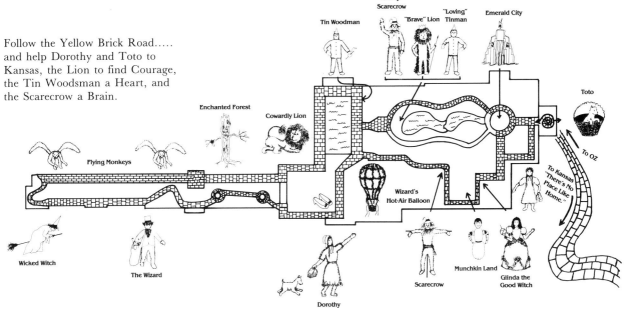

Follow the Yellow Brick Road.....
and help Dorothy and Toto to
Kansas, the Lion to find Courage,
the Tin Woodsman a Heart, and
the Scarecrow a Brain.

Layout plan for the Garden of Oz showing all the characters in position on the plan.

Creating the Wonderful Garden of Oz

L. Frank Baum, who wrote *The Wonderful Wizard of Oz* in 1900, was an avid gardener. Among his favored garden treasures were chrysanthemums, and to many he was known as the ''Chrysanthemum King.'' In 1986, a horticultural interpretation of his best-known story seemed almost essential!

Longwood's ''Wonderful Garden of Oz'' topiaries were characters of a story known to everyone. Each of the main characters was positioned at two different points along the Yellow Brick Road which led through the greenhouses. The first Scarecrow was lifeless and rather dull-witted, hanging on a pole along the garden path. His body was of ivy and straw. A raven sat on his shoulder.

A larger-than-life Toto was stationed in a 5-foot grapevine basket. His body was formed of cut yew greens woven through a wire frame, and a yellow bow replaced the ordinary dog collar.

The Making of the Wonderful Garden of OZ.

· **How are the topiary Oz characters made?**
1. Metal frames are custom built.
2. Large frames are fitted with plastic bags filled with syrofoam packing ''peanuts'' to reduce the weight of the finished topiary.
3. Frames are then webbed with a netting of fish line to hold sphagnum moss stuffing.
4. Moistened sphagnum moss is packed into frames.
5. Rooted plant cuttings are pinned into pockets of sphagnum moss at approximately 6-inch spacings.

· **How long did it take to plant 18 OZ topiaries?**
10 gardeners worked a total of 21 days.

· **How long did it take for plants to cover the figures?**
3 months from planting to the November display.

· **What plants grow on the topiaries?**

Dorothy

dress	500	Marie-Louise English Ivy (*Hedera helix* cv. Marie Louise)
head, legs, arms	42	Eva English Ivy (*Hedera helix* cv. Eva)

Toto

	144	Pin Oak English Ivy (*Hedera helix* cv. Pin Oak)

Glinda the Good Witch

dress	1008	Calico English Ivy (*Hedera helix* cv. Calico)
dress accents	36	Garland English Ivy (*Hedera helix* cv. Garland)
hair	72	Shamrock English Ivy (*Hedera helix* cv. Shamrock)
face, arms	72	Creeping Fig (*Ficus pumila*)

Scarecrow

body	720	Brokamp English Ivy (*Hedera helix* cv. Brokamp)
feet	12	Swicegood English Ivy (*Hedera helix* cv. 'Leo Swicegood')

Tin Woodman

	360	Misty English Ivy (*Hedera helix* cv. Misty)

Lion

body	700	Creeping Fig (*Ficus pumila*)
	40	Variegated Spider Plant (*Chlorophytum comosum* cv. Vittatum)

Wizard

body	144	California English Ivy (*Hedera helix* cv. California)
head, hands	24	Kobold English Ivy (*Hedera helix* cv. Kobold)
shirt	12	Little Diamond English Ivy (*Hedera helix* cv. Little Diamond)

Flying Monkeys

body	300	Creeping Fig (*Ficus pumila*)
wing, underside	144	Misty English Ivy (*Hedera helix* cv. Misty)
head, paws	52	Spetchley English Ivy (*Hedera helix* cv. Spetchley)

Wizard's Hot Air Balloon

framework	Grapevine (*Vitis* sp.)
balloon	Manda Crested English Ivy (*Hedera helix* cv. 'Manda Crested'

Toto in his basket.

The 6-foot-tall Tin Woodsman, made of a silvery ivy called 'Misty', had buttons made from rusty bolts; his hat, gloves, and axe were also rusty. The awkward and stiff pose left no doubt that this character was missing his heart.

The creature hiding in the chrysanthemums was a lion, but what a lazy pose! No courageous King of Beasts would ever be found in that position. Later this same character stood tall and wore a large Badge of Courage.

The second Tin Woodsman was shiny and full of life with a big red anthurium bloom for a heart. His brainy friend the Scarecrow stood tall and carried his diploma of wisdom.

Bonnet, basket, and pigtails left little doubt as to Dorothy's identity, particularly since Toto was following close behind. Her dress had detail and color variety through a combination of different ivies.

The Wizard was only 3½-feet tall, properly dressed in a dark green suit of *Hedera helix* 'California' with a frilly white shirt of 'Calico' ivy. A black top hat and wiry gray hair of Spanish-moss completed the picture. He carried a bag which included a crown, a badge of courage, an oil can, a heart, and a diploma. Later he could be spotted flying off in a great balloon made of grapevines trimmed with long-trailing and curly 'Manda Crested' ivy.

The four flying monkeys were made of 'Misty' and 'Spetchley' ivy and of creeping fig. The bodies, legs, and tails were small and required *Hedera helix* 'Spetchley', a small, dark green, tiny-leaved ivy with a flat growth habit to tightly outline each of the long extremities. The undersides of the 4-foot wings were planted with a silvery variegated ivy, and the tops were covered with creeping fig. Taking seven hours each to make, the monkeys were finely detailed in both color and texture and meticulously groomed.

The Tin Man and Scarecrow.

Dorothy, Toto, and the balloon.

One of the most successful topiaries, Glinda the Good Witch, from the Wonderful Garden of Oz.

The topiary crew took twenty-three hours to create Glinda, a fairy princess remembered from everyone's childhood. The frame of the skirt was made in two parts that fastened around the waist. Since weight was a major concern, the skirt was a double-walled structure that left the inner part of the topiary hollow. Chicken wire was shaped and fastened to the inside of the skirt frame. The 4-inch space between the two walls was filled with sphagnum moss to accommodate planting.

The entire frame was welded together before it was planted. A wooden circular platform on wheels, cut to fit exactly to the hem of Glinda's dress and attached to the outer circle of the skirt frame, ensured that the topiary weight was evenly distributed and well supported. The dress, sleeves, and skirt were made of variegated dark green and pure white curly ivy, *Hedera helix* 'Calico'. Its texture appeared like lacy chiffon around the large, full sleeves. Over nine hundred rooted cuttings of this ivy were used on the skirt alone. A wide belt with a long, trailing bow in the back was planted with a large, bold-textured ivy, 'Garland'. Large swags of 'Garland' were also planted around the bottom of the skirt.

The bodice parts of Glinda's form were covered with creeping fig. The flat habit of fig and the medium green color contrasted with the showy ivy sleeves and skirt. The face and neck were covered with smooth sheet-moss to help denote the facial features. The hair was of 'Shamrock' ivy. 'Shamrock' has small to medium-sized leaves and is a very shiny dark green with a lustrous sparkle.

In all, Longwood's Garden of Oz had eighteen topiaries made with sixty-nine hundred living specimens that required one hundred eighty-eight hours to stuff and plant. Numerous props included eyes, hats, a crown, axes, gloves, a diploma, ruby slippers, and even a heart. The success of the Oz display can be attributed to a team effort by Longwood's staff and to a stage cast of living plants.

One of the flying monkeys.

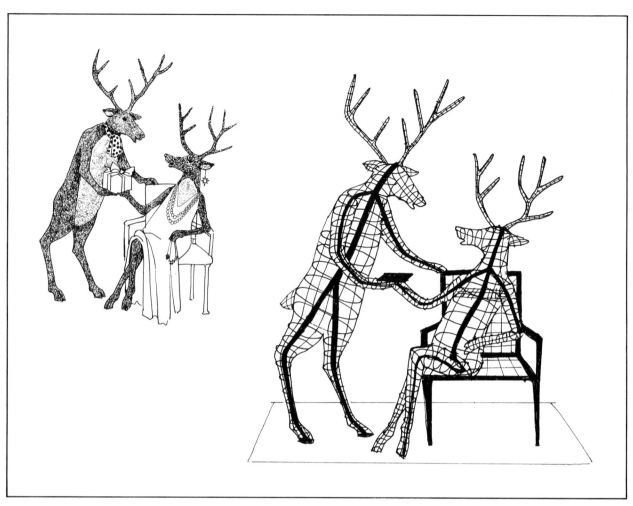

Frames for the seated and standing reindeer guests. Top left: As they will look planted and dressed.

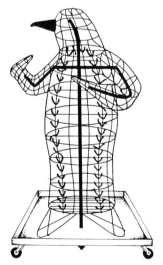

A drip pan with removable plug.

Icicles, Snowflakes, Reindeer, and Penguins

An elegant Christmas party was staged in topiary at Longwood Gardens in 1986. Reindeer in formal wear enjoyed cocktails around a sumptuous dessert table. Service was provided by a 7-foot penguin waiter and entertainment by two penguins at a piano and violin. These were Longwood's first costumed topiaries.

Creating this reindeer rendezvous required aesthetic and practical planning. How would topiaries look in the Music Room, an elegant, walnut-panelled salon adjoining the greenhouses and once used by the du Pont family for entertaining? Practical considerations included grooming, maintenance, and watering, all to be carried out in a dark room with a parquet wood floor that had to be protected from moisture. The topiaries would have to be moved for watering, and because of the number of people visiting during the holidays, maintenance could only be carried out after public hours.

A floor plan was made, and each topiary was designed to fit the planned position, facing the visitors as they passed through the Music Room. The animals were also positioned to interact with each other, enhancing the feeling of a real party in progress.

The first topiary was a green and white penguin waiter carrying a silver tray with a pastry and a linen towel draped over his right wing. His massive body needed extra support pipes in the frame to keep him upright and rigid, as the frame supported

Frames for the reindeer Host and Hostess, with two other drawings showing the completed figures.

several hundred pounds of wet moss and over eight hundred ivy plants.

The next two topiaries were guests exchanging traditional Christmas gifts. A lady reindeer was seated in a chair with her legs crossed. The frame-maker's challenge was to make her provocative, include the chair in the frame, and plan construction so that not only could she be planted but also dressed easily in an elegant costume. Areas that would be covered by the dress and chair were not planted to help protect the fabric and upholstery from water. A gentleman reindeer was positioned to lean forward slightly; his lady friend had her head tilted up with full attention on him.

Near the dessert table a reindeer hostess was elegantly dressed in a full-length strapless white gown with sparkling jewels to add glamour. Again, only part of the frame had to be stuffed and planted. Another reindeer guest held a top hat and cane. All the topiary deer, 7- to 8-feet tall, had full antler racks.

A drip pan with a removable plug was attached to the base of each topiary to catch any water that might seep out. Each base sat on a wooden platform with casters. The topiaries were undressed and rolled out into the nearby greenhouse for watering and grooming.

The completed figures of the reindeer Host and Hostess standing in the Music Room at Longwood Gardens.

Two penguins, a pianist and violinist.

The display area was kept cool for the five weeks during December and January when the topiaries were exhibited. Since these are cold months and the topiaries were not in the sun, watering was needed only once a week. Each Sunday after the last visitor left, the defrocked topiaries were rolled out and watered thoroughly. The plugs were removed from the drip pans, which drained overnight. Monday morning the drip pans were dried and the topiaries were groomed, dressed, and returned to their places on stage. The process took two people about four hours each week.

The dresses were designed to be easily removed. Each was lined with water-repellent material to prevent stains on the fabric. Patterns were made in advance so that the topiary team could stuff and plant around the costume in readiness for the final dress.

The sitting deer had to be dressed and undressed while attached to the chair. This required cooperation among frame-maker, topiary builders, and dressmakers. Both dresses and chair covers were made to attach with Velcro® fasteners in strategic places.

Ivies tolerant of low lighting were used on all characters. After five weeks on display, some ivies began to show signs of stress from poor light, but most remained remarkably fresh for the duration of the display.

Plants were carefully selected to interpret each character. The penguins needed

Another pair of reindeer – this time, the guests.

contrasting dark and light greens to achieve an authentic appearance. *Hedera helix* 'Shamrock' was used for the dark color and *Hedera helix* 'Calico' for the striking white contrast.

A finely textured small-leaf ivy, 'Pixie', was used for the green cover on the female deer. The small, variegated ivy 'Kolibri' was used on the chests. These ivies worked well together, and the fine leaf texture gave the ladies a feminine touch. The males were planted with the bigger-leaved, medium-green, textured ivy 'Curly Locks'. Their bellies were covered with the variegated ivy 'Eva'. It spreads quickly and in growth is very flat. The contrast between these two cultivars helped delineate the animals' features.

The costumes were completed with appropriate accessories including a large "diamond" ring, a feather boa, a diamond-studded silk ascot, a black bow tie, a real silk top hat, and even a shiny black cane.

On the party table were beautifully decorated desserts including delights from the forest and the sea to please every guest at the party. There were meringue mushrooms, cookies shaped like walnuts and pine cones, candied leaves, and other whimsical reindeer delicacies whipped into sugary treats. And for the penguins, mirrored trays were filled with make-believe seashells, each containing a silver pearl.

One seated and two standing penguins – the empty and planted frames for the 1986 Christmas party in the Music Room at Longwood Gardens.

TOPIARIES FOR CHRISTMAS 1986

CHARACTER	PLANTING HOURS	PLANT MATERIAL	NUMBER OF PLANTS
Penguin (waiter) Tray and food	28½	*Hedera helix* 'Shamrock' 'Calico' 'Witchtel'	600 200 12
Penguin (violinist) Violin and bow	20	*Hedera helix* 'Shamrock' 'Calico' 'Witchtel'	400 200 12
Penguin (piano player) Piano and stool	16	*Hedera helix* 'Shamrock' 'Calico' 'Witchtel'	400 200 12
Reindeer (lady hostess) Opera glasses, glass jewels, gown	5½	*Hedera helix* 'Pixie' 'Kolibri'	200 12
Reindeer (lady sitting) Jewels and gown	10½	*Hedera helix* 'Pixie' 'Kolibri'	300 12
Reindeer (man) Cane, top hat, ascot	12	*Hedera helix* 'Eva' 'Curly Locks'	144 650
Reindeer (man) Gift and ascot	12	*Hedera helix* 'Eva' 'Curly Locks'	144 650
TOTALS	104½		4,148

New Animals for an African Safari

Old frames were rejuvenated and used for fifty-seven characters in Longwood's 1987 Chrysanthemum Festival. Gardeners spent four hundred thirty-five hours stuffing, planting, drying, gluing, pinning, and pruning nine thousand seven hundred seventeen live plants and bushels of dried flowers, leaves, and moss to create Safari topiaries. By increasing the plant repertoire, it was possible to expand the display locations, create more detail on each figure, and bring many new and different plants to the visitors' attention.

A previously fig-covered indoor lion received a new coat so that he could be displayed outside. Two ivies from the Longwood ivy hardiness trials were used. The big, bold texture of 'Garland' was perfect for the mane. By contrast, the body was of 'Ritterkreuz', a small, finely textured cultivar. This topiary was planted and grown outdoors most of the summer, and by November it was stationed outside for display where it remained until mid-December with no visible damage. The topiary was left outdoors until mid-February when it was dismantled. At that time, there was very little winter damage to the ivy even though January and February are the coldest months in the Philadelphia area. By using these cultivars a breakthrough was made for outdoor portable stuffed topiary.

New characters were chosen to increase the use of color. The ivy 'Tussie Mussie', which takes on a subtle pink color during the winter months, was planted on three flamingos with painted pink legs and beaks. This ivy added more than a touch of authenticity.

Since Longwood's first major topiary display in 1984, topiary-making skills had improved a great deal. The first time a peacock was constructed it took thirty-five hours to plant and stuff the entire bird; this did not include the hours spent finding, testing, and learning to preserve the cut flowers and foliage used to decorate the tail. Three years later, it took only seven hours to stuff and plant the same peacock. This time cascading chrysanthemums were trained up and over the fan-shaped tail, requiring only a minimal amount of regular maintenance. Dried grass plumes gave the crucial feathery appearance needed.

The Lion planted with *Hedera helix* 'Garland' and 'Ritterkreuz'.

Very little damage to the ivies after almost a year outside.

The completed hippo being moved on a fork lift truck into the East Conservatory.

Hippo being slowly lowered onto supports positioned in the water. Note the black metal 4-inch band hiding the base.

Supports having final adjustment before animal is lowered into position.

Hippo now in position and ready for display.

In 1984, it took twenty-one hours to stuff and plant a 10-foot giraffe with sphagnum moss and creeping fig. In 1987, it took just as long, but time was saved in another way. The first year, the giraffe was built in two parts, then tediously joined together and secured when ready for display. In 1987, the frame was fastened together with extra support added before it was planted. Several hours were saved setting up the display and the fear that the giraffe would lose his head was eliminated. Other details, too, reflected Longwood's improved skills. Tails, wings, and crests on topiary birds were now accented with colorful and unusual plants, adding realism. Instead of asking the frame-maker for water birds, we now asked for specific types, like cattle egrets.

Previously, a topiary alligator had been displayed in water by building a platform in the pool; the alligator lay just above water level. In 1987, a topiary hippopotamus was designed especially to fit into the pool. He appeared to be floating half submerged, just as hippos do in the wild. This was a challenge to the frame-maker. Only half of the animal was topiary, and at the water level the frame was designed to have two bottoms. The first bottom kept the topiary moss and plants out of the water, while the second bottom rested on supports in the water. A black metal, 4-inch band was added to hide the base. This allowed the character to sit in the water but kept the plants suspended above the surface. Aquatic plants hid the underwater view.

A new touch of realism was water squirting from a life-size elephant. The frame included a hidden metal pipe housing a small plastic hose which carried water from the front foot up through the leg and body and out through the trunk. By positioning the elephant at the pool's edge, it was possible to pump water through the topiary and squirt it back into the pool. A timer was included so that the spouting was intermittent to add an element of surprise.

This charming koala bear sitting in a tree in the Acacia Passage at Longwood Gardens was planted with *Hedera helix* 'Spetchley'.

The River Lord Dragon - original sketch for the topiary, by Frank Sipala.

Topiaries for the Dragon's Garden

Although the River Lord Dragon, the star of the 1988 fall display, was grandiose and had to be displayed in water, it was his posture that presented a challenge. The lunging creature required counterbalance weights hidden from view. The frame included a base built to the depth of the pool so that the moss and plants were not in the water. As with the hippo, a band hid the space between the planted dragon and the water. Each body part was spaced to give the illusion that the sections were continuously united under water. The tail rose straight out of the pool and ended in a point.

So that the topiary could be moved readily, lifting points were welded onto the inner support structure. Heavy-duty loops made it possible to lift the parts with a small crane. The lifting points had to be located carefully so that balance was maintained after the topiary was completed.

Along with a massive head, face, and arms, this dragon had a pair of wings, each 4 feet long and 2 feet wide at the broadest point. They were covered with trained cascading chrysanthemums, grown on separate frames and added to the body when the dragon went on display. Openings were reserved in the body by an empty pot the same size as the wing pot. Inside the main body, the frame-maker fabricated a connecting point that locked the wing into place after it was added. This gave extra

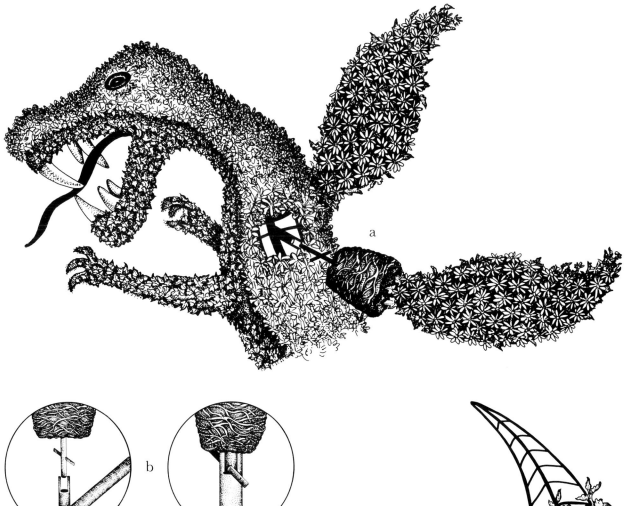

a) The chrysanthemum-covered wings being slotted into the pot-sized body cavities.
b) The wing being slotted and locked into the connecting point on the body frame.

support and prevented the wing from twisting or turning. The connecting point was a pipe welded to the wing frame with a larger pipe used as a sleeve attached to the body frame. It was critical that each wing remained stationary to keep the flower side up so that visitors saw hundreds of tiny yellow blooms, not the flowerless underside.

The base of each wing frame was built into a 10-inch clay pot with the connecting piece protruding through the drain-hole. This enabled the completed wing to neatly slip into place. While the chrysanthemum was being trained, the wing pot was placed into a second, much larger pot filled with sand. The wing was then able to stand upright, the anchor piece sticking through the first pot into the sand of the outer pot. Two sets of wings were made and grown for the dragon. Since the wings were right- and left-sided, one spare would not be sufficient; a set was essential.

To emphasize color and a variety of plant materials, *Alternanthera* 'True Yellow' was combined with Hedera helix 'Witchtel', a dark green ivy planted on the underside, and with 'Megumi', a yellow cascading chrysanthemum trained on the wings.

Over twelve hundred alternanthera plants were used on the River Lord Dragon. The yellow cultivar was outstanding in Longwood's conservatory setting. However, there were certain difficulties; Pennsylvania's climate does not allow the same growth

The wing growing on the frame.

The head and wings of the River Lord Dragon. The wings, massed with flowers, add color and texture.

The wings being slotted into postion.

Installing the tail section to complete the dragon.

The fearsome Earth Dragon among the palms in the Palm House at Longwood.

response from this plant as in Florida, where it is used extensively for topiary all year round. At Longwood, it was much slower-growing and the color less brilliant. We had to be cautious not to overwater in cool fall temperatures. A few disease problems arose from the cool, damp conditions.

Since alternanthera is not vining, good coverage requires frequent pinching, even with close spacing. Getting the plants to grow fast enough in our northern climate was a problem, and to complete coverage we had to add more plants in October.

Another creature, the Earth Dragon, had red and green spines, a combination of *Cryptanthus bivittatus* 'Ruby' and *Guzmania zahnii* 'Variegata'. Spanish-moss decorated his ivy-covered face. The body was planted with *Hedera helix* 'Eva'. Two cultivars of alternanthera were planted to create stripes on his underside, but it didn't grow as successfully as hoped. Alternanthera does best in full sun, and plants on the shaded underside areas were not as vigorous as the plants above. *Alternanthera* 'Variegated White' is slower-growing and smaller than 'Crinkle Red'. Planted together, the red cultivar overwhelmed the white.

Treasure Dragon standing guard on the Treasure Chest.

The Treasure Keeper Dragon, yet another monster, was bursting with color. The main plant on the body was *Euonymus fortunei* 'Gracilis', decorated here and there with *Cryptanthus bivittatus* 'Ruby'. The wintercreeper euonymus is white and green and develops a pink coloring during the fall. *Cryptanthus* 'Ruby' is as colorful as the gem. Brightly painted whiskers, fangs, spines, claws, and teeth made of glazing compound were added. This 6-foot-long creature was perched on a box holding ancient treasures.

Greeting visitors outdoors was the Fire Dragon towering 13 feet tall and spanning, serpent-style, 75 feet of lawn. The 35-foot-long frame was covered with cut greens and dried grasses and breathed fireworks on command.

Temple Foo Lions were designed to imitate sculpture. A minute wintercreeper euonymus was chosen for the covering, and the plants had to grow very flat and close to the frame to give a ''hard'' statuary look. The plants also had to be cold tolerant, as the figures were stationed in an unheated entrance foyer.

The 1988 exhibit also gave Longwood's gardeners the opportunity to create a Taj Mahal of cascading chrysanthemums. The facade of an Indian temple in chrysanthemums could be viewed through an extended palace garden of swirling fountains, flowering columns, and long turf panels, taking visitors on a journey to the East.

Like a life-size puzzle, frames covered with chrysanthemums that had been trained for almost a year were assembled to create the temple. There were twenty-two parts to the frame. Each part anchored onto the pots in an upright position, and instead of cascading downward, the chrysanthemums were trained up and over the frames. When the tubs of chrysanthemums were assembled onto the pipe racks for display, each row overlapped the row above to hide the pots. A red and gold fascia made of rigid plastic covered the bottom pots. The completed temple had bright red and gold trimmings and was topped with a styrofoam finial.

Foo Lions outside the Pierce-du Pont house.

Most amazing of all in 1988 was a 20-foot-tall topiary pagoda. It was built in twenty-two parts. Each of the first four tiers was made of five pieces (a base and four roof sections). The last tier was one piece with a detachable roof ornament crowning the top. The weight of the unplanted frames alone was over five thousand pounds.

More than a dozen gardeners helped plant six thousand four hundred forty rooted cuttings of 'Ritterkreuz' ivy to cover the towering topiary. It took two hundred and seventy-six hours. The pagoda was so large it had to be grown outdoors until it was ready for display.

Assembly and installation required three days and plenty of hands. The frame-maker built the frame so that each part could be planted separately and then put together. Each piece of the frame was numbered and labelled for easier assembly. The

Constructing the Pagoda top, showing the white polystyrene filler, the moss and plants.

Sections of the Pagoda stuffed and planted.

A section of soil had to be excavated to hold the base for the Pagoda.

Bottom section of Pagoda being positioned on the wooden platform.

Fourth tier of Pagoda being installed.

Final adjustments to top.

An engineering feat - the magnificent Pagoda, each section slotted together.

four roof sections bolted to the upright part, and each tier bolted to the last as it was stacked. Small empty pots marked the spots where the frame would eventually be bolted together. These areas were left unplanted so that we could install the bolts, then they were filled in and covered over.

A special foundation was built for the pagoda. The base was 8 feet square and 4½ inches thick, made of wood rather than concrete because it was a temporary structure. It was anchored 2 feet into the soil with screw anchors, two anchors at each corner, and steel brackets were welded across each corner for stability.

Near the corners, where the pagoda legs met the platform, there were 6-inch-high, 14-inch by 14-inch squares. The steel plates on the bottom of the pagoda legs were bolted onto these platforms with 12-inch by ¾-inch bolts.

The site chosen was in the conservatory next to the pool. The turf was carefully removed, and the area was excavated so that the base would be level and recessed below the surface of the lawn. When the pagoda was in position and completely assembled, the lawn was replaced over the buried wooden foundation.

An irrigation system consisting of three ¾-inch black poly-pipes ran up inside one corner, one line servicing each of the top three tiers. Each pipe was connected to soaker hoses positioned to give complete coverage to the roof area. At the base, hose bibs were installed for quick hose connections. As each tier was irrigated, the water was allowed to run until the roof was saturated and the wall sections were soaked. The bottom layers were easily watered from the ground.

Tiny white lights traced the entire outline of the temple, and special oriental bells hung from each upturned eave. The 20-foot temple was topped with an authentically duplicated roof ornament.

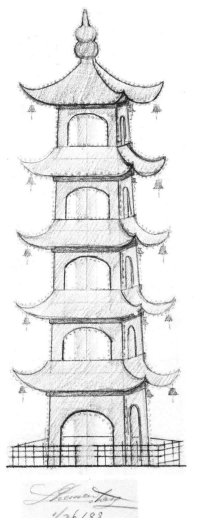

Original sketch for the Pagoda.

185

2. Topiaries for Children and the Children's Garden

A simple outline frame covered with ivy

Children can be successfully involved with topiary if they start with simple shapes. Each project should be carefully monitored for safety, and no project should require tools or equipment too advanced for a child to use.

Catherine Eberbach, Associate Administrator of Children's Education at The New York Botanical Garden in the Bronx, has spent several years developing garden programs for children. She emphasizes that in a topiary class designed for youngsters, visual demonstration and allowing children to use their imaginations are important. Children must understand the mechanics of their topiary projects, such as how to make the frame stand up in the pot and where to put the plants.

If children are making the frames, they should first draw their ideas on paper. By drawing and discussing the building of the topiary, the children will more easily understand the task at hand. The drawing will also help them shape the wire when they are ready to begin the frame. Technicalities like height, size, where to join the wires, and what to do with areas too narrow to hold their shape after the plants are added can be resolved before the project starts.

Plastic-coated electrical wire is ideal for frame making. It is heavy enough to hold a shape but flexible enough for children to bend. The brightly colored coating on electrical wire makes the frames fun even before they are covered with plants. For trained-up topiary, the children must leave about a 10-inch piece of wire at the base of their frame shape so they can secure it to the pot. Praise and encouragement are important to children even if their frames are not perfect. Plants will soon cover crooked or bent spots.

Always choose healthy plants. For trained-up topiary, select a plant with two long runners which will grow up and around in two directions and provide the quick coverage needed for a child's relatively short attention span. Choose flexible plants that are easy to bend but will not break, plants that will enhance the frame and not hide the shape.

An outline butterfly frame covered with chicken wire and anchored into the pot.

Have children put ideas for topiaries on paper first. This will give them a better understanding of the project.

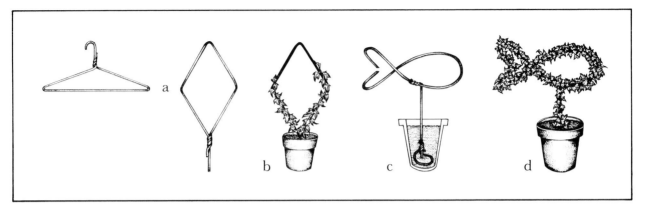

a) Using a wire coat-hanger, start with a simple shape.
b) Train the vine up the frame and secure with twist-ties.
c) Simple frame anchored into the pot, eventually to be covered by an ivy growing up from the pot.
d) The finished topiary does not take a long time to achieve so it is very suitable for eager young children!

Tabletop Topiary

For young children a simple, quick, "work together" project is best. Start with a coat hanger and ask the child for shaping ideas. Try something requiring a few pulls and bends on your part. Do not cut the wire and leave sharp edges. Help the child to bend the hook over on the hanger, then push the bent hook into the bottom of a small pot. The frame will stand firmly when soil is added to the pot. Add the plant. The runners can be loosely wrapped around the frame and tied gently into place. Twist-ties are ideal for children and will hold the plant securely along the frame.

Older children, more skilled in shaping, can make more complicated frames. Buy a wire gauge the child can safely handle, but avoid wire that is too stiff. Children get frustrated when it is too difficult to make or recognize a shape.

Loose ends should be taped together with electrical tape to prevent sharp edges, or electrical wire caps can be used to join the wires together. With a little planning, the caps can end up being the nose, tail, or toes of the new creature.

Adding a coating of chicken wire will turn an outline topiary into a one-dimensional frame that a plant can cover completely. These projects are longer term. Children get a chance to understand how the plant grows and where the new shoots come from along the stem. The project will require more maintenance such as tying, pruning, and cleaning. Even house plants and topiary vines get brown leaves that have to be removed. Children quickly learn that this is a normal process for green plants. The frame shape may be permanent, but the plants will be changing all the time. It is not long before children begin to notice how the vine grows toward the light. It's fun to watch what happens as the plant is rotated each week.

Watering and misting over the topiary will be the most fun for children. The first needs for plants are water and sunlight. Show children how bright sunny days affect how much water a plant needs – and what happens if you forget to water the plant. Lots of gardening skills can be developed from one window topiary project.

a) Wire cap used to join wire.
b) On complicated figures, loose ends can be joined with electrical tape or wire caps.

187

Two mini-pigs from Longwood Gardens.

These mini-ducks planted with creeping fig would be a suitable project for children.

Small turtle: Three-dimensional frame stuffed with sphagnum moss. A creeping fig is planted into the top. This plant will eventually cover the entire frame. With help, children could make this type of topiary and learn to care for it as well. See page 192, Pre-made Frames.

Teddy Bears picnic exhibited by The Ivy Guild.

This delightful floral topiary was created for the Chelsea Flower Show in 1990. Children would enjoy making these animals.

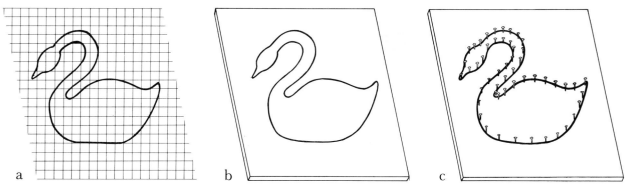

A topiary frame made from a jig.
a) Sketch the design on paper first.
b) Transfer the design onto the plywood.
c) Hammer in nails evenly spaced around the design. Bend the wire around the nails and fasten ends together.

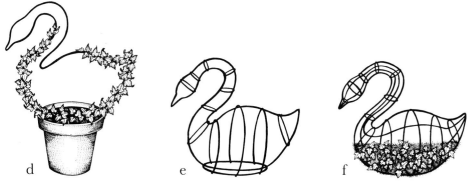

d) Add a base rod to the frame then anchor into the pot. Fill the pot with planting medium, then add the plant.
e) Turn the one-dimension frame into a 3-D shape by adding circles and a few support wires.
f) This frame is now ready for stuffing and planting.

For aspiring carpenters, mechanics, and engineers, a topiary with a frame made from a jig will be fun. You will need a scrap piece of plywood, marking pen or crayon, a few nails, some stiff but pliable wire, wire-cutters, and pliers for bending. Consider safety eye protection for you and your child, and always supervise the use of tools and equipment.

Sketch the design on paper first so that obvious difficulties can be corrected before transferring the design to the board. Hammer in the nails, following the markings. Help your child decide how far apart to space the nails, and try to use enough so that all the design details will be incorporated into the frame.

After the nails are in place, loop the wire around the first nail, bend and shape the wire around the outside of the remaining nails until you complete the outline, then fasten the two ends together with tape or by twisting. You may want to consider investing in a soldering gun for more advanced projects. Add a base to the frame and anchor it into the pot. The topiary is now ready for planting.

This one-dimensional frame can easily be turned into a 3-D frame. Just add assorted circles at right angles to the existing wire outline. Tie or solder them into position; a few cross pieces of wire may be added for support. This frame can be anchored to a pot, and the plant can be trained up and around the structure, or it can be stuffed with sphagnum moss as described for tabletop topiary. Children want to see results quickly, so don't make the frame too big.

Pre-Made Frames

If you are choosing a pre-made frame for a child, select one such as a ball or simple animal shape. Avoid forms that have small areas to stuff. The "One-Plant Stuffed" method is easiest and will give the quickest results. Block letters or geometric shapes can be easy and fun. Animal or bird shapes can be dressed up after planting with grass plumes, flowers, eyes, or feathers. Plan a walk to collect acorns for eyes and noses, or stems, nuts, and seed pods for tails and ears. Remember, wet moss is heavy, so small topiary is best.

Topiary can be done in stages, so have fun ordering the frame or shopping for the supplies. Stuff one day and add the plants the next. It does not need to be started and finished all in one session.

Dried Topiary

When collecting things, don't overlook dried topiary projects. A one-dimensional butterfly frame with chicken wire may look great covered in autumn leaves. Try making a dried standard. Position a stick or branch into the bottom of a pot filled with sand or plaster. Push a styrofoam ball firmly onto the top of the stem and let the children glue the collected materials to the ball. For those who are not able to collect in the wild, most garden centers have large selections of dried flowers and other materials.

Older children may enjoy planning a small garden to grow special "everlasting" flowers to use later on topiary. Keep the garden small the first year and help children understand how to dry the plants in the autumn. They will have plenty of flowers and seed pods for winter topiary projects from just a few plants.

a

b

c

a) Cover a chicken-wire frame with colorful fall leaves.
b) Mouse: A pre-made frame can be filled with crumpled newspaper, covered with sheet moss, and decorated with collected twigs, nuts, and seeds.
c) Collected materials from the wild or from the garden make wonderful dried standards.

Above: A surprise for parents - children will love making this mock ice cream soda.
a) A topiary ice cream float made with carnations.
b) Floral topiary animals made by using floral foam for the base.

Fresh Flowers

Start with five or six carnations in almost any color, a plastic glass, two straws, and one fake cherry. Put them all together and you have a topiary ice cream float. Youngsters will love teasing their parents with this unique party decoration.

Try making a floral animal. Set an Oasis® Igloo Holder (a small, rounded piece of floral-foam that comes in a plastic cage) on a tray or plate. Demonstrate how to add flowers tightly spaced to cover and create an animal body. The body shape is the same for almost any small creature, but its identity is established by inserting small cardboard cut-outs for ears and tails then adding button eyes. Try rabbits, cats, mice, hedgehogs, porcupines, and even imaginary animals. Experiment with coverings such as weeds, evergreen clippings, vegetables, or colorful foliage plants.

Young children enjoy doing projects with adults. The floral foam wreath filled with greens and flowers and the traditional ''florist topiary'' are both basic designs that children will understand and can participate in constructing.

Party Topiaries

Intriguing topiaries can be developed for a child's birthday party. Mini-topiary frames filled with special treats and toys can be used as individual party favors or presents. After the party, each child takes his topiary favor home as a keepsake.

Consider a turtle party with a large turtle for the center filled with fresh flowers and mini-turtles to mark each guest's table place. Turtles are a good choice, as they are well balanced on four feet and their basic outline is easily recognized without the need to add detailed features. The frames are designed and made in two parts. The lid (turtle shell) is hinged on one side so that it can open. Covering the topiaries with fiber-backed sheet moss makes them somewhat permanent and children can enjoy them for several months. The bodies can be decorated by gluing fresh flowers onto the moss. Later, the flowers are easily removed. The head and tail shapes are carved from Oasis®, fixed to the frame, and decorated with fresh flowers. You may wish to choose flowers that will dry and remain attractive. The legs are covered by wrapping with raffia strips.

Consider decorating topiaries with items found naturally. Dried flowers and leaves are more permanent. For specific suggestions for creative plant materials, see the sections ''Dried Topiary'' and ''Topiary and Flowers'', (page 128 and 132).

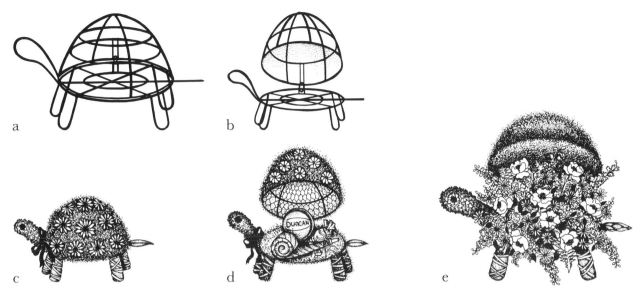

a   b

c   d   e

Party topiaries that open.

a and b) Hinged frame - closed view, open view.

c) This party favor is covered with sheet moss and decorated with fresh or dried flower.

d) The same party favor opened and filled with special treats.

e) Large turtle filled with fresh flowers.

Original Children's Garden at Longwood with topiary giraffe.

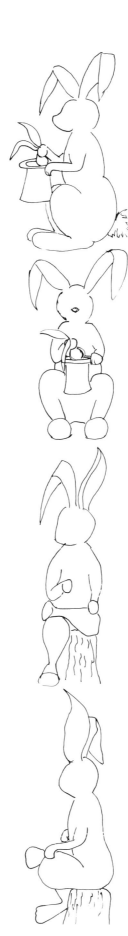

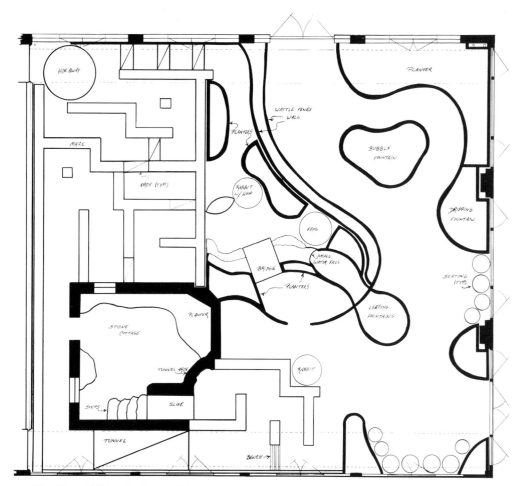

The New Children's Garden Plan, by M. Mizdail Allinson and C. Eberbach.

The Children's Garden

In April 1987, Longwood unveiled a 36- by 38-foot indoor garden for children. All the garden elements were scaled to child size. The major points of interest were a pool, several fountains, an elevated tree-house, a tea-garden and maze, and topiaries – four bears, two giraffes, and several birds. Some of these animal topiaries directed children towards activities. The topiaries identified and highlighted the points of interest, and for younger children they stimulated imaginary play. The 3-foot-high topiary maze walls, planted with ivy, created the "paths to adventure." With parents in sight, youngsters could retreat to nooks and corners to hide and play.

The ivy 'Gold Dust' was chosen for the speckled topiary giraffes. The bears were covered with *Polystichum tsus-simense,* table fern. The fern made the bears look fuzzy and cuddly and at the same time added another plant texture to the design.

The animals were large enough to be focal points of the garden and still be in scale with children. Each animal was carefully located with space left for the youngsters to become involved with the character. The first bear fished in the pool. The second bear sat in the tree-house, peeking through the rails surveying the entire garden. The bear stationed at the entrance to the maze and tea-garden held a sign for adults which read "Kids Only." Once inside the high-walled tea-garden, children found another topiary bear sitting at a party table, and they joined the party. Many conversations went on behind these walls of privacy.

The original Children's Garden was planned and designed to be a temporary display for one year. After three successful years, it was decided to replace it with a new Children's Garden covering the same area. The new garden will remain at least five years and incorporates all the best features of the preceding design. There are birds, frogs, and rabbit topiaries encouraging youngsters to join in on the fun and, of course, to learn!

The original Children's Garden at Longwood was a great success. It included a maze and topiary animals, a viewing platform, and tree house.

"Kids Only" Bear in the Children's Garden.

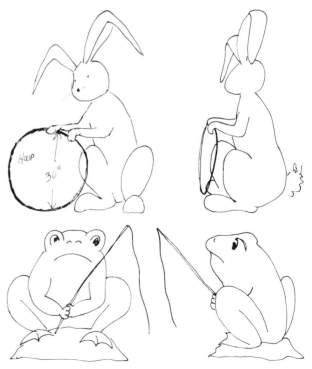

All drawings of the New Children's Garden topiary characters are by Mary Mizdail Allinson.

3. Interiorscaping, Outdoor and Turn-About Topiaries

Wherever plants are used to decorate commercial interiors, topiaries can provide noteworthy accents. Stuffed topiary has begun to show up in many interiorscapes. The more progressive mall management corporations have found that topiaries among the planted settings help make shopping an entertaining experience.

The secret of growing successful topiaries in these locations is to choose plants best adapted to each individual situation. If a fig tree does well in a foyer, then a fig standard will be successful, or if ivy is a good groundcover in a shopping mall, an ivy trained on a trellis or frame can be as good and even more interesting. Specimen topiaries in containers can be treated like any other potted plant as far as cultural maintenance is concerned, although special care may be needed to maintain the regimented shape.

Planning Topiary for Interiorscapes

Jenny Lloyd, owner of Jenny Lloyd Interior Landscaping in Darlington, England, says plants used in offices and work areas can be functional as well as enjoyable. For example, plants and particularly topiaries can act as dividers, giving each person's work area privacy.

Topiary birds used to decorate the fireplace for a wedding.

196

Landscape designer Deborah Reich uses topiary to add interest to her New York apartment.

This Meadowbrook patio topiary could be used successfully in a conservatory or garden room.

To use topiary effectively indoors, consider the size and decor of the area. Keep the topiary in scale with the setting. Standards fit nicely in classically designed areas, while topiary horses, pigs, and sheep might suit a shopping area with a country flavor. A modern decor calls for geometric shapes and abstract topiaries that could be trained up a frame.

Color is important in public settings, and several designers are developing topiaries that can incorporate colorful seasonal plants. Jeff Brees of Gardenworks in Coloma, California, has designed a stuffed topiary bear holding a honey pot which can be filled with fresh flowers or colorful live plants. Depending on conditions, plants with colorful foliage can also be planted into stuffed topiary. Hot, dry, and bright locations could be ideal for colorful succulents, which require less watering and usually less grooming.

Position indoor topiaries in conspicuous locations and do not crowd them into small areas or among other large plants. A giraffe should not be standing up to his neck in understory vegetation. Use topiaries for emphasis.

Always locate the topiary to be easily accessible for routine maintenance. If a gardener has to climb over or remove other plants to carry out maintenance, care will soon become minimal.

The basic considerations for adding plant topiaries to often less-than-ideal environments are water, light, temperature, humidity and good air circulation. These are the same elements that must be considered when any plant is used in an interiorscape. Numerous books on house plants and interiorscapes discuss these basic considerations, but there are some unique requirements when using topiaries indoors which should be clarified.

The single most important consideration in deciding what type of topiary to use is watering. What are the water requirements of the topiary? What are the site limitations and what happens to excess water? Stuffed topiary should be located where it can be watered regularly. Even if the topiary can easily be wheeled to a suitable area for watering, there is always some dripping afterwards. Planting beds are ideal locations in which to water topiary, but drip trays under containerized topiaries can also provide adequate floor protection.

Determine what light intensity the topiary will receive. If natural light is available, consider obstructions and establish how many hours of light are received per day, and at what time of day. Natural light can be supplemented or replaced by artificial light. If artificial light is already part of the setting, check the number of hours per day it is on and if it continues into evenings, weekends, and holidays.

Inside most buildings, the temperature ranges from 65° to 75° F., which is adequate for most plants used in interior displays. Temperature may be regulated according to the hours of human use per day and altered on weekends, so ensure that the topiaries will not be subject to sudden or frequent climatic changes. Plants in entrances can get repeated blasts of outside air drastically different from indoor temperatures. Only the toughest plants can survive such treatment.

Most plants can adjust to the lower humidity levels in buildings, but some sites offer advantages. Pools and fountains add moisture to the air, and planted beds and groupings of plants also raise the humidity since the soil mass will constantly give off moisture. Humidifiers or water trays under container plants can also help. Stuffed topiary has a slight advantage, since the moss acts as a water reservoir to raise the immediate humidity.

Stuffed topiary should be planted in such a way as to minimize the watering requirements. If vining plants can be planted into a container or bed and trained up the form, they will be less likely to dry out. Other long vines can be planted into the largest body area and trained out over the thinner areas, which dry out more quickly. (For more details refer to Large-Scale Stuffed Topiary on page 80).

Interiorscape topiaries may need special bases for anchoring into beds or containers to provide stability and safety. Hide any unattractive mechanics such as concrete or metal supports and growing tubs in attractive containers, or underplant them with foliage plants for cover. In planting beds, the topiary base can be totally recessed into the soil.

Watering Systems

Some growers have added watering systems to stuffed topiaries using plastic pipes with Chapin spaghetti tubing and weighted emitters inside the topiary. These systems can direct water to areas that dry out most often. Determining how many emitters are needed and just where to locate them requires careful planning. One problem is getting water evenly distributed throughout the moss. More water flows down than is absorbed upward. Getting sufficient water above the emitter locations may mean that the moss and plants below become too wet.

One grower has experimented with a submersible soaker hose. This delivers water through the stuffed topiary internally, but again, gravity causes anything below the perforated hose to be saturated long before the areas above are moist.

Longwood has used flat hoses, with holes evenly arranged along the top, to spray water out like a lawn sprinkler on the upper surface of the topiary. The water is evenly distributed and percolates downward, soaking the topiary thoroughly. The drawback is that the hose is visible in most situations and can be awkward to attach to many shapes.

Even though none of these systems can yet do the entire watering job, they may be the answer for hard-to-reach areas, and they can reduce the amount of time required for manual watering.

Transporting Topiary

Barbara Gallup of Totally Topiary in Stockton, New Jersey, is an expert on how to move topiaries for interiorscaping jobs. She recommends that when designing a frame, you should always add carrying handles for larger forms. The larger the topiary the more hands and handles will be needed. Hollow pipes are welded into the frames, providing a channel through the body of the finished character. A smaller pipe is slipped through this channel, creating easy-to-use handles and ensuring proper weight distribution.

Wrapping topiaries in protective plastic bubble wrap or styrofoam insulation blanketing provides protection. Always lay the topiaries down in the truck for transporting, perhaps on a foam rubber mattress for padding. Large bags of kitty litter, strategically placed and wedged into the topiaries, will keep things firmly in place.

Since the weather cannot be controlled, in winter heat up the vehicle before loading the topiaries and keep the heaters blowing until temperatures are stabilized. Keep the doors closed between trips while loading and unloading, both in winter and summer. Do not allow plant-covered topiaries to sit for prolonged periods in a closed van without air conditioning. Never subject living topiary to wind and weather by transporting it in an open truck.

When loading, plan the position of all the characters in the truck or van before the first piece goes in to avoid having to take topiaries in and out several times; otherwise, the arms, legs, tails, and other extremities may be damaged. If deliveries must be made to more than one location, load the topiaries accordingly.

Transporting topiary: The body section, of a horse by Richard Lyon in New Zealand.

Maintenance

Maintenance of topiaries in an indoor setting is no more difficult than grooming and caring for other plants. Start with properly grown topiaries that have been gradually acclimatized to the new environment and the job will be made easier.

Spend a few hours regularly trimming and grooming. Remove dead leaves, pinch, trim, and pin weekly. It will be surprising how little time maintenance actually takes if incorporated into a routine.

Interiorscape companies contracted to maintain displays often rotate the plants to ensure the best appearance at all times. Likewise, by having back-up topiaries and by switching them at regular intervals, those on display always look their best. This is particularly important if the display location does not meet the minimum light requirements. The topiaries could be exact duplicates or different characters, but each should be suited to the setting. You can use different characters to change the exhibit on a regular basis, perhaps with the season or holidays.

Ultimately, the success of topiaries in the interiorscape is in the hands of the people who maintain them. Properly trained individuals with a positive attitude make a big difference. Ideally, the same person should care for the topiaries regularly. All plants,

These classical shapes were displayed at Longwood in 1977.

Topiary swans and cranes planted with creeping fig at Owings Mills Town Center in Owings Mills, Maryland.

Harvey at the Fourth of July celebrations.

but particularly topiary, need a regular routine, with even and consistent care. A well-trained technician with an interest in the job will be quick to spot a problem and capable of caring for topiaries in most situations.

Bob Beck, staff horticulturist at Owings Mills Town Center in Maryland, says that in caring for stuffed topiaries in a public location one should start with the highest quality plants and topiaries. The sooner the maintenance technician becomes familiar with the topiary, the sooner he will overcome "topiary fears." It is important to examine topiaries to determine watering needs and to show restraint when fertilizing. Over-fertilizing vine-covered, stuffed topiary will only result in more pinching and pruning. Good grooming and proper sanitation practices will cut down on disease and insect problems.

After several years of caring for topiaries in a shopping mall, Bob has developed some ideas about the people who use shopping areas and how they feel about his topiaries. In the past, most maintenance technicians have been encouraged to do the public tasks before or after business hours, partly to make the job easier and also to give people the idea these areas are always perfect. Bob finds that visitors are very interested in the plants and topiaries and how he cares for them. They ask questions and seem to enjoy the topiaries more once they understand the mechanics. People do less damage to the topiaries when they can ask him if the plants are real or if there is a frame inside rather than poke and prod to investigate for themselves. Topiaries should be located where people can inspect them closely without trampling other plantings. Topiaries should be the focal points of the display.

Dee McGuire of McGuire Interior Plant Design and McGuire's Topiary Sculptural Design in Baltimore, Maryland, has been involved with interiorscape maintenance for fifteen years, and she and her husband Patrick design and build topiaries. Demand has exploded for topiaries in many of her interior locations. She attributes much of the success to Patrick's artistic abilities. A sculptor by profession, he develops life-like frames. She feels the public's attitude towards horticulture is becoming more sophisticated. People have always found great satisfaction in art and gardening. Topiary, she says, is the perfect marriage of the two!

George H. Manaker, author of *Interior Plantscape,* says decorating with plants is not a fad but is here to stay. Public interest in topiary, coupled with our increasing knowledge of plants which can be grown successfully indoors, has led to experimentation which shows there are plants that can be shaped or grown on frames for almost any interiorscape.

Outdoor Topiary

Container plants have been groomed and shaped throughout garden history. Today, topiaries adorn porches, decks, and patios and occupy focal points in many gardens. They are often in classic shapes like spheres, cubes, cones, cylinders, or pyramids, or they are pruned into cloud forms commonly called "poodles."

Standards are very popular in containers. Flowering standards are often grown all year yet displayed only during their flowering peak. Others, such as adult ivy standards, are permanent parts of a garden's design.

Uniquely detailed topiaries can be classic in style or whimsically fun-filled. Gardeners can entertain and amuse visitors with a plant-filled cat on the fence or a moss-filled horse in the pasture.

J. Liddon Pennock, of Meadowbrook Farm near Philadelphia, gives a vertical dimension to his gardens with topiary pyramids and an assortment of other classic shapes. He uses pairs of ivy cones planted in urns to flank the paths leading from one garden room to the next. These topiaries frame the well-planned vistas for which his garden is noted.

Topiaries can be used as sculpture in the garden and are usually a less expensive investment. Jeff Brees of Gardenworks in Coloma, California, accents his frames with decorative, hand-wrought copper, lead, and brass trim, creating one-of-a-kind pieces of garden art for outdoor use in the San Francisco area. In a roof-top sculpture garden, his topiary horses join bronze, steel, and granite works of art.

Cliff Finch, owner of Finch's Zoo in Friant, California, supplies topiary to shopping complexes, small business, private homes, and even to celebrities, such as giraffes for Michael Jackson. He concentrates on frames used as pruning guides for woody plants growing in the ground, but many are left in the containers for years and are used as portable topiary in the landscape.

Topiaries become advertisements when a company's name or logo is formed from living plants. Cliff Finch has topiary letters flanking the entrance of his business that spell out THE ZOO. A topiary elephant sat for years in front of the Elephant Bar and Grill in southern California.

Free-standing containers supporting trellis-work (or trellises) can be useful in the outdoor garden as portable screens. City gardeners can use topiary screens to provide privacy. Container topiaries are easy to move about to change the setting.

Portable outdoor topiaries are beginning to appear in commercial districts as well, particularly in the milder areas of California. The Horton Plaza shopping center in downtown San Diego has several whimsical characters on the main terrace that are at least 10 feet tall. They are large container topiaries with creeping fig growing up and over the frames.

On Pier 39 in San Francisco, topiary has been used outside since 1981. Carousel topiary characters are mounted in large containers planted with annuals. Ivy, also planted in containers, grows up and covers over the carousel animal topiaries, which appropriately surround a real merry-go-round. Since color is a main emphasis on the Pier, other topiaries incorporate displays of changing annuals. An ivy-covered, bathtub-sized basket is one of the most outstanding topiaries and is filled with color all year long.

In many regions, container or portable topiaries can be grown outdoors year-round. In others, topiaries must be brought indoors for the winter. If you can't leave container plants outdoors during the coldest months, chances are you won't be able to leave topiaries out either.

With stuffed topiaries, the plants may survive the winter if the body mass is large

This lion's spider plant mane did not survive outside in winter.

A similar lion but with a *Lirope* mane was left outside from mid December to early April. By early April the *Lirope* began to re-grow.

enough. At Longwood, (1990 USDA Plant Hardiness Zone 6b) we planted a larger-than-life lion with two ivies, *Hedera helix* 'Garland' and 'Ritterkreuz'. These two cultivars were used because they had performed well in our hardiness trials. We left the topiary outdoors in 1987 from July until mid-February with little winter damage to the ivies.

A chance experiment with outdoor stuffed topiary involved wintercreeper euonymus on another lion. This topiary was on display in a greenhouse until mid-December then was placed outside where it had no water or protection until spring. In early April, the body of euonymous was still alive and had already started to send out new growth. There was only minimal dieback on the tip of the nose and the front paws where the roots had the least protection.

In climates that have cold winters, submerging a topiary container into the soil or mulching the tub will help protect the plants. At Longwood, pyracanthas (normally hardy here when growing in the ground) have been planted in fiberglass tubs and grown in frames during the summer and fall. As winter approaches, the containers are grouped together in a protected area between buildings. A small wire fence is arranged around the group of tubs. Leaves are used to loosely fill in around the containers up to 3 inches above the soil level. All the plants come through the winter uninjured despite single digit temperatures.

Of course, the biggest advantage to container topiaries in the garden is that they are portable. A marginally hardy plant may need to be moved indoors for part of the season, but its special qualities can make it a valuable garden addition the rest of the year. Remember, though, that many hardy plants need a dormant season. Try to provide each topiary with a seasonal cycle as natural as possible.

Gardeners in warmer climates may have to protect outdoor stuffed topiaries from too much sun and heat. In hot, dry climates, stuffed topiary will need plenty of water. If the topiary is small, watering may be required several times per day. Plan the size according to your ability to provide this living garden sculpture with its daily requirements.

Swans add decoration to the Peirce-du Pont fountain.

Close-up of three-tiered standard from the square garden at Meadowbrook.

Marvelous color and shape combinations fill Liddon Pennock's Meadowbrook garden.

The square garden at Meadowbrook with topiary cones and tiered standards. Two young rosemary standards can be seen in the background.

Ivy hearts with stylised flower decoration.

Left: A pair of Turn-Abouts add decoration and emphasis to a front door.
Right: Proposed layout for an enclosed garden using turn-about topiary for emphasis and decoration. The layout was designed by Thomas J. Brinda of Callaway Gardens.
a) Bas relief or trellis Palladian arch or cut stone mural. Annuals at base.
b) Peegee hydrangea standards
c) Annuals in window box
d) Door
e) Fountain with topiary sculpture
f) Twelve squares indicate topiary

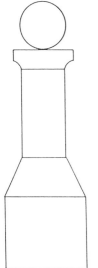

Classical shape for this turn-about.

Turn-About Topiaries

For those gardeners who have always wanted a traditional topiary garden but cannot wait twenty, thirty, or maybe fifty years, "Turn-Abouts" can be used to make an instant topiary display. This new concept combines classic style with modern methods.

Turn-Abouts are simply portable stuffed topiaries framed in classical shapes. Each topiary is built in parts that can be interchanged as desired. For example, a five-section topiary could have a square base, pyramid-shaped column, shelf, and a sphere at the top (see diagram). The frame is made in five parts, each fitting into the next by dowels that slip into a pipe sleeve.

Another possibility illustrated here is a pyramid done in three parts: a cubed base, an obelisk mid-section, and a small, pointed, pyramid top. The parts can be mixed and matched with other styles, and any number of combinations can be made.

An entire Turn-About garden could be designed with traditional shapes differing from usual outdoor topiary only by their ability to be moved. Imagine a chess garden with movable pieces.

This type of topiary is perfect for city gardens which are often small rectangular or square allotments totally enclosed by a fence or wall. Classic shapes in topiary can easily be added to an already formal garden layout. By rearranging the sections from time to time, you can maintain interest.

Artists impression of the turn-about garden.

PLANT LIST

American		English	
Trellis	*Clematis* 'Nelly Moser'	Trellis	*Hedera helix* 'Gloire de Marengo'
Palladian arch	*Hedera helix* 'Ritterkreuz'	Palladian arch	*Hedera helix* 'Glacier'
Center annual beds	Mixed planting of *Petunia* x *hybrida* 'Light Pink Pearls' *Petunia* x *hybrida* 'Azure Pearls' In 4 corners of bed, planting of 1 *Salvia farinacea* 'Victoria'	Center annual beds	*Catharanthus roseus* 'Morning Mist' (underplanted for spring bloom with *Tulipa* 'Blizzard')
Side flower beds	*Geranium sanguineum* var. *striatum* 'Splendens' In front of Palladian arch planting of 3 *Salvia farinacea* 'Victoria'	Side flower beds	*Astrantia major* (underplanted with *Lilium regale*)
Hedge	*Berberis thunbergii* cv. 'Kobold'	Hedge	*Taxus cuspidata* 'Densiformis'
Side beds groundcover	*Liriope platyphylla*	Side beds groundcover	*Sarcococca hookeriana* var. *humilis*
Bases of Pee Gee	*Hosta fortunei* 'Albomarginata'	Bases of Peegee	*Hosta* 'Francee'
Window box	*Hedera rhombea* 'Variegata' *Petunia* x *hybrida* 'Light Pink Pearls' *Pelargonium* (white cultivar) *Lobelia erinus* cv. 'Blue Moon'	Window box	*Petunia* x *hybrida* 'White Cascade' planted with *Hedera helix* 'Lalla Rookh'

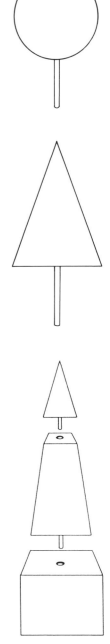

Each piece fits into the next by dowels that slip into the pipe sleeves.

207

A newly planted topiary. Ball: *Hedera helix* 'Gold Child'. Collar: *Hedera helix* 'Shamrock'. Pyramid: *Hedera helix* 'Pixie'.

The forms now well grown in and ready for display.

Pyramids with a ball of *Hedera helix* 'Gold Child' on either side of the steps at the Pierce-du Pont House.

Point: *Euonymous fortunei* 'Longwood'. Middle: *Euonymous fortunei* 'Longwood'. Base: *Euonymous fortunei* 'Gracilis'.

Completed pyramid ready for display

Flanking the door of the Peirce du Pont House are a pair of pyramids with bird finials.

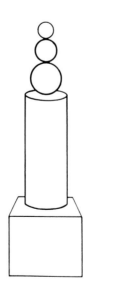

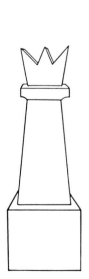

Classic finial forms such as crowns, balls, and obelisks can be replaced with whimsical characters such as cats, dogs, and birds, or a favorite animal or shape. For special parties, the tops could be replaced with floral arrangements or flowering plants.

Size and height can be altered by adding or subtracting the parts. In a new garden with young plants, the topiaries could grow along with the garden.

The frame design is basically the same as that used for the large-sized stuffed topiaries, with an internal skeleton and an outer wire shape suitable for stuffing and planting. Since the topiaries are intended to be moved around readily, it is important to minimize weight by limiting the stuffing. This is the perfect situation for a double-walled frame (see illustration). Double walls are much easier to construct for geometric shapes than for animal shapes. The thickness between the walls should be 3 to 5 inches; any thinner and the topiary will dry out continuously.

The center support pipe is the connecting sleeve. Each pipe should be aligned in the center of the topiary section frame. If not, the final composite may be off balance and look peculiar. The length of the dowel protruding below each interchangeable part should be long enough to keep the construction stable; if it is too long, it may be awkward to assemble, especially when adding the top pieces.

Geometric topiary garden specimens are often shaped according to specific formulas. These same guidelines should be followed when making Turn-About frames. On a vertical character with sloping sides, the incline is called a batter. The ideal batter is 2 to 4 inches of slant for every 1 foot of height. This formula will give the portable shapes the same classic proportion as old outdoor specimens. Hedges and walls with batters should be identical so that when lined up they will have a uniform appearance. Keep horizontal lines level in planting these topiaries.

Handles on the frame can be very helpful. They should be attached to the main structural support. Only add as many as needed and try to locate them in less noticeable areas.

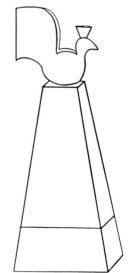

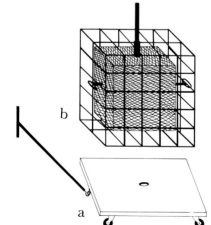

Left and above: An assortment of top pieces and line drawings of turn-abouts.
a) The base can be metal or heavy plywood. Castors aid in mobility. The handle is designed to attach easily.
b) The larger components have a double-walled frame and carrying handles.

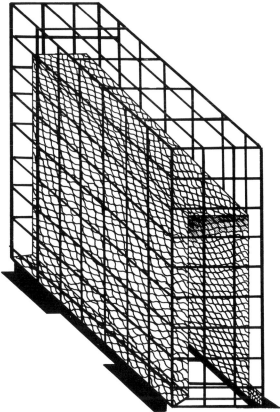

Above: Moss and plants being added to the hedge frame.
Right: A portable topiary wall or hedge frame. Double walled to reduce weight.

The base is important and requires custom design. A metal or heavy plywood platform should be made to fit exactly under the base section of the topiary. If plywood, it should be ¾-inch thick and an exterior grade. Paint the platform black so that it is less obvious. Attach four high-quality castors to the base at each corner to add mobility. Moving the completed topiary will be much easier if the castors roll freely. Purchase them with stops so they can be locked into place while on display.

The platform base should have a hole in the center of the bottom so that each dowelled topiary piece will be centered and secure. Remember to build the base up high enough so that the dowel can protrude through the bottom without hindering mobility. Add wooden blocks at the corners between the platform and the castors if necessary.

To make the topiaries easy to move around, add a detachable wagon handle to the base. A simple T-shaped handle that attaches quickly will do the job.

Stuff the double-walled topiary with damp sphagnum moss which must be packed tightly and evenly to prevent uneven drying. Hollow topiaries dry much faster than filled forms. Fillers and soil are not needed.

It is best to coordinate the plants used on the individual parts so that pairs and

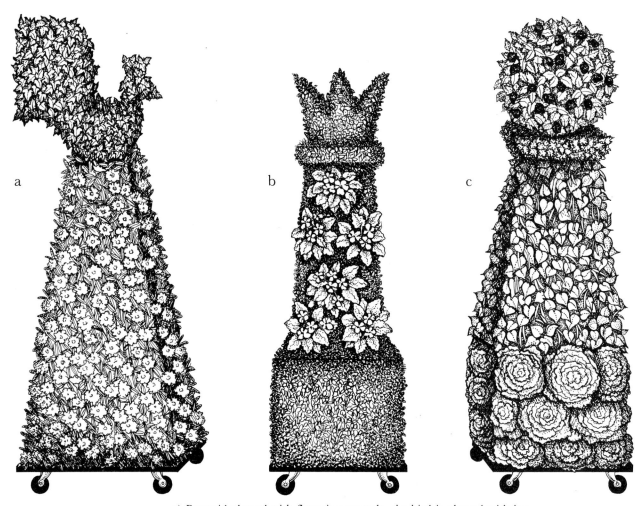

a) Pyramid planted with flowering annuals, the bird is planted with ivy.
b) Body planted with Ficus pumila, potted primulas added for decoration. Remember to reserve places in the turn-about with empty pots for the pot plants.
c) A celebration of vegetables: From top to bottom, strawberries, herbs, beans, lettuce or cabbage.

An example of pots in position to hold added flowering plants.

multiples match. For example, all the bottoms should be made of the same plants. The next section up should be different from the bottom, but it should match its equivalent on the other topiaries. This repetition helps tie the total garden design together.

Turn-Abouts open the way to an extraordinary plant selection. Not only can they be covered with plants normally suggested for stuffed topiary, but they also offer the opportunity of several plantings per section in one season. For instance, Turn-Abouts can be planted totally with vegetable plants. Imagine a tower of red and green lettuces, all types of cabbages, or strawberries. Apartment dwellers could enjoy their favorite salad and have gardening artistry on the patio at the same time.

Over the past few years, gardeners have been looking for practical but satisfying ways to horticulturally complement today's lifestyles. Many people no longer have the time or space for large, traditional plantings of vegetables, annuals or perennials, or specialty gardens, and Turn-Abouts offer an alternative.

Remember, the more compact the growth habit of the plant, the better the outline silhouette will be. In early spring, roll the Turn-About out onto the patio and plant it with frost-hardy vegetables; a rotation of lettuce could be planted on the base for several weeks. Once the danger of frost is past, one or more sections could be planted with early annuals. A truly dedicated gardener will have one part filled with herbs to use all season long. As different crops are harvested, summer flowering crops can be planted. At the base, a few climbing beans could be trained up the vertical structure.

A dramatic effect created by this grouping of Turn-About topiaries.

Another possibility is to plant the entire shape with a cover of ivy or creeping fig, reserving spots with empty plastic pots for an assortment of flowering plants. The flowering pots could be changed seasonally, from primulas in the spring to poinsettias for Christmas.

Many plant collectors like to place their rare indoor specimens outdoors during the summer months. The problem is that the plants are often forgotten outdoors and dry out, or it is impossible to arrange them attractively. And as spring turns to intense summer, they may need to be relocated to a shady area. Adding these plants to a Turn-About will solve these problems.

There are a few basic growing tips that are important with Turn-Abouts. Rotate the entire character on a regular schedule to provide light to all sides and to keep the plants growing at an equal rate. Do not push one side tightly against a wall or into a corner. This will not only restrict light and water to parts of the topiary but also can cause heat build-up from poor air circulation to quickly burn some of the plants.

Rotate the individual sections on the stack every few weeks. This will keep them from rooting into each other. In some cases, it may be necessary to grow sections separately so that each piece fills in and covers completely.

Always consider the cultural needs of each plant when combining more than one on a unit. All plants on a topiary should be compatible with one another as well as with the local environment.

Part IV
Elements of Topiary

1. Topiary Frames

2. Plants for Topiary

3. Plant Chart

4. Ivy Chart

1. Topiary Frames

Topiary frames range from simple, homemade supports to very ornate structures, from delicate 4-inch animals to buildings 22 feet tall or dinosaurs stretching 40 feet. Styles vary as much as the people who make them; many frames are works of art in their own right. Selecting the best construction method and choosing the right frame-maker are determined by topiary size, style, and special features.

Frames for all the types of topiary covered in this book include products that most gardeners would not think of as topiary supports. The florist industry produces frames made of plastic and Oasis® floral foam for floral topiaries. Oasis® and Sahara® floral foams are also available in block form and can be carved to create topiary shapes.Another popular frame combines several materials into a wreath base.

There are plastic topiary frames filled with dry moss. Soaked in water a few hours, they are ready to plant. Wooden stick figures have been used for outdoor topiaries and for containers. Even something like a lightweight aluminium wire hoop intended for needlework can be used as a frame (perhaps shaped like a teddy bear).

The frame for a 30-foot ivy bear at the Village of Alder Creek in Oregon's Mt. Hood Corridor was originally an old cedar tree stump with cedar boards added for appendages. Restoration after the bear toppled in 1984 included a new steel tower frame and extra shaping of angle iron.

The role the frame will play for a topiary will affect its construction. A frame can be used as a planting guide or as a pruning guide. Smaller stuffed topiaries usually need the frame for shape only. On the other hand, large stuffed forms need frames for shape and to support the weight of the structure.

Planting Guides

Vining plants that are trained up use the frame as a skeleton. Often flat, the frame needs to support only slightly more than its own weight, since wet moss (which is heavy) is not needed for this type of topiary. Often, vining plants develop a woody stem and begin to support themselves. Even if the frame is three-dimensional, the weight of the plant is insignificant until the topiary reaches about 8 feet in height.

Since vining plant topiaries are either silhouettes or outlines of shapes, details in the frame will not have to be as exaggerated as for stuffed topiary. Nevertheless, it is important to consider eventual plant growth when designing these frames so that features are not lost. Such frames are usually more stylized than the frames for stuffed topiary. Frames used as training guides can extend upward in a formal pattern or can create a path for plants to cascade down.

Pieces of wire not part of a frame are sometimes used to train individual branches into a desired shape, as with bonsai. Eventually, these wires may be removed and the woody stems will retain the form.

Pruning Guides

Frames developed as pruning guides are structures which surround the plants as they grow. When growth exceeds the limits set by the frame, the plant is sheared off. These frames usually don't support the plants, and often the plants are not attached to them. The structures should be anchored into the soil or onto the containers to keep them stable in windy weather. Securing the frames will also prevent movement that could result in pruning errors. These types of frames can be used for outdoor garden or container topiary.

A selection of topiary frames from a simple heart to an elaborate three-tiered standard.

A topiary frame: constructed with two hanging baskets.

Shaping

Small tabletop-sized frames are used to give shape to stuffed topiary. They also act as containers to hold the growing medium as well as the plants. Often, these frames depict small animals or birds, but even a wire hanging basket used to create a ball or bell can become a topiary frame. They need to be strong, durable, and well defined. Weight becomes a major factor when the specimens are people-sized, or the main body holds a thickness of moss that exceeds 12 to 18 inches. Beyond this thickness, reinforcement in the frame becomes essential for maintaining the shape and posture of a stuffed and planted topiary.

Large Shaping and Support Frames

When giraffes stretch 10 feet or penguins stand taller than men, the frames are more than a shape and a planting container. They must support several times their own weight and reflect finely detailed characteristics without sagging. As the topiary reaches these impressive sizes, weight becomes critical. One cubic foot of wet moss squeezed to the non-dripping point weighs about 33 pounds.

As size and weight increase, so do other considerations. Safety is important. Balance and posture must be well planned. Mobility should be considered before frame construction begins. Large creations often require an interior skeletal structure for support, balance, and mobility after planting.

Pagoda Frame

The 22-foot-tall pagoda displayed at Longwood Gardens in the fall of 1988 is Longwood's tallest stuffed topiary to date, and its frame required special planning, construction, and assembly. Every aspect of the pagoda frame was custom designed. This project brought the art of topiary to the level of architectural engineering. The frame was made of angle iron and constructed like a multi-story building. Before planting, the frame weighed 2½ tons. It had five tiers, each progressively smaller than the last. Four of the tiers were designed and manufactured in five pieces each; the top was one unit. The entire building was comprised of twenty-two pieces including the ornate top adornment. Each piece was permanently numbered by the welder for easier assembly. The tiers were separated for planting then, when grown, stacked for display.

Structural soundness required adequate building materials, a heavy-duty base, and anchoring. Even the strength of the conservatory floor had to be considered. Safety is particularly important when presenting a display of this size to the public.

Specialized Frames

Non-living topiaries can be covered with materials such as dried flowers, dried or preserved leaves, mosses, spices and seeds, and vines or twigs. Each coating requires a different support. Often, regular topiary frames can be covered with chicken wire, wire screening, nylon mesh, or any pliable surface suitable for adding various topiary coverings. Longwood's butterflies and apple trees (p.144) are two examples.

The Weathermaker Dragon's head, ready for a covering of dried material.

This partially stuffed rabbit was constructed with chicken wire. The unfinished leg or arm clearly shows this technique. Ears, legs, and arms can be made and planted, then attached.

Frame Selection

When selecting a frame, consider character interpretation. If the frame itself cannot be recognized immediately as the object being portrayed, then once plants are added, it will be even harder to identify. Definition, interpretation, and movement are three words often used to describe design elements of a superior frame. These artistic qualities become even more important as the frames become larger and details are magnified. If these components are not part of the frame before planting, they will not appear later.

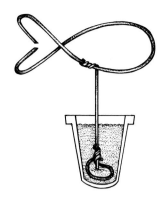

From a practical standpoint, make sure there are no sharp edges. The wire joints should be secure. The wire gauge must be suitable for the size and style of the topiary. For stuffed topiary frames the spacing between the wire must be large enough to allow filling and planting but close enough to keep the stuffing snugly in place. The wire structure should be three dimensional and provide a form. Often, smaller shapes will have arms, legs, ears, and wings that are just a flat outline and difficult to stuff. There are remedies for this situation with smaller frames, but as size increases, it becomes increasingly difficult to cover the flat appendage with plants. Choose or design a frame that is plantable but not bulky in appearance.

Mechanical needs must be considered. Balance, mobility, and structural support become more critical as the topiary increases in size. Free-standing topiaries must remain standing after they are filled with wet moss. Lifting points or provisions for moving need to be part of the internal structure. A life-size elephant standing on four legs cannot be transported by lifting from under his belly; he must be lifted by placing the stress on the internal support skeleton. The outer topiary wire cannot support excessive weight. Its function is for design shape and characterization.

Another practical consideration is maintenance. The frame needs to be made from a gauge of wire that will hold up for the duration of the topiary display. Thin wire rusts through quickly and should not be used for long-term topiaries. Most topiary frames made of steel rods should be rust-proofed and painted before use. This is particularly important for moss-filled frames that will be continually covered and in a damp environment. If the frame is cleaned and repainted regularly to protect it from rust, the life of a steel structure can be extended for several years.

The material used to build a frame can make it virtually permanent. Stainless-steel is more durable than steel rods. A stainless steel frame at Longwood which was made in 1968 still looks new even though it has been planted most of the past twenty years. If a project needs to remain in use for several years, consider using stainless steel, even if the price for the frame construction is considerably higher. It should last longer and require less attention and so be less expensive in the long run. Understand the expectations for each topiary and decide if the frame you have chosen will hold up.

Outdoor topiary frames used for pruning guides are sometimes made of flat strips of aluminium. These last indefinitely. Always anchor the frames securely to the ground. Such frames are not rigid so they can become distorted if not secured.

Homemade Frames

Making topiary frames at home can be as simple as reshaping a coat hanger into a circle or a geometric shape, then bending over the hook and using it to anchor the new frame into a flower pot. This can be used with a potted vining plant. Alternatively, an inverted wire hanging basket can be attached to the top of a sturdy stake to make an umbrella frame.

Wire is available in all gauges and lengths. With a little experience, mechanical minds can develop skills with metal working and make high-quality small- to medium-size frames. Choose methods for joining metals together, from soldering to portable welding, depending on your ability and resources. Joints can be made on smaller frames by wrapping with wire or strong tape. There are also small clamps available to hold frames together.

To develop your frame-making style, use real-life models or study photos of your subject. Put a sketch on paper and use it as a construction guide. A basic outline shape of wire can be developed into a stuffable frame by adding loops and circles to the

Simple shaping to create a topiary frame.

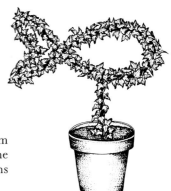

design. Your first project should be an easy subject. Before long, you will find a system that works best for you and progress to more intricate shapes and characters. The Complete Book of Topiary (see Gallup in book list) gives specific plans and directions for several topiary projects to get you started.

Chicken wire frames that can easily be made at home deteriorate faster than metal fabricated frames but they are inexpensive and easily manipulated. Shape the main body and connect the edges forming the seam by bending over the wire of the unfinished margin onto the matching edge. Appendages can be shaped from smaller pieces of wire mesh and attached to the main body.

With chicken wire more than with any other material, it may be necessary to add a support inside as the size of the frame increases. This can be of hard styrofoam, pipe, or wood strips. Without support, chicken wire frames sag and lose the desired shape when wet moss is added.

Openings must be left for stuffing a chicken wire topiary with moss. Usually, this type of frame is completely stuffed before the plants are added. Newly rooted cuttings can be planted by making a small hole in the moss through the mesh with a dibble. If the root balls are larger than the wire openings, holes must be cut into the wire. Each cut leaves sharp edges, and caution is needed to protect hands from scratches and punctures.

Liddon Pennock, founder of Meadowbrook Farm near Philadelphia, shapes forms from poultry wire, attaches them to containers of trailing ivy, then allows the ivy to cover the frames with long runners.

Style of Frames

Each framemaker brings his or her own style to the frame. At Longwood, our craftsmen have built frames for every type of topiary grown in the Gardens. During the early years, all of the frames were made in-house. Recently, outside professional firms helped fill our needs. Two firms have provided many of our most-talked-about frames. Both companies have developed special styles at our request. Topiary Inc., in Tampa, Florida, makes most of our small tabletop frames and many of our pieces up to 6 feet tall. Longwood Manufacturing Corporation in Kennett Square, Pennsylvania, makes most of our larger topiary frames.

Topiary Inc.

Carole Guyton and Mia Hardcastle started building topiaries in 1975. They began with a few very small animals and now make thousands of tabletop-size topiaries and hundreds of custom-ordered topiaries. Their frames and finished topiaries have reached every corner of America and beyond. Carole is the horticultural wizard and has perfected the technique of stuffed and planted topiary. Mia Hardcastle is a mechanical engineer and has developed the frame-making. As Mia creates a frame, Carole makes sure it will be workable. In 1983, when we started to plan Longwood's first major topiary display, we commissioned Topiary Inc. to produce thirty frames for us.

Topiary Inc. prefers to make topiary frames no taller than 5 feet; if they are larger they are hard to handle and difficult to ship. A portable spot welder is used. It is designed to weld sheet metal, weighs about twenty pounds, and plugs into a 200-volt clothes dryer outlet. Trigger-operated and easy to hold, it costs less than $400.

Plant growing up the frame.

14-gauge wire is used for the Topiary Inc. frames.

A simple jig is made using an outline drawing on plywood with nails and flexible wire.

A portable spot welder is used by Mia Hardcastle of Topiary Inc. for frame making.

Mia Hardcastle welding a frame.

After making a prototype, Mia develops a jig so that hundreds of nearly identical frames can be made by each of her part-time frame-makers. Each employee is supplied with an electric welder and is instructed in metal crafting by Mia.

For small frames, a jig is made by tracing the pattern onto a ½-inch piece of plywood, then tacking 6-gauge finishing nails about 2 inches apart along the outline. Flexible wire is then bent around the jig and spot-welded together. A 3-D figure can be made from this outline by adding a series of wire circles. Each size circle has its own mold, ranging from juice cans, bottles, and pipes to a vacuum hose! Ninety percent of their stock topiary frames are made on these wooden pattern boards.

Various wire and rod sizes are used to make the frames. The smallest are made of 14-gauge wire. These very tiny characters are generally not planted, since the thin wire will not hold up under repeated watering. Mia uses 12-gauge wire for many tabletop topiaries and feels it will last seven to eight years, even outdoors. Her frames of substantial size or for custom work are made of 10-gauge wire. One-quarter-inch steel to ¾-inch steel reinforcement bar is used for support in large frames. Straight lengths of wire are rigid and are used for straight parts of the frame. Coiled wire is more flexible and is easier to use for curves and rounded shapes, especially on a jig.

To give extra strength and increase the frame life, Topiary Inc. brazes the joints on larger frames. This gas-welding process uses a copper welding rod and adds an extra coating to the original electrically-fused joint. These brazed joints can be recognized by the copper-colored coating at each intersection.

Topiary Inc. paints all of its frames, and Carole has developed a dipping procedure to allow paint to reach every spot on the frame. She uses a thick paint mixture, giving the frame better protection from rust. Each frame is hand dipped in a large paint drum

Mia Hardcastle with the Longwood Gardens swan.

Treasure Dragon at Longwood. This frame is typical of the high quality work done by Topiary Inc.

Penguin and reindeer frames were the first large frames that Joe Piacentino built for Longwood.

Completed reindeers on display.

and hung to air dry.

Larger frames are spray painted, with particular attention to covering each joint since these are important areas of support. (At Longwood, frames are electrostatically sprayed with two coats of rust-proofing and two coats of paint.)

Longwood Manufacturing Corporation

Many of Longwood's larger frames have been made by Longwood Manufacturing Corporation, a company located near the Gardens but without any affiliation. Topiary welding is done by Joseph (Joe) Piacentino, the youngest of four brothers who run the business.

Although industrial fabrication is LMC's orientation, in 1986 the Gardens asked them to build frames for three penguins (one playing a piano, one playing a violin, and one serving desserts) and for four formally dressed reindeer (one sitting in a chair with her legs crossed wearing a strapless evening gown). The brothers exploded with laughter! Now, nothing the Garden asks for surprises them. Both parties work together closely to plan each new topiary, starting with basic drawings. The physical and mechanical needs are discussed in detail. The first frames started with detailed professional drawings and full-scale paper layouts; now the Gardens only has to supply a quick sketch!

Past experience has taught us that it is important for the frame-maker to understand the display position. We provide dimensions for the topiary, the display site, and the specific posture of the topiary figure. Often Joe comes to Longwood for on-site inspection and a better understanding of the projected display. He is now able to produce life-like frames which are not just simple characterizations but realistic sculptures. He studies photos of typical body structures before he begins to work.

To construct a large topiary frame, LMC starts with the base. Weight and balance must be considered. Should it have a solid base or stand on one foot? Will it be able to stand alone or will the frame need supports or anchors? Joe cautions that a large topiary figure must be properly anchored. Longwood's life-size elephant is a good example. The body weight created such tremendous pressure on the four free standing legs that after a year it was necessary to go back and add base strips of steel to tie the feet together, eliminate movement, and give the elephant stability.

It is best if each topiary can be free standing, unencumbered by support rods and pipes, although some life-like body positions can create an unbalanced situation. Wherever possible, LMC adds counterbalances hidden inside the body.

The skeleton is the interior structure that supports the frame, wet moss, and plants. Depending on the frame size, LMC uses ½-inch round stock or solid steel rod, steel pipe 1 to 2 inches in diameter, or, for extra-large structures like a pagoda, angle iron to make the skeleton. Pipe is Joe's preference because it is easier to bend and shape. Pipe is usually strong enough to stand by itself and to hold up the finished topiary. It attaches readily to the base, and it is easy to add the shaping wire to what is essentially a stick figure.

The real artistry starts with the wires used to create the figure's shape. Joe uses ⅛-inch round stock wire in straight lengths and 10-gauge flexible wire. The straight lengths are used for the ''ups and downs'' and the coiled wire is for shaping the outline, circle areas, and more detailed parts like fingers and toes.

Joe's step-by-step formula for developing a large topiary:

1. Base - construct one solid base or legs and feet
2. Skeleton - build with a stick figure for strength
3. Profile - develop the outline
4. Circles - make for head, body, arms, and legs
5. Draping - cover with wire mesh
6. Details - construct nose, mouth, etc.
7. Mechanics - attend to lifting points and extras
8. Clean-up - undertake visual inspection
9. Protection - paint with rust-proofing, etc.

Constantly referring to pictures and drawings, Joe develops a visual image into a 3-D character. After the basic shape is formed, he adds the mesh which holds the plants, moss, and filler within the frame. The size of mesh used varies according to location on the frame. Bottoms and undersides need tightly spaced mesh, while areas not working against gravity can be generously spaced. On large topiary, the mesh spacing can range from 2 inches square to 12 inches square. Joe knows that the person planting must be able to reach into the middle of every topiary. Very small tabletop topiaries need only enough space to get fingers and sometimes a hand inside. Larger frames may require arm-deep access. Occasionally, frames have been designed with a large access area for filling the center of the topiary.

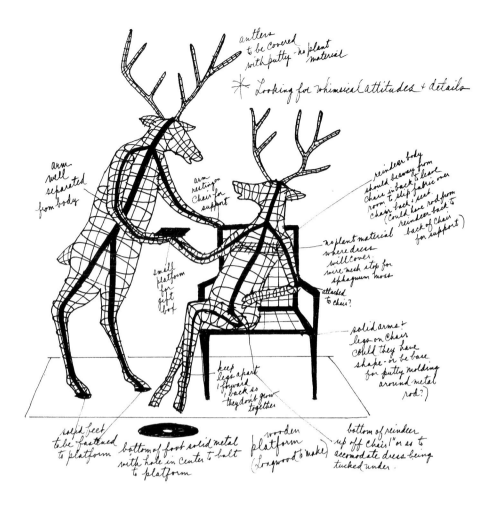

To decrease weight, it is possible to create a double wall so that the topiary center can remain empty. To do this, Joe uses a very fine mesh for the inner wall against which the moss is packed. Wire netting with a mesh stronger than chicken wire is used for these areas. The outer cover of wire is the same as for any other frame. When a double wall is used, Joe allows a minimum of 4 inches between the walls. Thinner walls allow the moss to dry too rapidly, increasing maintenance.

Details such as noses, fingers, ears, and wings are added after the figure has taken shape. If something like antlers or long teeth are added, it may be necessary to include a center support to stabilize and hold the weight.

Extras such as chairs and piano benches have become intricate parts of some frames, and they may become the base. Other additions may be nothing more than a small shelf to hold a plant or decorative prop. For one large penguin, Joe added extra wire supports to help hold a violin under his chin. A large elephant had a pipe added inside from toe to trunk; a hose was connected, and the animal was able to squirt water.

Topiaries that cannot be moved about easily or that must be lifted over obstacles need lifting points as design features on the inner frame. LMC tries to determine a balance point for the finished topiary. The weight distribution, once the frame has been planted, depends on the posture of each topiary and on how the topiary has been stuffed. Has it been uniformly stuffed? Has styrofoam filler been added evenly to all parts of the topiary?

The lifting points are loops or hooks added to the main skeleton structure so that chains or straps can be attached for lifting by a fork-lift or crane. Provision in the planted areas must be made to allow access to these points.

Before being painted, the entire frame is inspected and each joint checked to be sure it is secure. Sharp points and rough edges are eliminated, improving safety for the gardeners. Sharp points left on the frame can result in serious injury, since these areas are often hidden in the sphagnum moss.

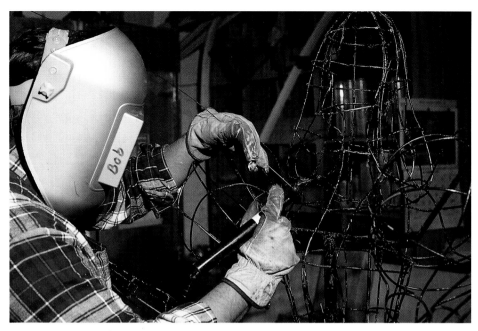

Bobby Nead of Longwood Gardens repairing the large Glinda frame from the Garden of Oz. Note the protective mask and gloves.

The welding process LMC uses is quite different from that used by Mia Hardcastle of Topiary Inc. Mia's small, hand-held welder heats two wires electrically, melting them together. This is excellent for constructing small topiary frames. LMC uses equipment designed for industrial work. Their method feeds a third wire onto the joints of the frame, adding increased strength to the area. This is similar to Mia's added step of brazing each joint, but LMC is able to do it all in one process.

Longwood Frames

Since 1955 when Longwood set up a fully equipped metal-working shop, frames have been made by Longwood's staff. The first frames were all used for chrysanthemum topiary. Many of these were made with ¼-inch stainless steel.

Bob Nead, who works in Longwood's metal shop, has made 10-inch squirrels and 70-foot fire-breathing dragons. He is often asked to make changes in topiary frames or modify an old frame for a new display. He makes weak frames strong, collapsed topiary stand again, and even totally rebuilds old frames. As the frames are removed from display, they are sent to Bob for inspection and repair before they go to the paint shop for a new coat, then storage.

Bob Nead uses many different metals - steel, stainless steel, wrought iron, and aluminium. His shop is equipped for any job and includes a Tig® welder and a Mig® welder.

The Big Dragon, a giant creature flowing in and out of the lawn during Longwood's 1988 Chrysanthemum Festival, was built by Bob Nead. He estimates there were one hundred and fifty to one hundred seventy-five hours invested in making the frame, which was built using ¼-inch rods in 20-foot lengths. He did not use any coiled wire, and since the Dragon was planned for dried material, no internal skeleton support structure was needed. In all, Bob used 1,000 feet of rod.

Jim Silvia

Another notable frame-maker is Jim Silvia of Middletown, Rhode Island. He created the trend-setting topiaries, (a human-size ivy-covered rabbit, owl, and deer), which were featured in *House and Garden* magazine in 1984. Jim's background is metal-

An elegant outline by Kenneth Lynch and Sons for the rooster frame.

Reindeer frames in the conservatory at Longwood Gardens.

working, and he owns and operates a welding shop. For topiary frame-making, he uses an industrial-type welder and works with 3/16- to ¼-inch rod. His frames range from tabletop sizes up to human-size figures. The heavier wire makes his frames strong without the use of an interskeletal frame.

Jim's artistic ability helps him to achieve detailed characters. Frame-makers are often not able to capture the graceful features of animals and birds when working with heavy wire. The end result can be stiff, robot-like characters.

His *House and Garden* characters had frames made of ¼-inch rod covered with chicken wire. He has also done frames that did not require any covering. White-tailed deer topiaries he made for a garden center near his home were so realistic that they were often mistaken for the real thing when viewed from a distance. Jim has made water birds, rabbits, deer, and geometric frames. Many have been used for special wedding decorations and as specimen pieces for sun rooms and patios. He has created frames for the Duke Gardens Foundation in New Jersey and a Mad Hatter for the Whitney Museum in New York.

Kenneth Lynch & Sons

Kenneth Lynch & Sons, Inc., of Wilton, Connecticut, was one of the first companies in America to make topiary frames, and they still produce elegant frames today. They carry a line of formal geometric frames, whimsical frames, and combinations of lead characters with topiary tails. Their hardbound catalog is a gardener's treatise.

Recently, Ernesta Drinker Ballard of Philadelphia gave Longwood one of the first frames made by Kenneth Lynch for a stuffed topiary. The 3½ foot-tall rooster was constructed of stainless steel in 1968 and is still in excellent condition. He has been remade and planted with the original ivy cultivar, *Hedera helix* 'Shamrock', and is once again on display, this time at Longwood.

2. Plants for Topiary

Longwood has developed the following chart lists which include a wide range of plants appropriate for container-grown or stuffed topiary. Since not every possibility could be included, plants were selected and grouped to give the reader a better understanding of the suitable types. The descriptive characteristics indicate the most important factors for topiary as well as the basic environmental requirements.

Standards trained on their own root systems and topiaries pruned into shapes without frame supports require plants that develop woody stems. These include tropical plants unable to tolerate frosty temperatures. Non-tropical plants have been grouped together. Further investigation may be necessary to establish their hardiness in your area.

Leaf size is important for all types of topiary, but particularly so for small-scale projects. It is equally important to know the flowering and fruiting habits of each plant because these aspects can add surprise and special beauty to a topiary. Sometimes these elements actually make the plant undesirable because the color is wrong, or the fruit is messy, or both flowers and fruits encourage insects.

The categories of topiary marked after each plant indicate the styles best suited for that plant. By combining the horticultural characteristics with the topiary categories, the reader should develop a clear picture of how to use the plants.

To save space on the chart, each plant is listed only by its generic name. Multiple category markings indicate that the plant genus or one of its species is versatile and could be used for several topiary styles.

In the "How To's" for each style, some information has been included about plant selection. Understanding the factors involved will give the reader the information needed to make the best choice.

It is difficult to decide which factor to consider first, since each topiary character may have more than one important factor. At Longwood, the plant selection process for stuffed topiary usually starts by reviewing plants that best represent the topiary character, and from there we decide if all the required conditions have been met.

Check list for choosing plants:

Size	Growth rate
Color	Growth habit
Leaf shape	Compatibility
Flowering habit and timing	Cost and availability

Size and Texture

The plant size needs to be scaled to the topiary. For very small tabletop topiary, use a small plant with small foliage so that the frame shape is not lost under large leaves or thick stems. Sometimes large topiary characters need to be graceful, so large, bold-textured plants might not work. Massive structures may need a tiny plant for definition of detailed characteristics. Often, it is important to contrast large plants with small ones to accent features such as faces, hands, and feet.

Life-size elephants and hippopotamuses could be covered with larger plant material with less delicate growing habits. An advantage of a large-leafed plant is that it quickly covers greater areas. The texture is important. A leathery, 3- to 4-inch leaf would represent the hide of an elephant better than a tiny fern-like leaf.

Color

Explore the colors of foliage as well as flowers. Colorful foliage can make a vivid topiary. Silver, blue, gold, red, and yellow hues in foliage are all available.

We have only begun to use flowers for topiary but the possibilities are exciting. Longwood's use of cascading chrysanthemums is a fine example of topiaries in bloom.

Choose plants with colors that interpret the character, such as silver for the Tin Woodsman or pink for flamingos. If you are using two or more colors, will they complement each other? Before the colors have been chosen, consider the display location.

Leaf Shape

Leaf shape can greatly enhance a topiary. A peacock's tail feathers are best represented by feather-like palm fronds. Small lanceolate-shaped ivy leaves work nicely as bird feathers. Table fern makes a dramatically hairy gorilla. Succulent rosettes are superb for scaly, hard-shelled creatures. And one of the best lion manes is the grass-like foliage of the spider plant.

Flowering Habit and Timing

If you are planning to use a particular plant for its flower color, make certain it will be in bloom at the time of the display. Consider the cultural requirements for flowering to occur. Will temperature and light requirements be fulfilled? Walt Disney World Resort® in Orlando, Florida, uses flowering wax begonias for fall topiaries with great success. But at Longwood during the fall season, the temperatures would be too cool and the light intensity not strong enough for begonias to flower. Use flowers that bloom normally under your conditions for your topiary display. Flowering annuals can be great in early summer, ornamental vegetables can be the answer for summer and early fall, and, at Longwood, the chrysanthemum is perfect for November.

Growth Rate

Sometimes the best plant for a particular topiary character is slow growing, and time becomes the deciding factor. If you are not in a rush, use that slow-growing choice. If the topiary must be ready quickly, choose the fastest growing plant available.

Growth Habit

Each topiary style requires plants with specific growth habits. Stuffed topiary needs plants that will spread and cover the moss-filled frame. Some plants cover because the growth habit is spreading, vining, and self-branching. Other plants such as wax begonias and alternantheras work well because they branch readily if pinched or clipped. Plants that do not send out new side shoots readily should be avoided for stuffed topiary. A vining or trailing plant generally works best for topiaries trained along a frame.

This charming little horse, using Ceropegia and Ophiopogon, is from Chicago Botanic Garden.

Tropical bird. The plant material is ivy 'Kobold' and purple passion plant.

The lion shows an excellent use of plants: body creeping-fig mane spider plant.

Compatibility

Don't overlook compatibility. Will different plants be happy together on a topiary? Do they have the same watering, temperature, and care requirements? Will they thrive in the environment of their final destination? Will it be effective to have a tropical plant representing a desert animal? Does this plant really make people think of that character? By considering as many factors as possible, you will develop the best characterization for each topiary.

Excellent use of material for this topiary poodle at Chicago Botanic Garden. The plants are *Sedum lineare* 'Variegatum'.

Another exotic bird. The plant material is Acorus and ivy.

Hippo planted with Alternanthera and Begonia. Walt Disney World Resort® in Florida.

PLANT CHART

PLANT NAME	Woody	Non-woody	Trailing or vining	Succulent	Tropical	Temperate	Deciduous	Evergreen	Annual	Perenial	LEAF SIZE (INCHES) -1"	1-2"	2"+	Variegated foliage	Foliage color	Ornamental flower
Abies	*					*		*		*		*				
Abutilon	*		*		*			*		*		*	*	*		*
Acacia	*					*	*	*		*	*	*		*		
Acalypha	*				*			*		*		*				*
Acorus		*				*		*		*		*		*		
Aeonium		*		*	*			*		*		*				
Ajuga		*				*		*		*		*		*	*	*
Allamanda	*		*		*			*		*		*				*
Aloe		*		*	*	*		*		*		*		*		
Alternanthera		*			*			*	*		*	*		*	*	
Azalea	*					*	*	*		*	*	*		*		*
Begonia		*			*			*	*	*	*	*	*		*	*
Berberis	*					*	*	*		*	*	*		*	*	*
Bougainvillea	*		*		*			*		*		*				*
Brassica (o)	*					*		*	*			*			*	*
Brugmansia	*				*			*		*		*				*
Buddleia	*					*	*	*		*		*				*
Buxus	*					*		*		*	*					
Callistemon	*					*		*		*		*				*
Camellia	*					*		*		*		*				*
Carex		*			*	*		*		*		*			*	
Ceropegia		*	*	*	*		*	*		*	*			*	*	*
Chlorophytum		*			*			*		*		*		*		
Chrysanthemum (c)	*		*			*	*			*		*	*			*
Chrysanthemum (p)	*					*	*			*		*	*			*
Cissus		*	*		*		*	*		*			*			
Citrus	*					*		*		*		*	*			*
Clematis	*		*			*	*	*		*		*				*
Clerodendrum	*		*		*		*	*		*		*				*
Coleus	*	*			*			*	*	*		*		*	*	*
Convolvulus		*	*			*	*	*	*	*		*				*
Coprosma	*					*		*		*	*	*		*	*	
Cotoneaster	*					*	*	*		*	*	*				*
Cotula		*	*			*		*		*	*					

(o) Ornamental cabbage
(c) Cascading
(p) Pot

PLANT CHART

PLANT NAME

Ornamental fruit	STUFFED FRAME Mini	STUFFED FRAME Tabletop	STUFFED FRAME Large	Accent plant	Wreath	Ball	Column	PRUNED TO SHAPE -2'	PRUNED TO SHAPE 2-6'	PRUNED TO SHAPE 6'+	TRAINED ON FRAME -2'	TRAINED ON FRAME 2-6'	TRAINED ON FRAME 6'+	Trained standard	Grafted standard	PLANT NAME
												*	*	*		Abies
							*		*	*			*			Abutilon
										*			*	*		Acacia
														*		Acalypha
		*	*	*		*										Acorus
																Aeonium
		*	*		*	*	*									Ajuga
							*							*		Allamanda
		*	*													Aloe
		*	*	*	*	*	*									Alternanthera
											*	*	*	*		Azalea
		*	*	*	*	*	*	*	*							Begonia
*												*	*			Berberis
							*							*		Bougainvillea
			*											*		Brassica (o)
														*		Brugmansia
														*		Buddleia
											*	*	*	*		Buxus
														*		Callistemon
													*	*		Camellia
				*												Carex
	*	*	*					*	*							Ceropegia
		*	*		*	*										Chlorophytum
			*		*				*	*						Chrysanthemum (c)
		*	*		*	*					*	*	*	*		Chrysanthemum (p)
		*	*		*	*			*	*				*		Cissus
*													*	*	*	Citrus
									*	*						Clematis
										*				*		Clerodendrum
			*		*	*	*	*	*	*		*	*	*		Coleus
									*	*				*		Convolvulus
											*	*		*		Coprosma
*									*	*	*	*		*		Cotoneaster
	*	*	*		*											Cotula

231

PLANT CHART

PLANT NAME	Woody	Non-woody	Trailing or vining	Succulent	Tropical	Temperate	Deciduous	Evergreen	Annual	Perenial	-1"	1-2"	2"+	Variegated foliage	Foliage color	Ornamental flower
Cotyledon		*		*	*			*		*				*		
Cryptanthus		*			*			*		*			*	*	*	
Cupressus	*					*		*		*	*				*	*
Cymbalaria		*	*			*		*		*	*					*
Cytisus	*					*	*	*		*	*					
Echeveria		*		*		*		*		*				*		*
Erica	*					*		*		*	*				*	*
Eugenia	*				*			*		*		*	*		*	*
Euonymus	*		*			*	*	*		*	*	*	*	*	*	
Euphorbia	*		*	*	*	*	*	*		*		*	*	*	*	*
E. pulcherrima	*				*			*		*			*	*	*	
Evolvulus	*		*		*			*		*	*				*	*
x Fatshedera	*					*		*		*				*		
Faucaria		*		*	*			*		*				*		
Ficus	*		*		*	*	*	*		*	*	*	*	*		
Fittonia		*	*		*			*		*	*	*	*	*		
Fortunella	*					*		*		*				*		*
Fuchsia	*		*			*	*	*		*	*	*	*			*
Gardenia	*				*	*		*		*		*	*			*
Gasteria		*		*	*			*		*				*		
Grevillea	*					*		*		*				*		*
Guzmania		*			*			*		*			*	*	*	*
Haworthia		*		*		*		*		*	*	*	*		*	
Hedera	*		*			*		*		*	*	*	*	*	*	*
Hoya	*	*	*		*	*		*		*	*	*	*	*	*	*
Hydrangea	*		*			*	*	*		*				*		
Iboza	*				*			*		*			*			*
Ilex	*					*	*	*		*	*	*	*	*		
Impatiens		*			*			*	*	*			*		*	*
Ipomoea		*	*		*		*	*	*					*		*
Jasminum	*		*		*	*	*	*		*		*	*	*		*
Juniperus	*		*			*		*		*	*					
Lagerstroemia	*					*	*	*		*				*		*
Lantana	*		*		*			*		*		*		*	*	*

PLANT CHART

PLANT NAME

Ornamental fruit	STUFFED FRAME			Accent plant	Wreath	Ball	Column	PRUNED TO SHAPE WITH OR WITHOUT FRAME (FEET)			TRAINED ON FRAME (FEET)			Trained standard	Grafted standard	PLANT NAME
	Mini	Tabletop	Large					-2'	2-6'	6'+	-2'	2-6'	6'+			
			*	*												Cotyledon
		*	*	*	*	*										Cryptanthus
													*			Cupressus
		*	*		*											Cymbalaria
											*	*	*	*		Cytisus
		*	*	*	*	*										Echeveria
											*	*		*		Erica
*											*	*		*		Eugenia
		*	*						*	*	*	*		*		Euonymus
									*	*	*	*		*		Euphorbia
				*		*	*							*	*	E. pulcherrima
									*	*				*		Evolvulus
														*	*	x Fatshedera
	*	*		*												Faucaria
	*	*	*		*						*	*		*		Ficus
	*	*			*											Fittonia
*														*		Fortunella
*					*	*	*	*	*	*	*	*	*	*		Fuchsia
											*	*		*		Gardenia
				*												Gasteria
														*		Grevillea
				*												Guzmania
	*	*	*	*												Haworthia
*	*	*	*	*	*	*	*	*	*	*	*	*	*	*	*	Hedera
				*				*	*	*						Hoya
						*	*							*		Hydrangea
												*		*		Iboza
*											*	*	*	*		Ilex
				*		*	*									Impatiens
										*						Ipomoea
									*	*				*		Jasminum
		*	*	*						*		*	*	*		Juniperus
														*		Lagerstroemia
						*	*		*	*				*		Lantana

PLANT CHART

PLANT NAME	Woody	Non-woody	Trailing or vining	Succulent	Tropical	Temperate	Deciduous	Evergreen	Annual	Perennial	LEAF SIZE (INCHES) -1"	1-2"	2"+	Variegated foliage	Foliage color	Ornamental flower
Laurentia		*	*			*			*	*	*					*
Laurus	*					*		*		*		*				
Lavandula	*					*		*		*	*				*	*
Leptospermum	*					*		*		*		*				*
Ligustrum	*					*	*	*		*		*			*	
Liriope		*				*		*		*				*		*
Lonicera	*		*			*	*	*		*				*		*
Lysimachia		*	*			*		*		*	*				*	
Macfadyena	*		*		*			*		*				*		*
Malus	*					*	*			*				*	*	*
Mandevilla	*		*		*			*		*					*	*
Mentha		*				*	*			*	*					
Metrosideros	*		*			*		*		*				*		*
Mikania		*	*			*	*	*		*				*		
Muehlenbeckia	*	*	*			*		*		*	*					
Myrsine	*					*		*		*		*				*
Myrtus	*					*		*		*	*					
Neohenricia		*	*	*	*			*		*	*					
Nerium	*					*		*		*				*		*
Nertera		*	*			*		*		*	*					
Olea	*					*		*		*		*				*
Ophiopogon		*				*		*		*				*		*
Pachyphytum		*		*		*		*		*				*		
Pachystachys	*				*			*		*				*		*
Pelargonium (zonal) (Geranium)	*					*		*		*	*	*	*	*		*
Pelargonium (Ivy Geranium)		*	*			*		*		*	*	*	*	*		*
Pellionia		*	*		*			*		*		*	*	*	*	*
Petrea	*		*		*			*		*				*		*
Petunia		*	*		*				*			*		*		*
Picea	*					*		*		*	*					
Pilea		*			*	*		*	*	*		*		*	*	
Pinus	*					*		*		*		*	*			

234

PLANT CHART

Ornamental fruit	STUFFED FRAME			Accent plant	Wreath	Ball	Column	PRUNED TO SHAPE WITH OR WITHOUT FRAME (FEET)			TRAINED ON FRAME (FEET)			Trained standard	Grafted standard	PLANT NAME
	Mini	Tabletop	Large					-2'	2-6'	6'+	-2'	2-6'	6'+			
								*	*	*						Laurentia
												*	*	*		Laurus
											*	*	*	*		Lavandula
									*	*		*	*	*		Leptospermum
												*	*			Ligustrum
			*	*												Liriope
									*	*						Lonicera
	*	*	*		*											Lysimachia
									*	*						Macfadyena
														*		Malus
									*	*						Mandevilla
	*	*	*													Mentha
										*				*		Metrosideros
	*	*	*		*											Mikania
	*	*	*		*	*		*	*	*						Muehlenbeckia
											*	*	*	*		Myrsine
											*	*	*	*		Myrtus
	*	*														Neohenricia
														*		Nerium
	*	*														Nertera
*												*	*	*		Olea
		*	*	*												Ophiopogon
		*	*	*	*	*										Pachyphytum
														*		Pachystachys
				*		*	*				*	*	*	*		Pelargonium (zonal) (Geranium)
					*	*	*	*	*	*				*		Pelargonium (Ivy Geranium)
		*	*	*	*											Pellionia
									*	*				*		Petrea
		*	*		*	*										Petunia
													*	*		Picea
		*	*													Pilea
													*	*		Pinus

235

PLANT CHART

PLANT NAME	Woody	Non-woody	Trailing or vining	Succulent	Tropical	Temperate	Deciduous	Evergreen	Annual	Perennial	-1"	1-2"	2"+	Variegated foliage	Foliage color	Ornamental flower
Pittosporum	*				*	*		*		*				*		*
Plumbago	*		*		*			*		*		*				*
Podocarpus	*					*		*		*		*				
Polystichum		*				*		*		*			*			
Poncirus	*					*	*			*		*				*
Portulaca		*	*	*		*			*		*					
Portulacaria		*	*	*		*	*			*	*					
Pyracantha	*					*		*		*		*				*
Rhododendron	*					*		*		*		*	*			*
Rosa	*		*			*	*			*		*				*
Rosmarinus	*		*			*		*		*	*				*	*
Sagina		*	*			*		*	*	*	*				*	
Salvia	*				*	*	*	*	*	*		*				*
Schefflera	*				*			*		*		*				
Scirpus		*			*	*		*		*		*				
Sedum		*	*	*		*		*		*						
Selaginella		*	*		*	*		*		*	*					
Sempervivum		*		*		*		*		*		*	*		*	
Senecio	*	*	*	*	*	*		*	*	*		*	*		*	*
Serissa	*					*		*		*	*					*
Solanum	*				*			*		*		*		*		*
Soleirolia		*	*			*		*		*	*			*	*	
Taxus	*					*		*	*	*	*					
Teucrium	*	*				*		*	*	*						*
Thuja	*					*		*		*	*					
Thunbergia	*		*		*			*		*		*				
Thymus	*		*			*		*		*	*			*	*	*
Tibouchina	*				*			*		*		*	*			*
Tillandsia		*	*		*	*		*		*	*	*	*	*	*	*
Tropaeolum		*	*			*			*			*				*
Ugni	*					*		*		*	*					*
Verbena	*	*	*		*	*	*	*	*	*				*		*
Westringia	*					*		*		*	*					

PLANT CHART

Ornamental fruit	Mini	Tabletop	Large	Accent plant	Wreath	Ball	Column	Pruned -2'	Pruned 2-6'	Pruned 6'+	Trained -2'	Trained 2-6'	Trained 6'+	Trained standard	Grafted standard	PLANT NAME
*											*	*	*	*		Pittosporum
							*		*	*				*		Plumbago
												*	*	*		Podocarpus
		*	*	*	*	*	*									Polystichum
*														*		Poncirus
	*	*	*													Portulaca
		*	*	*												Portulacaria
*									*	*		*	*			Pyracantha
												*	*	*		Rhododendron
*									*	*				*	*	Rosa
								*	*	*	*	*	*	*		Rosmarinus
	*	*	*													Sagina
														*		Salvia
															*	Schefflera
		*	*	*												Scirpus
	*	*	*	*												Sedum
	*	*	*													Selaginella
	*	*	*	*	*	*										Sempervivum
		*	*		*			*	*	*				*		Senecio
											*			*		Serissa
*												*	*	*		Solanum
	*	*	*													Soleirolia
												*	*			Taxus
											*	*				Teucrium
												*	*	*		Thuja
									*	*						Thunbergia
	*	*	*													Thymus
														*		Tibouchina
		*														Tillandsia
						*			*	*						Tropaeolum
*												*		*		Ugni
					*	*								*		Verbena
												*	*	*		Westringia

Ivy

Ivy is the plant most often used for portable and container topiary. One commercial greenhouse in California reports growing more than forty thousand ivy topiaries each year. Ivy trees at Christmas are popular, and stuffed topiaries covered with fancy Hedera have become fashionable.

Ivy is indispensable to the gardener looking for easy-to-grow, dependable plant sculptures. Most cultivars of Hedera are tolerant of a wide range of light and temperature conditions. Bob Beck, a horticulturist living in Owings Mills, Maryland, refers to ivies on topiaries as "user friendly." He feels they readily lend themselves to all the bending, twisting, pinning, pinching, and cultural conditions that topiaries must endure. The truth is there is at least one cultivar of ivy for every topiary need.

The single most important factor that makes ivy so popular for portable and container topiary is the speed with which many of the cultivars grow. Unlike traditional outdoor topiary requiring twenty to thirty years, these newer styles are nearly instantaneous. Whimsical characters are amusing as soon as they are built, and within a few months, stuffed critters of ivy are completely covered. And even the worst catastrophe (such as forgetting to water for weeks) can be quickly corrected by replanting.

The ivy chart points out characteristics important for topiary use. Each of the ivies has been growing at Longwood for a minimum of two years. Many of the cultivars have been used on topiary, and the others have been evaluated for use. By combining the facts about each cultivar with the suggested styles, you should be able to select an ivy suitable for any project.

Pierot Classification

The American Ivy Society has adopted the Pierot System of Classification as a consistent and convenient way to identify ivy. The system was developed by Suzanne Pierot in her work, The Ivy Book, The Growing and Care of Ivy and Ivy Topiary.

The eight-category system classifies leaf shapes found among ivy as follows:

M	=	Miniatures	B-			C	=	Curlies
H	=	Heart-shaped	F	=	Bird's foot	I-I	=	Ivy-ivies
F	=	Fans	V	=	Variegateds	O	=	Oddities

Suzanne describes "Miniatures" as "plants with the majority of leaves under one half an inch; and plants with the majority of leaves about one inch but because they are so delicate, slender, and finely cut, they appear to be miniature." The "Variegateds" include any ivy with more than one color in the foliage. "Oddities" are cultivars that do not fit elsewhere.

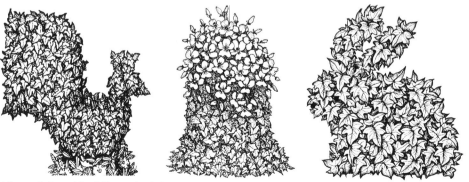

Above: Ivies with different leaf sizes for these topiaries.

The Ivy Chart

Each of the Hedera cultivars has been coded by the Pierot Classification to help identify the plant. On the ivy chart, the growth habit has been divided into categories starting with "Trailing" and "Upright." Trailers are best for most styles of topiary, but ivies pruned into a shape without a frame require an upright woody stem. If a plant is marked in both categories, the habit would be upright but not woody and eventually it would flop over and trail.

Self-branching ivies are best for stuffed styles because they will cover quickly, but ivies trained on a frame, particularly small items, are better if they branch only with pinching. However, there are some ivies that will develop only one shoot per stem no matter how many times they are pinched.

The lengths of the internode (the area between leaves on the stem) and petiole (the leaf stem), noted in general terms on this chart, are important for topiary work because ivies with short internodes and petioles cover surfaces better and help to define the shapes, almost like tight-fitting clothing. On the other hand, long spaces between leaves and stem create an open, vining appearance. Long petioles make the leaves stand out from the topiary, and on small topiaries the definition of shape can be lost. For some ivies, neither category has been marked, indicating the ivy is average in appearance and could be suitable for any type of topiary.

a b c d e

a) Ivy – not self-branching. If pinched, it may produce one or two breaks.
b) Ivy – readily self-branching.
c) Ivy – self-branching if pinched.
d) Ivy – short internodes.
e) Ivy – long internodes.

Leaf color is important and will often determine cultivar selection. The chart indicates the shades of green as well as variegations. In some cases, an ivy will fall into more than one category. The following examples help explain the designations:

1. An ivy marked "Medium Green" and "Variegated Green and White" indicates two colors – medium green and white.

2. An ivy marked "Dark Green" and "Variegated Green and White" indicates two colors – dark green and white.

3. An ivy marked "Dark" or "Medium Green" and "Variegated Gray and White" indicates three colors – green, gray, and white.

Ivies suitable for topiaries growing at Ivies of the World in Florida.

Frog using *Euonymous fortunei* 'Minima' and *Hedera helix* 'Calico'.

The green herons are planted with *Hedera helix* 'Green Feather'. The cattle egrets are *Hedera helix* 'Denmark'.

Plants including ivies used for topiary.

A marking for "color" indicates that there are possibilities other than those above, including: gold, gold and green, gold turning green, red stems, and winter colors, usually ranging from light pink to dark purple-black. These color distinctions will be useful when selecting ivy for topiary.

Leaf sizes have been divided into the same three categories used in the general chart. There are many cultivars that are larger than two inches, but their use would be limited to the grandest projects. By contrast, detailed information about leaf size is very important when choosing ivies for frames under 6 feet. Do not use ivies too large for the frame size. Remember to scale the ivy to the topiary.

Ivy – leaf size: 2 inches or more, 1 to 2 inches, under 1 inch.

American Ivy Society

All of the ivies on this chart have been verified by The American Ivy Society. Unfortunately, there are many ivies in the trade that are improperly labelled. Nonetheless, this chart should serve as a guide for plant selection.

The American Ivy Society (AIS) is dedicated to encouraging the use of proper nomenclature among commercial growers. AIS offers an identification service, and there are many reputable and dedicated growers who are having their ivies verified. These ivies will be identified in catalogs by an American Ivy Society number (AIS 00-000) after the name. The American Ivy Society will provide a list of commercial members upon request as well as general ivy information. Write to:

The American Ivy Society
PO Box 520
West Carrollton, OH 45449

For ivy growers and information in Great Britain:

The British Ivy Society
14 Holly Grove
Huyton
Merseyside
L36 4JA

Variegated ivy.

IVY CHART

IVY NAME	Pierot Classification	GROWTH HABIT							COLOR						LEAF SIZE (INCHES)	
		Upright	Trailing	Readily self-branching	Self-branching if pinched	Non self-branching	Internodes & Petioles - short	Internodes & Petioles - long	Medium green	Dark green	Variegated green & white	Variegated gray & white	Other colors	Winter color	1" or less	1-2"
Hedera azorica cv. Variegata	V,F		*			*					*					
Hedera canariensis	H		*			*		*		*						
Hedera canariensis cv. Gloire de Morengo	V		*			*		*		*		*				
Hedera colchica cv. Sulphur Heart	H		*			*		*		*			*			
Hedera helix cv. Ambrosia	V	*	*				*					*			*	
Angularis-Aurea	V		*			*		*		*			*			
Anne Marie	V		*		*				*			*				
Appaloosa	V,C		*	*					*		*					
Asterisk	BF		*	*					*							
Astin	O,C	*			*				*							*
Big Deal	O,F		*	*					*							
Boskoop	C		*	*				*	*							*
Brokamp	BF		*			*				*						
Buttercup	V		*			*				*			*	*		*
Caecilia	V,C		*		*				*			*				
Calico	V		*	*			*				*	*				*
California	C		*		*		*		*							*
California Fan	F,C		*	*					*							*
California Gold	V,C		*	*			*			*			*			*
Carolina Crinkle	C		*	*						*						*
Cascade	I,C		*	*			*			*					*	
Chester	V		*			*		*		*		*				
Chicago	I		*	*						*						*
Christian	M,H		*			*		*								*
Cockle Shell	F		*	*					*							*
Congesta	O	*				*	*			*					*	
Conglomerata	O,C	*				*	*			*					*	
Curly Locks	C		*		*			*	*					*		
Curvaceous	V,C		*	*					*			*		*		
Cyrano de Bergerac	O		*		*			*	*							

242

IVY CHART

Topiary Style & Size — columns: 2" or more (leaf size, inches); Mini stuffed; Tabletop stuffed; Large stuffed; Accent plant stuffed; Wreath; Balls; Bells; Columns. Trained on Frame (Feet): 2' or less; 2'-6'; 6' or more. Pruned to Shape With or Without Frame (Feet): 2' or less; 2'-6'; 6' or more. Grafted standard.

2" or more	Mini stuffed	Tabletop stuffed	Large stuffed	Accent plant stuffed	Wreath	Balls	Bells	Columns	Trained 2' or less	Trained 2'-6'	Trained 6' or more	Pruned 2' or less	Pruned 2'-6'	Pruned 6' or more	Grafted standard	IVY NAME
*			*	*							*					*Hedera azorica* cv. Variegata
*		*	*					*			*					*Hedera canariensis*
*		*	*							*	*					*Hedera canariensis* cv. Gloire de Morengo
*			*								*					*Hedera colchica* cv. Sulphur Heart
									*	*						*Hedera helix* cv. Ambrosia
*										*	*					Angularis-Aurea
*		*	*													Anne Marie
*		*	*												*	Appaloosa
*	*	*			*			*							*	Asterisk
			*									*				Astin
*			*												*	Big Deal
									*	*	*					Boskoop
*			*								*					Brokamp
										*	*					Buttercup
*			*	*		*	*	*		*	*					Caecilia
	*	*	*	*	*	*	*	*							*	Calico
*	*	*	*	*	*										*	California
	*	*	*	*						*					*	California Fan
	*	*	*	*	*			*							*	California Gold
	*	*	*	*	*			*							*	Carolina Crinkle
	*	*			*	*		*							*	Cascade
										*	*					Chester
		*			*	*	*	*							*	Chicago
		*	*													Christian
			*						*	*	*					Cockle Shell
												*	*			Congesta
												*	*			Conglomerata
*			*								*					Curly Locks
*	*	*	*	*	*			*								Curvaceous
*											*					Cyrano de Bergerac

IVY CHART

IVY NAME	Picrot Classification	Upright	Trailing	Readily self-branching	Self-branching if pinched	Non self-branching	Internodes & Petioles - short	Internodes & Petioles - long	Medium green	Dark green	Variegated green & white	Variegated gray & white	Other colors	Winter color	1" or less	1 - 2"
Dealbata	V		*			*				*	*					*
Deltoidea	H		*		*		*			*				*		*
Denmark	M, V		*		*		*		*			*			*	
Diana	O		*		*		*		*							*
Dragon Claw	C		*		*		*		*					*		
Duck Foot	M, BF		*	*			*		*						*	
Elegantissima	V		*			*		*		*	*			*		*
Elfenbein	V		*			*		*				*				
Emerald Globe	O	*		*			*			*					*	
Ester	V		*		*		*		*			*			*	
Eva	V		*	*			*		*			*			*	
Fallen Angel	O	*	*	*			*		*							*
Fan	F		*	*					*							*
Fantasia	V		*		*			*	*		*					
Fiesta	C		*			*		*	*							
Filigran	C	*	*		*		*			*						*
Fluffy Ruffles	C		*		*			*	*							
Galaxy	BF		*	*					*							*
Garland	H		*	*			*			*						
Gavotte	H		*	*			*			*						
Gertrud Stauss	V		*	*					*			*				*
Glacier	V		*		*				*			*		*		*
Gold Graft	V		*		*		*		*				*	*		*
Gold Dust	V		*		*					*			*			*
Gold Heart	V		*			*		*		*			*	*		*
Gold Child	V		*		*				*				*	*		
Green Feather	BF		*		*		*			*					*	
Green Ripple	F		*		*					*						*
Harrison	I		*			*		*		*				*		*
Helena	V, BF		*	*			*		*		*					*
Helvetica	H		*			*		*		*						*
Hibernica	I		*			*		*		*						

IVY CHART

LEAF SIZE (INCHES)	TOPIARY STYLE & SIZE								TRAINED ON FRAME (FEET)			PRUNED TO SHAPE WITH OR WITHOUT FRAME (FEET)				IVY NAME
2" or more	Mini stuffed	Tabletop stuffed	Large stuffed	Accent plant stuffed	Wreath	Balls	Bells	Columns	2' or less	2'-6'	6' or more	2' or less	2'-6'	6' or more	Grafted standard	
									*	*	*					Dealbata
		*	*	*					*	*	*					Deltoidea
		*	*		*			*								Denmark
			*		*			*								Diana
*			*	*		*		*							*	Dragon Claw
	*	*	*		*											Duck Foot
										*	*					Elegantissima
*										*	*					Elfenbein
												*	*			Emerald Globe
		*	*		*				*	*					*	Ester
		*	*	*	*	*									*	Eva
		*		*								*				Fallen Angel
		*	*	*		*									*	Fan
*				*			*			*	*					Fantasia
*				*												Fiesta
				*					*							Filigran
*				*											*	Fluffy Ruffles
				*					*	*	*					Galaxy
*			*	*		*		*							*	Garland
*			*	*		*		*							*	Gavotte
		*	*	*	*	*										Gertrud Stauss
		*	*		*		*			*	*				*	Glacier
		*	*		*	*	*								*	Gold Graft
*			*	*											*	Gold Dust
									*	*	*					Gold Heart
*			*	*				*							*	Gold Child
		*	*						*	*	*					Green Feather
		*	*	*											*	Green Ripple
										*	*					Harrison
		*	*		*											Helena
										*	*					Helvetica
*										*	*					Hibernica

IVY CHART

IVY NAME	Picrot Classification	GROWTH HABIT							COLOR						LEAF SIZE (INCHES)	
		Upright	Trailing	Readily self-branching	Self-branching if pinched	Non self-branching	Internodes & Petioles - short	Internodes & Petioles - long	Medium green	Dark green	Variegated green & white	Variegated gray & white	Other colors	Winter color	1" or less	1-2"
Holly	O		*		*					*						*
Ingrid	V		*	*			*			*		*				*
Innuendo	BF, V		*	*			*			*	*					*
Irish Lace	BF		*		*		*			*						*
Ivalace	M,C		*		*		*			*						*
Jack Frost	C,V		*		*				*					*		
Jersey Doris	V		*		*				*				*			
Jubilee	M,V		*	*			*		*			*		*	*	
Kolbold	M		*	*			*			*				*		
Kolibri	V		*	*			*			*	*					*
Kurios	O	*	*			*		*		*						
La Plata	M, BF		*	*			*		*					*		
Lalla Rookh	C		*		*			*	*							
Lemon Swirl	V,C		*	*			*			*		*				*
Leo Swicegood	BF		*	*			*		*						*	*
Lilliput	M	*			*		*			*					*	
Little Diamond	M,V		*	*			*			*		*	*			*
Lustrous Carpet	C,V		*		*				*			*				*
Manda Crested	C		*	*						*			*			
Manda Fringette	C,F		*		*			*		*						*
Maple Leaf	BF		*		*			*	*							
Merion Beauty	M	*	*	*			*		*						*	
Midas Touch	V		*	*			*			*		*				*
Midget	M, BF		*	*			*			*					*	
Mini Ester	M,V		*		*		*			*		*			*	
Minigreen	M, BF		*	*			*			*					*	
Minor Marmorata	V		*			*		*	*	*		*	*			*
Miss Maroc	O,C		*		*				*							*
Misty	M,V, BF		*	*					*			*		*	*	

246

2" or more	Mini stuffed	Tabletop stuffed	Large stuffed	Accent plant stuffed	Wreath	Balls	Bells	Columns	Trained 2' or less	Trained 2'-6'	Trained 6' or more	Pruned 2' or less	Pruned 2'-6'	Pruned 6' or more	Grafted standard	IVY NAME
		*	*		*	*									*	Holly
		*	*	*	*										*	Ingrid
		*	*		*											Innuendo
		*	*		*				*	*					*	Irish Lace
		*	*	*	*			*	*	*					*	Ivalace
*			*	*		*									*	Jack Frost
*			*	*			*								*	Jersey Doris
	*	*	*	*		*									*	Jubilee
	*	*				*										Kolbold
		*	*	*	*											Kolibri
*													*			Kurios
	*	*														La Plata
			*	*		*				*	*				*	Lalla Rookh
		*	*	*	*	*									*	Lemon Swirl
		*	*	*	*											Leo Swicegood
												*				Lilliput
		*	*	*	*	*										Little Diamond
		*									*					Lustrous Carpet
*			*	*		*									*	Manda Crested
*			*								*				*	Manda Fringette
*			*	*						*	*				*	Maple Leaf
	*	*			*											Merion Beauty
		*	*	*	*	*		*							*	Midas Touch
	*	*			*											Midget
	*	*													*	Mini Ester
		*													*	Minigreen
				*				*		*	*					Minor Marmorata
		*	*		*			*							*	Miss Maroc
		*	*	*	*	*		*							*	Misty

IVY CHART

IVY NAME	Pierot Classification	GROWTH HABIT							COLOR						LEAF SIZE (INCHES)	
		Upright	Trailing	Readily self-branching	Self-branching if pinched	Non self-branching	Internodes & Petioles - short	Internodes & Petioles - long	Medium green	Dark green	Variegated green & white	Variegated gray & white	Other colors	Winter color	1" or less	1-2"
Needlepoint	BF		*	*			*			*					*	*
Neptune	F		*			*		*	*							
Nice Guy	V, BF		*		*				*				*			
Paper Doll	V		*			*		*	*			*				*
Parasol	C		*		*		*		*							*
Peacock	I		*			*				*					*	
Pedata	BF		*			*				*					*	
Perkeo	H	*		*			*		*							
Perle	V		*	*			*				*	*			*	*
Pin Oak	BF		*	*			*		*						*	*
Pirouette	C	*	*		*		*		*							*
Pittsburgh	I		*		*				*							
Pittsburgh Variegated	V		*		*				*		*					
Pixie	M, BF		*	*			*		*							*
Plume d'Or	BF		*	*				*	*							*
Ralf	H		*	*			*		*							*
Rauschgold	V		*		*								*			*
Ritterkreuz	BF		*	*			*		*							*
Romanze	C		*		*				*							
Russelliana	O	*				*	*		*						*	
Sagittaefolia Variegata	V		*	*			*		*			*				*
Schimmer	I		*	*					*							
Serenade	V		*		*				*			*				*
Shäfer Three	V		*		*		*		*			*				*
Shamrock	BF		*	*			*		*							*
Shannon	BF		*		*				*							*
Silver King	V		*	*			*		*			*		*		*
Sinclair Silverleaf	M, V	*	*	*			*		*		*		*		*	
Spear Point	BF		*	*				*	*							*

248

IVY CHART

Topiary Style & Size | Trained on Frame (feet) | Pruned to Shape With or Without Frame (feet)

Leaf size 2" or more	Mini stuffed	Tabletop stuffed	Large stuffed	Accent plant stuffed	Wreath	Balls	Bells	Columns	Trained 2' or less	Trained 2'-6'	Trained 6' or more	Pruned 2' or less	Pruned 2'-6'	Pruned 6' or more	Grafted standard	IVY NAME
		*	*		*	*		*							*	Needlepoint
*										*	*					Neptune
				*					*	*	*					Nice Guy
*										*	*					Paper Doll
		*	*	*	*			*							*	Parasol
									*	*	*					Peacock
									*	*	*					Pedata
				*		*									*	Perkeo
		*	*	*	*											Perle
		*	*		*										*	Pin Oak
		*	*													Pirouette
*			*			*	*	*							*	Pittsburgh
*		*	*			*	*	*							*	Pittsburgh Variegated
		*	*	*	*	*									*	Pixie
									*	*	*					Plume d'Or
			*		*			*							*	Ralf
		*	*		*	*		*							*	Rauschgold
		*	*	*	*	*		*	*	*	*				*	Ritterkreuz
*		*	*		*			*							*	Romanze
												*	*			Russelliana
		*		*					*	*						Sagittaefolia Variegata
*			*	*	*	*	*	*							*	Schimmer
		*	*	*	*	*	*	*							*	Serenade
		*	*	*	*			*							*	Shäfer Three
		*	*	*	*			*							*	Shamrock
									*	*						Shannon
		*	*	*	*	*	*	*	*	*					*	Silver King
	*	*														Sinclair Silverleaf
									*	*						Spear Point

IVY CHART

IVY NAME	Pierot Classification	Upright	Trailing	Readily self-branching	Self-branching if pinched	Non self-branching	Internodes & Petioles - short	Internodes & Petioles - long	Medium green	Dark green	Variegated green & white	Variegated gray & white	Other colors	Winter color	1" or less	1 - 2"
Spetchley	M, BF		*	*			*			*					*	
Spinosa	M,H	*		*			*		*							
Star	BF		*	*					*							*
Sterntaler	V		*		*				*			*				*
Stift Neuberg	V		*			*				*	*					*
Stuttgart	C		*	*			*			*						*
Succinata	V		*			*				*			*	*		*
Sulphurea	V		*			*		*	*				*			
Tear Drop	H		*	*						*						*
Telecurl	C		*	*			*			*						*
Tenerife	V		*		*				*				*	*	*	
Thorndale	I		*			*		*		*						
Tobler	BF		*		*					*						*
Touch of Class	I		*	*			*		*							*
Triton	F		*		*			*		*						
Tussie Mussie	V, BF		*	*						*	*			*		*
Ustler	C		*	*					*							*
Very Merry	M	*	*	*			*		*						*	
Wichtel	BF		*	*						*						*
William Kennedy	M,V		*	*			*					*		*	*	
Williamsiana	V		*		*			*		*		*	*	*		
Wingertsberg	H		*			*		*		*				*		*
Zebra	V,F		*		*				*		*			*		
Hedera nepalensis			*			*			*							*
Hedera nepalensis cv. Marbled Dragon	V		*			*				*						*
Sinensis	H		*			*		*	*							
Suzanne	BF		*			*			*							*
Hedera pastuchovii	H		*			*		*		*						
Hedera rhombea	H		*			*				*						*
Hedera rhombea cv. Pierot	I		*			*				*					*	
Variegata	V		*			*				*	*			*	*	

IVY CHART

Leaf Size (inches) 2" or more	Mini stuffed	Tabletop stuffed	Large stuffed	Accent plant stuffed	Wreath	Balls	Bells	Columns	Trained 2' or less	Trained 2'-6'	Trained 6' or more	Pruned 2' or less	Pruned 2'-6'	Pruned 6' or more	Grafted standard	IVY NAME
	*	*	*	*	*				*							Spetchley
			*													Spinosa
		*	*	*	*			*								Star
			*	*	*	*	*	*							*	Sterntaler
			*		*											Stift Neuberg
			*	*	*			*							*	Stuttgart
								*	*	*						Succinata
*									*	*	*					Sulphurea
		*	*	*					*	*	*				*	Tear Drop
		*	*	*	*			*	*	*	*					Telecurl
	*	*		*				*	*							Tenerife
*										*	*					Thorndale
		*							*	*						Tobler
		*	*		*	*		*							*	Touch of Class
*										*	*					Triton
		*	*	*	*	*		*							*	Tussie Mussie
		*	*		*	*		*							*	Ustler
	*			*	*											Very Merry
		*	*		*	*		*							*	Wichtel
	*	*	*		*				*							William Kennedy
*			*	*		*										Williamsiana
										*	*					Wingertsberg
		*	*	*					*							Zebra
				*						*	*					*Hedera nepalensis*
									*	*	*					*Hedera nepalensis* cv. Marbled Dragon
*										*	*					Sinensis
									*	*						Suzanne
*										*	*					*Hedera pastuchovii*
									*	*						*Hedera rhombea*
									*	*						*Hedera rhombea* cv. Pierot
									*	*						Variegata

SOURCES

Plant Suppliers

Allen C Haskell Horticulturist
787 Shawmut Avenue
New Bedford, MA 02746
508-993-9047
Ivies

Angelwood Nursery
12839 McKee School Road
Woodburn, OR 97071
503-634-2233
No mail order sales
Ivies

Anglo Scandinavian
Greenhouses, Inc.
PO Box 1099
Windermere, FL 34786
407-886-7108
Wholesale ivies

W Atlee Burpee Co
300 Park Avenue
Warminster, PA 18974
215-674-4900
Seeds, plants, supplies, ivy

Butterfield Laboratories
RD 5, Box 386
Bridgeton, NJ 08302
609-451-3861 Fax 609-451-3861
Custom tissue culture
Cascading chrysanthemums

Evergreen Nursery
1220 Dowdy Road RT 4
Athens, GA 30606
404-548-7781
800-521-7267
Ivies, ground covers

Gilson Gardens
3059 N Ridge Road
PO Box 277 (US RT 20)
Perry, OH 44081
216-259-4845
216-258-5252
Ivies

Green Leaf Enterprises, Inc.
17 W. Main Street
Leola, PA 17540
717-656-2066
Wholesale ivy

Ivies of the World
PO Box 408
Weirsdale, FL 32195
904-821-2201
Ivies

The Ivy Guild
PO Box 371
835 Simonds Road
Williamstown, MA 01267
413-458-5701 Fax 413-458-5703
Ivies wholesale

King's Mums
PO Box 368
Clements, CA 95227
209-759-3571
Cascading chrysanthemums

Logee's Greenhouses
141 North Street
Danielson, CT 06239
203-774-8038
Ivies

Longwood Gardens, Inc
Museum Shop
PO Box 501
Kennett Square, PA 19348-0501
No mail order sales
Ivies

Meadowbrook Farm
1633 Washington Lane
Meadowbrook, PA 19046
215-887-5900
Ivies

Merry Gardens
PO Box 595
Mechanic Street
Camden, ME 04843
207-236-2121
Ivies

Roberta Moffitt
PO Box 3597
Wilmington, DE 19807
302-655-8012
Dried plant material

Schubert Nursery, Inc.
PO Box 858
Half Moon Bay, CA 94019
415-726-2618
Ivies

Stoneboro Nurseries, Inc.
RD 2
Stoneboro, PA 16153
814-786-7991
Wholesale
Ivies

Sunnybrook Farms Nursery
PO Box 6
Chesterland, OH 44026
216-729-9838
216-729-7232
Catalog $1.00
Ivies retail

Sunnyslope Gardens
8638 Huntington Drive
San Gabriel, CA 91775
818-287-4071
Cascading chrysanthemums

Vine Acres Nursery, Inc.
PO Box 317
Clarcona, FL 32710
407-886-5900
Wholesale ivies

Waterloo Gardens
136 Lancaster Avenue
Devon, PA 19333
215-293-0800
and
200 North Whitford Road
Exton, PA 19341
215-363-0800
Ivies

Topiary Suppliers

Allen C Haskell Horticulturist
787 Shawmut Avenue
New Bedford, MA 02746
508-993-9047
Topiary

Angelwood Nursery
12839 McKee School Road
Woodburn, OR 97071
503-634-2233
Topiary

Badger's Earthscapes
PO Box 2407
La Mesa, CA 92044
619-466-8569
Finished topiary

Cliff Finch's Zoo
16923 N. Friant Road
PO Box 54
Friant, CA 93626
209-822-2315
Frames
Finished topiary

The Connoisseur's Garden
3144 E. Shadowlawn Ave, NE
Atlanta, GA 30305
404-233-3248
Outdoor topiary

The Cottage Garden
3166 Maple Drive, NE
Atlanta, GA 30305
404-233-2050
Party settings and fantasy topiary

Creative Topiary
5223 SW Illinois Street
Portland, OR 97221
503-245-6409
Finished topiary - retail

Deborah Reich & Associates Ltd
Landscape Architecture and
Topiary
25 Schermerhorn Street
Brooklyn, NY 11201
718-643-6146
Finished topiary
Garden design
Party settings
Frames

**Delaware Valley Wholesale
Florist, Inc.**
520 Mantua Boulevard North
Sewell, NJ 08080-1096
609-468-7000 Fax 609-468-5576
800-852-8052
Floral supplies

Forrest Products Packaging Co
5180 Center Street NE
Salem, OR 97301
503-378-1333
Sphagnum moss and related products

Frenchwyers
PO Box 131655
Tyler, TX 75713
214-597-8322
Frames

Gardenworks
PO Box 216
Markleeville, CA 96120
916-694-2515
Custom frames

Green Animals Topiary Garden
380 Cory's Lane
Portsmouth, RI 02840
401-683-1267
Topiary and topiary related items

Green Treasures
250 Old Grumman Hill Road
Wilton, CT 06897
203-762-8198
Custom topiary

Hon Grown
PO Box 2135
Forks, WA 98331-0828
206-374-9267
Dried materials

Irene's Topiary
3045 W. Academy
Sanger, CA 93657
209-875-8447
Frames and finished topiary

The Ivy Guild
PO Box 371
835 Simonds Road
Williamstown, MA 01267
413-458-5701 Fax 413-458-5703
Ivy topiary wholesale

Logee's Greenhouses
141 North Street
Danielson, CT 06239
203-774-8038
Topiary standards

Longwood Gardens, Inc
Museum Shop
PO Box 501
Kennett Square, PA 19348-0501
No mail order sales
Finished topiary

Longwood Manufacturing Corp.
816 E. Baltimore Pike (Route 1)
Kennett Square, PA 19348-1890
215-444-4200
Custom frames

Manfred Schickenberg
Ivy Topiary
154 Princeton Avenue
Half Moon Bay, CA 94019
415-728-3817
Ivy topiary

McGuire Topiary and Sculptural Designs
6219 Burgess Avenue
Baltimore, MD 21214
Office: 301-426-1267
Studio: 301-244-0096
Frames and finished topiary

Meadowbrook Farm
1633 Washington Lane
Meadowbrook, PA 19046
215-887-5900
Finished topiary
Topiary supplies

Merry Gardens
PO Box 595
Mechanic Street
Camden, ME 04843
207-236-2121
Finished topiary

The Mosser Lee Company
Box 437
Millston, WI 54643
Sphagnum-moss, spanish-moss

Nature's Alley
108 N. Santa Cruz Avenue
Los Gatos, CA 95030
408-354-4221
and
3020 Middlefield Road
Redwood City, CA 94063
415-367-9772
Topiary supplies
Finished topiary

Noah's Ark Topiary
PO Box 10213
Largo, FL 34643
813-393-8830
Finished topiary

O'Farrior Topiary
117 E. Whitcomb Avenue
Glendora, CA 91740
818-963-3568
Frames
Finished topiary

The Potted Plant
3165 E. Shadowlawn Avenue, NE
Atlanta, GA 30306
404-233-7800
Finished topiary and topiary
containers

Renny-The Perennial Farm
60 Thompson Mill Road
Wrightstown, PA 18940
212-598-0550
Finished topiary

River Oaks Plant House
3401 Westheimer
Houston, TX 77027
713-622-5350
Finished topiary
Custom topiary

Schubert Nursery, Inc.
PO Box 858
Half Moon Bay, CA 94019
415-726-2618
Finished topiary

Spring Topiary Farm
25510 Spring Ridge Drive
Spring, TX 77386
713-292-5808
Custom topiary

Topiary Art Works
PO Box 574
Clearwater, KS 67026
316-584-2227 Fax 316-584-2227
Frames
Finished topiary

Topiary by Lucky
DBA Pat Stewart
1830 Jacks Creek Pike
Lexington, KY 40515
606-263-2215
Frames
Finished topiary
Specializes in horses

Topiary Inc.
41 Bering Street
Tampa, FL 33606
813-254-3229
Finished topiary
Frames
Wholesale

Totally Topiary
Box 191
Stockton, NJ 08559
609-397-2314
Custom topiary

Topiaries Unlimited
RD 2 Box 6
Pownal, VT 05261
802-823-5080
Custom frames

Waterloo Gardens, Inc.
136 Lancaster Avenue
Devon, PA 19333
215-293-0800
and
200 North Whitford Road
Exton, PA 19341
215-363-0800
Finished topiary
Topiary supplies

Wilmington Florist Exchange
PO Box 1166
Third & Church Sts.
Wilmington, DE 19899
302-652-3456
Wholesale and retail
Floral supplies

Supplies

Nursery and Greenhouse Supplier (Wholesale)

Garden Center (Retail)

Farm & Garden Supplier (Wholesale and Retail)

Soil Amendments:
Soilless mixes
Peat moss
Terragreen
Vermiculite
Sphagnum moss

Supplies:
Raffia
Horticultural black cloth
Rubber budding strips
Green twisties
String
Soil test kits
Wire hanging baskets
Misting spray pump bottles
Wire wreath frame
Straw wreath frame

Tools:
Clippers
Shears
Gloves
Grafting knife

Chemicals:
Fertilizer
Liquid fertilizer
Growth retardants (e.g., B-Nine, Arest, Cycocel)
Insecticidal soap
Horticultural oil
Bacillus thurengiesis - BT (e.g., Dipel)
Insecticides
Fungicides
Rooting hormones

Floral Suppliers:
Wreath frames
Straw wreath frames
Floral spray plastic coat
Floral foams (e.g., Oasis®, Sahara®)
Floral stem tape
Floral adhesives
Floral spray (e.g., Crowning Glory)
Sheet moss
Spanish-moss
Dried flowers & leaves

Hardware or Building Suppliers:
Insulation foam sheets
Insulation foam spray
Latex glazing compound
Green coated wire

Paper Supplier:
Styrofoam packing peanuts

Taxidermist:
Glass eyes

Sewing Supplier:
Fun eyes

Sporting Goods Supplier:
Fish line

Supermarket:
Clear floor wax

Bibliography

Allen, Oliver E. and Time-Life Editors. 1978. *Pruning and Grafting.* Time-Life Books, Alexandria, Virginia. 160 pp.

Anonymous. 1984. *Frog Frolics.* Merrimack Publishing Company, New York. 14 pp.

Baker, Margaret. 1969. *Discovering Topiary.* Shire Publications, Tring, Herts. 64 pp.

Baker, Martha, ed. 1977. *The World of Cactus and Succulents and Other Water Thrifty Plants.* Ortho Books, Chevron Chemical Company, San Francisco, California.

Barrett, W. A. 1868. *Flowers and Festivals or Directions for Floral Decoration of Churches.* Rivingtons, London, Oxford and Cambridge. 176 pp.

Berrall, Julia S. 1966. *The Garden: An Illustrated History.* Viking Press Inc., New York, New York. 388 pp.

Boyd, Nancy Long. 1983. *The Pine Cone Book.* Prospect Hill, Baltimore, Maryland. 80 pp.

Brook, Wallace. 1984. *Growing and Showing Chrysanthemums.* David and Charles, London. 68 pp.

Brooklyn Botanic Garden Editorial Committee. 1958. *Gardening in Containers - A Handbook.* Brooklyn Botanic Garden, Brooklyn, New York. 14 (1).

Clark, Virginia. 1961. *The New Book of Wedding Flowers, Decorations, and Etiquette.* Hearthside Press Inc., New York. 192 pp.

Clarke, Ethne and George Wright. 1988. *English Topiary Gardens.* Clarkson N. Potter, Inc. Distributed by Crown Publishers Inc., New York. 166 pp.

Clevely, A. M. 1988. *Topiary.* William Collins Sons and Co. Ltd, London. 128 pp.

Creekmore, Betsey B. 1970. *Making Gifts from Oddments and Outdoor Materials.* Hearthside Press Inc., New York. 224 pp.

Crisp, Frank. 1966. *Mediaeval Gardens.* Hacker Art Books, New York, New York. 2Vols.

Curtis, Charles H. and W. Gibson. 1985. *The Book of Topiary.* Charles E. Tuttle Company Inc., Rutland, Vermont. 80 pp.

Cutler, Katherine N. 1964. *How to Arrange Flowers for all Occasions.* Doubleday, Garden City, New Jersey. 256 pp.

DeWolf, Gordon P., ed. 1987. *Taylor's Guide to Shrubs.* Houghton Miffin Company, Boston. 479 pp.

Dirr, Michael A. 1983. *Manual of Woody Landscape Plants.* Stipes Publishing Company, Champaign, Illinois. 826 pp.

Eberbach, Catherine. 1988. *Garden Design for Children.* Master's Thesis, University of Delaware, December.

Ecke, Paul Jr., ed. 1976. *The Poinsettia Manual.* Paul Ecke, Encinitas, California. 205 pp.

Gallup, Barbara and Deborah Reich. 1988. *The Complete Book of Topiary.* Workman Publishing, New York. 318 pp.

Graf, Alfred Byrd. 1957. *Exotica.* Roehrs Company Inc., East Rutherford, New Jersey. 643 pp.

Hadfield, Miles. 1971. *Topiary and Ornamental Hedges.* A. and C. Black Ltd, London. 100 pp.

Harry, William Cleaver. 1930. *The Art of Floral Designing.* A. T. De La Mare Company Inc., New York. 178 pp.

Heieck, Ingobert. 1980. *Hedera Sorten.* Grtnerei Abeti Neuberg, Stiftweg 2, Heidelberg. 134 pp.

Hill, Susan. 1986. *Through the Garden Gate.* Hamish Hamilton Ltd, London.

Hixson, Bill. nd. *Christmas Decorations.* np. 63 pp.

Joosten, Titia. 1988. *Flower Drying with a Microwave Technique and Projects.* Lark Books, Asheville, North Carolina. 72 pp.

Kramer, Jack. 1971. *Container Gardening Indoors and Out.* Doubleday and Company Inc., Garden City, New Jersey. 157 pp.

Lacey, Geraldine. 1987. *Creating Topiary.* Garden Art Press, Northiam, East Sussex. 147 pp.

Lamb, Edgar and Brian. 1955. *The Illustrated Reference of Cacti and Other Succulents.* Volume I. Blandford Press, London. 311 pp.

Lamb, Edgar and Brian. 1957. *The Illustrated Reference of Cacti and Other Succulents.* Volume II. Blandford Press, London. (312)-580 pp.

Lamb, Edgar and Brian. 1963. *The Illustrated Reference of Cacti and Other Succulents.* Volume III. Blandford Press, London. (581)-896 pp.

Lamb, Edgar and Brian. 1966. *The Illustrated Reference of Cacti and Other Succulents.* Volume IV. Blandford Press, London. (896)-1212 pp.

Lamb, Edgar and Brian. 1978. *The Illustrated Reference of Cacti and Other Succulents.* Volume V. Blandford Press, Poole, Dorset. (1212)-1498 pp.

Laurie, Alex. 1930. *The Flower Shop.* Florist's Publishing Company, Chicago, Illinois.

Liberty Hyde Bailey Hortorium. 1976. *Hortus Third.* The Macmillan Publishing Company Inc., New York. 1290 pp.

Lloyd, Nathaniel. 1925. *Garden Craftsmanship in Yew and Box.* Ernest Benn Ltd, 8 Bouverie St, London. EC4. 36 pp & 54 plates.

Lynch, Kenneth. 1979. *Garden Ornaments.* Canterbury Publishing Company, Canterbury, Connecticut. 400 pp.

Manaker, George H. 1987. *Interior Plantscapes: Installation, Maintenance and Management.* Prentice-Hall Inc., Englewood Cliffs, New Jersey. 324 pp.

Martin, Tovah. 1989. *Once Upon a Windowsill.* Timber Press, Portland, Oregon. 313 pp.

Mead, Chris and Emelie Tolley. 1985. *Herbs: Gardens, Decorations, and Recipes.* C. N. Potter, New York, New York. 244 pp.

Oliver, Libbey Hodges and Betty Hundley Babb. 1981. *Colonial Williamsburg Decorates for Christmas.* The Colonial Williamsburg Foundation, Williamsburg, Virginia. 80 pp.

O'Neill, Sunny. 1981. *The Gift of Christmas Past.* American Association for State and Local History, Nashville, Tennessee. 145 pp.

Ortho Books Editorial Staff. 1975. *Container and Hanging Gardens.* Ortho Books, Chevron Chemical Company, San Francisco, California. 95 pp.

Otis, Denise. 1978. *Decorating with Flowers.* Harry N. Abrams Inc., New York, New York. 244 pp.

Paul, Raj S. *Installations Manual.* Branching Out Inc., Houston, Texas. 23 pp.

Pierot, Suzanne. 1974. *The Ivy Book.* Macmillan Publishing Company Inc., New York. 164 pp.

Pulbrook and **Goulds.** 1982. *Flowers for Special Occasions.* Batsford Ltd, London. 95 pp.

Rose, Peter Q. 1980. *Ivies.* Blandford Press, Poole, Dorset. 180 pp.

Rowley, Gordon. 1978. *The Illustrated Encyclopedia of Succulents.* Crown Publishers Inc., New York, New York. 256 pp.

Ruffin, Lisa and Leonard Tharp. 1986. *An American Style in Flower Arrangement.* Taylor Publishing Company, Dallas, Texas. 231 pp.

Scanlon, John and Bruce Palmer, eds. 1968. *Album of Designs: Funeral Flowers.* Florist's Publishing Company, Chicago, Illinois. 96 pp.

Scott-James, Anne and Osbert Lancaster. 1977. *The Pleasure Garden.* Gambit, on Meeting House Green, Ipswich, Suffolk. 128 pp.

Simmons, Adelma Grenier. 1987. *The Caprilands Wreath Book.* Clinton Press of Tolland, Tolland, Connecticut. 194 pp.

Simmons, Adelma Grenier. 1989. *Country Wreath from Caprilands*. Rodale Press, Emmaus, Pennsylvania. 192 pp.

Sunset editors. 1979. *New Western Garden Book*. Lane Publishing Co., Menlo Park, California. 512 pp.

The Florist's Review, ed. 1940. *The Designer's Notebook*. Florist's Publishing Company, 508 South Dearborn St, Chicago, Illinois. 95 pp.

Tijia, B.O., ed. 1986. *Commercial Poinsettia Production in Florida*. University of Florida, Gainsville, Florida. 60 pp.

Van Allsburg, Chris. 1979. *The Garden of Abdul Gasazi*. Houghton Mifflin Company, Boston, Massachusetts. 32 pp.

Van Rensselaer, Eleanor. 1957. *Decorating with Pods and Cones*. D Van Nostrand Co. Inc., Princeton, New Jersey. 179 pp.

Zabar, Abbie. 1988. *The Potted Herb*. Stewart, Tabori, and Chang, New York. 103 pp.

Articles

Ackerson, Cornelius. 1963. "Chrysanthemums in Japan." *The Garden Journal*, March-April: 38-42.

A Gardener's Notebook. "Shape a Plant." *Women's Day*, 4/2/1985: 94-95.

Allen, Oliver E. 1987. "Training a Standard Lantana." *Horticulture*, 85 (8): 30-31.

Anonymous. 1989. "Displaying with Drieds." *Florist's Review*, 180 (7): 10.

Anonymous. 1988. "The Art of Topiary." *Mid-Atlantic Country*, March: 96-98.

Anonymous. 1987. "Topiary Treasures." *Colonial Homes* 13 (6): 72-79.

Anonymous. 1986. "Sibley Center Works Its Plants Into Shape." *Callaway Gardens Newsletter*, Summer.

Anonymous. 1985. "Topiary: The Gardeners Art." *Creative Ideas for Living*, January: 56-57.

Anonymous. 1980. "Open Face Planters." *Sunset*, 164 (4): 112-113.

Anonymous, 1978. "The Blooming Bronx." *Time*, March 27: 74.

Anonymous. 1976. "Topiary Fun for Artist and Gardener Alike." *Popular Gardening Indoors*, 1 (4): 35-39, 82.

Anonymous. 1976. "You can Grow a Topiary." *The Ivy Bulletin*, Winter: 14-15.

Anonymous. 1974. "Will a Growing Dog Bark?" *House Beautiful*, : 62-63, 38-39.

Anonymous. 1970. "Why Not Raise a Seal...Stuff a Goose! Be a Garden Sculptor...Try Topiary." *Under Glass*, September-October: 13.

Anonymous. "Floral Columns." *Callaway Gardens, Home Horticulture Pamphlet*.

Anonymous. "Topiary: Living Sculpture." *Callaway Gardens, Pamphlet*.

Ballard, Ernesta Drinker. 1968. "Have Fun with Topiary Ivies." *Horticulture*, 46 (2): 26-27.

Bechtel, John. 1987. "Mother Nature Takes Second Place To Katy Warner." *Grit Magazine*, V. 6, Jan: 3.

Berrisford, Judith. 1988. "North Wales and the Lakes." Flora, 80: 14-17.

Blau, Teri. 1988. "A Wreath of Greens." Horticulture, 66 (12): 56-57.

Boles, Daralice D. 1989. "High-Tech Topiaries." Progressive Architecture 3: 123-124.

Borland, Jim. 1989. "Wild Petunia." Greenhouse Manager, 7 (10): 62-64.

Brown, Ross. 1988. "Carrying on in the Cold." *Interior Landscape Industry*, 5(12): 50-53.

Bruno, Barbara. 1983. "Decorating for a Christmas Victorian." *The Green Scene*, 12(2): 3-5.

Buckler, James R. and Kathryn Meehan. 1989. "Victorian Gardens: A Horticultural Extravaganza." *Smithsonian Institution Office of Horticulture, Promotional Publication.*

Campbell, Ilay. 1988. "From Cottage Garden to Tropical Forest." *The Garden.* 113 (9): 401-411.

Cappoccia, Cathy. 1980. "The Smithsonian Institute: New Keeper of the Floriculture Heritage." *Florist,* February: 39-45.

Clark, Cecily. 1973. "Nail Scissors for Pruning." *The Green Scene,* July 2 (6): 16-19.

Clevely, Andi. 1989. "Offshoots." *British Homes and Gardens,* February: 26-27.

Constable, Frank. 1985. "Topiary: Mutilation or Work of Art?" *The Garden.* 110 (8): 364-366.

Cosgrove, Tom. 1989. "Health Officials Warn of Sphagnum Moss Fungus Disease." American Nurseryman, 169 (2): 13-15.

Cox, David G. 1985. "Bud Grafting Ivies." *Ivy Journal,* 11 (1): 51-55.

Crain Penniman, Mary. 1986. "Make Your Own Plant Critter." *Callaway Gardens,* Pine Mountain, Georgia. Summer Newsletter.

Creech, Dr. John L. 1985. "Three Fall-Blooming Flowers Color Japan's October." *American Nurseryman,* 162 (6): 40-43.

Cronin, Evelyn. 1979. "Do It Yourself Topiary." *Light Garden,* 16: 92.

DuVal, Dagney. 1986. "Flights of Fancy." *Interior Landscape Industry,* 3 (5): 40-45.

Eberbach, Catherine. 1987. "Exhibiting a Childish Way." *Journal of the Interntional Association of Zoo Educators,* 18: 8-12.

Eberbach, Catherine. 1987. "Gardens: From a Child's View Interpretation of Children's Art-Work." *Journal of Therapeutic Horticulture,* 11: 9-16.

Egan, Christine. 1977. "You're a What? Topiarist." *Occupational Outlook Quarterly,* 21 (1): 30-31.

Emmet, Alan. 1988. "Family Trees." *House and Garden,* 160 (11): 194-199, 230.

Enterline, John L. 1987. "The Victorian Christmas Ivy." *The Ivy Journal,* 13 (3): 5-6.

Evan, Morgan. 1969. "Topiary Gardening." *California Horticultural Journal,* 30 (1).

Ewing, Jerry. 1976. "Try Topiary." *Plants Alive,* 4 (5): 36.

Feature. 1989. "Wedding Ideas: Ivy Wreath." *Florist's Review,* 180 (2): 52.

Fell, Derek. 1985. "The Maze at Deerfield." *The Green Scene,* 13 (3): 4-6.

Forcade, Tim. Photographer. 1988. "A Design for Every Door." *Florist's Review,* 179 (7): 42-47.

Gallup, Barbara S. and Deborah A Reich. 1986. "Portable Topiary." *American Horticulturist,* 65 (4): 28-33.

Gallup, Barbara S. and Deborah A Reich. 1986. "The Philadelphia Story: Indoor Topiary." *The Green Scene,* 14 (4): 7-10.

Garbarino, Steve. 1986. "Taking Shape." *Gardens and Landscaping,* September-October: 106-108.

Goulart, Francis Sheridan. 1989. "Six Steps to Top-Notch Topiary." *The Herb Quarterly,* 41: 12-13.

Grampp, Christopher. 1988. "The Well-Tempered Garden: Gravel and Topiary In California." *Landscape,* 30 (1): 41-47.

Gregory, Jeff. 1979. "Three Types of Topiary." *House Plants and Porch Gardens,* 4 (6): 66-72.

Hadfield, Miles. 1956. "Topiary Work." *Features of Old Gardens: Gardeners Chronicle & Gardening Illustrated,* 14 (22): 578

Hammer, Patricia. 1986. "Tabletop Topiary." *Ivy Journal,* 12 (3): 42-46.

Hammer, Patricia. 1986. "Topiaries at Longwood Gardens." *Ivy Journal,* 12 (2): 34-37.

Hammer, Patricia and Patricia Wellingham-Jones. 1986. "Longwood Garden's Holiday Treat." *Ivy Journal,* 12 (1): 7-9.

Hays, R. M. 1986. "Training Plant Standards at Longwood Gardens." *Longwood Gardens Inc., Kennett Square, PA*

Heiser, Charles B., Jr. 1985. "Topiary in Tulcan." *American Horticulturist,* 64 (4): 28-31.

Howland, Joseph E. 1988. "A Wild Idea in the Marketing Kingdom." *Nursery Manager,* 4 (11): 67

Jalics, Kristi. 1988. "Oasis." *The Green Scene,* 17 (2): 28-30.

Jones, Michael P. "Background Information on Mt. Hoods "Ivy Bear"." *Cascade Geographic Society Pamphlet.*

Johnson, Norman Kent. 1985. "Table-Top Topiaries." *Creative Ideas For Living,* January: 58-59.

Johnson, Peter H. 1979. "A Living Wreath." *House Plants and Porch Gardens,* 4 (10): 69-72.

Kent, Betsy. 1977. "How to Have Well-Behaved Animals in Your Garden with Topiary." *Flower and Garden,* 21 (6): 32-34, 37.

Klein, William M. 1986. "Chelsea 1986." *The Garden.* 111 (9): 424-432.

Korab, Balthazar. 1984. "A Gift to a Garden." *House and Garden,* 156 (12): 92-96.

LaRosa, Jim. 1988. "Flower Tower." *The Green Scene,* 17 (1): 33.

Lyon, Jean M. 1988. "Wreaths For All Seasons." *Herb Quarterly,* 39: 19-21.

Maguire, Eileen. 1989. "Tree Whimsy." *American Nurseryman,* 169 (11): 69-76.

Martin, Tovah. 1988. "Boxwood's New Faces." *Garden Design,* 7 (3): 83-87.

Martin, Tovah. 1988. "Standardizing: Training Plants to a Formal Shape." *Fine Gardening,* 2: 57.

Martin, Tovah. 1983. "Standards of Excellence." *Horticulture,* 61 (5): 15-21.

Marx, John H. 1958. Longwood Gardens Inc., October-December Quarterly Report: 14.

Mackenzie, Clodagh. 1957. "Dinosaur at Bombay." *Gardeners Chronicle & Gardening Illustrated :* 141 (18): 481.

McCarthy, Mary. 1983. "The Indomitable Miss Brayton." *House and Garden,* 155 (12): 140-145.

McKay, John A. 1986. "Topiary in Tulcan." *The Garden.* 111 (6): 280-340.

Miller, Don. 1988. "Searching for Begonias in Ecuador." *The Begonian,* 55 (November-December): 199-200.

Moneysmith, Marie. 1980. "Smithsonian Institution's Horticulture Exhibit Opens to Rave Reviews." *Florist,* September: 47-52.

Moretz, James. 1982. "Almost 100 Years Ago." *Southern Florist and Nurseryman,* February 11: 17.

Neustadtl, Sara Jane. 1982. "Shear Whimsy." *Horticulture,* 60 (10): 31-35.

Paterson, David. 1981. "Topiary the Old Way." *Plants and Gardens: Handbook on Pruning,* 37 (2): 29-30.

Pennsylvania Horticultural Society Collection. 1984. "PHS Christmas Exhibits." *The Green Scene,* 13 (2): 14-21.

Pepper, Jane. 1980. "Building a Garden." *Plants Alive,* January, 8 (1): 14-19.

Rear-Admiral Phillips, Neill. 1967. "Topiary." *The Boxwood Bulletin,* 6 (4): 50-53.

Phillips, Neill. 1960. "Topiary." *The Horticultural Society of New York Inc. Bulletin,* 10 (10): 7-8.

Pierot, Suzanne Warner. 1975. "The Fun and Art of Ivy Topiary." *American Horticulturist,* 54 (3): 8-11.

Pleronck, Mitch. 1983. "Four Suits in Topiary." *Flower and Garden,* 27 (5): 52.

Rackemann, Adelaide. 1987. "Lilyturf." *Horticulture,* 65 (8): 42-43.

Rackemann, Francis M., Jr. 1984. "Ladew Topiary Gardens." *American Horticulturist,* 63 (4): 24-27.

Radeloff, Ken. 1989. "Jimmy Paolini: A Prince Among Green and Growing Subjects." *The Green Scene,* 17 (3): 4-7.

Randall, Colvin. 1988. "Poinsettia Tree Standards." *The Green Scene,* 17 (2): 4-5.

Reath, Sally. 1980. "Topiary You Can Make." *Plants Alive,* January, 8 (1): 20-24.

Reed, Christopher. 1986. "In Christopher Lloyd's Garden." *Horticulture,* 64 (3): 36-45.

Reich, Deborah. 1988. "The Children's Garden." *The Green Scene,* 16 (4): 14-18.

Rogers, Charles. 1981. "Decorating Churches at Christmas." *The Green Scene,* 10 (2): 11-13.

Rogers, Charles. 1980. "Deck the Halls." *The Green Scene,* 9 (2): 13-16.

Rosen, Elyssa. 1988. "Industry Profits Through Child-Orientated Promotions." *Market Letter,* March: 1-2.

Sallee, Kay. 1989. "Fine Topiary at Noah's Ark." *Nursery Manager,* 5 (3): 92-99.

Schenk, George. 1989. "New Zealand's Changeful Carexes." *Pacific Horticulture,* 50 (1): 48-54.

Shapiro, Charlotte B. 1982. "Historic House Christmas Tours in Fairmount Park: The 10th Annual Tour." *The Green Scene,* 11 (2): 26-33.

Shigo, Cathleen. 1988. "Tips on Topiary." *Long Island Gardening,* December: 4.

Shimizu, Holly. 1986. "Herbs as Topiary." *The Business of Herbs,* 4 (1): 6-7.

Simpson, Babs, ed. 1988. "A Main Line Treasure: Waterloo Garden's Founder Jimmy Paolini Creates Living Art." *Main Line Community Magazine,* December: 4-5, 10-11, 13.

Society of American Florist. 1965. "FIC Plan Effective at Hoover Funeral." *The American Florist,* February-March: 7-8.

Street, Julianne R. 1981. "Preparing for Christmas in the Herb House." *The Green Scene,* 10 (2): 3-7.

Tait, William. 1988. "Hedges." *The Garden.* 113 (1): 5-11.

Temple, Dorothy. 1988. "Easy Herbal Topiaries." *Flower and Garden,* October 31 (6): 80-81.

Thompson, Dave. 1989. "Definitions of Topiary." *Longwood Gardens Inc. Continuing Education,* April.

Thompson, Dave. 1989. "History of the Longwood Topiary Collection." *Longwood Gardens Inc. Continuing Education,* April.

Thompson, Dave. 1986. "Notes on Topiary Collection." *Longwood Gardens Inc. Continuing Education,* September.

Vadukul, Max. 1988. "The Cutting Edge." *House and Garden,* 160 (6): 114-115.

Van Pelt Wilson, Helen. 1960. "All England is a Garden - Here Are My Favorites." *Flower Grower,* 47 (2): 64-69.

Whitman, Bob. 1988. "Cryptanthus Topiary." *Cryptanthus Society Journal,* 3 (4): 36-37.

Williams, Betsy. 1988. "Wreath Making, Part I: Gathering Materials to Dry." *The Joy of Herbs,* 1 (1): 7, 19-20.

Zabar, Abbie. 1988. "One Man's Eden: Allen Haskell and His New England Nursery." *Hortus: A Gardening Journal,* 2 (1): 78-85.

Zlotky, David. Photographer. 1989. "Summer Parties." *Florist's Review,* 180 (5): 39-42.

Newspapers

Anonymous. 1972. "Topiary: Living Sculpture." Women's World, *The Sunday Star,* Washington DC, March 26.

Anonymous. 1974. "Show House." *The Sandspur,* Tampa, Florida: 32 (3): 16.

Ascher, Amalie Adler. 1976. "An Indoor Menagerie from Bent Wire and Plants." *The Sun,* Baltimore, Maryland, Sunday, December 19.

Cunningham, Ann. 1977. "The Making of a Champion Plant." *Philadelphia Inquirer,* Philadelphia, Pennsylvania, April 10.

Curletti, Rosario. 1959. "At Montecito: Gala Garden Party Slated." *Los Angeles Times,* Los Angeles, California, July 26.

Deitz, Paul. 1984. "Rockefeller Center Gets A Topiary Zoo." *The New York Times,* New York, August 16.

Fitch, Daisy. 1988. "Menagerie Takes Shape in Stockton Greenhouse." *Evening Times,* Trenton, New Jersey, April 24.

Foerstner, Abigail. 1988. "Space-Saving Topiary." *Chicago Tribune,* Chicago, Illinois, July 17.

Garrett, Elaine. 1987. "2 Davis Islands Women 'Cut' Topiary Business into Shape." *The Tampa Tribune,* Tampa, Florida, Thursday November 19: 21H-27H.

George, Linda E. 1987. "Topiary Animals Abound at Longwood Display." *The Village News,* Oxford, Pennsylvania, November 18.

Hyche, Jerald. 1988. "Portable Topiary Promises Plants With Bit of Whimsy." *The Tampa Tribune,* Tampa, Florida, April 22: 6F-7F.

Newton, Roger. 1979. "Topiary Dates Back to Romans." *The Tampa Tribune-Times,* Sunday, September 2.

Rackemann, Francis. 1980. "Topiary Steed Popular at Conservatory." *Evening Sun,* Baltimore, Maryland, July.

Rackemann, Francis. 1979. "Gardening: Her Topiary is a Year-round Delight." *Evening Sun,* Baltimore, Maryland, November 21.

Schmidt, Peggy. 1985. "Christmas at Conestoga House." *The Sunday News,* Lancaster, Pennsylvania, November 17.

Spollen, Patricia. 1963. "Ivy and Ingenuity Star at Christmas Time." *The Sunday Bulletin,* Philadelphia, Pennsylvania, June 15.

Spraker, Eileen C. 1988. "Hobby Blooms into Business for Flower Lover." *Evening Journal,* Wilmington, Delaware, August 18: D1, D8.

Spraker, Eileen C. 1987. "A Garden of Tiny Delights." *Sunday News Journal,* Wilmington, Delaware, May 3: G1

Index by Chapter

AMERICAN TOPIARY HISTORY
Topiary Gardens:
Colonial Williamsburg, Virginia 14, 15
Deaf Park School, Columbus, Ohio 16
Filoli, Woodside, California 15
Green Animals Privet Zoo, Portsmouth, Rhode Island 16, 17
Hecker Pass, Gilroy, California 16, 17
Hunnewell Estate, Wellesley, Massachusetts 15
Ladew Gardens, Monkton, Maryland 14, 15
Vizcaya, Miami, Florida 16, 17
Circus Trees 16, 17
Victorians and Portable topiary:
Tovah Martin *'Once upon a Windowsill'* 18
James Moretz, American Floral Art School, Chicago, Illinois 18
Set pieces 18, 19
Role of Horticultural Societies 22, 23, 24, 25, 26
American Ivy Society 24, 25
Suzanne Warner Pierot, *'The Ivy Book'* 24, 25
Topiary businesses 25
Rockefeller Center 26
Ivy Bear 26
Rear-Admiral Neill Phillips 26
Lotusland 27
The Walt Disney Company 27

TOPIARY AT LONGWOOD GARDENS 28
Pierre du Pont 28
Traditional outdoor topiary 28
David Thompson 29
Cascading Chrysanthemums 28, 29
Chrysanthemum Festivals 33, 34
Cut greens 33
Frames 30, 31, 32, 33
Large-scale topiaries 32, 33, 34
Rockefeller Center 32, 33, 36
Callaway Gardens, Georgia 36

CASCADING CHRYSANTHEMUM TOPIARIES
Japanese Influence 38
Animals and life-size dolls 38
Kiky-ningyo 38
Tatami-mat straw 38
Longwood Chrysanthemum topiary 39
Chrysanthemum Propagation 40
Stock plants and tip cuttings 40
Propagation and soil mixes 40
Lighting 40
Temperature 40
Balls 39, 42, 43, 44, 45
Columns 46, 47
(For Callaway Gardens method see Page 162)
Arches 47
Cloud-Form 39, 48
Curtains and Collars 48, 49
General Care and Fertilizer Recommendations 51
Insects and diseases 52, 53

TABLETOP TOPIARIES 55
Tools and supplies 55
Frames, plant and fern pins 56
Watering 57
Pruned or Free-Form Topiaries 58, 59, 60
Trained-Up on a Frame 60, 61
Stuffed 62, 63, 64
One-plant Stuffed 65
Unrooted Cutting 66
Maintenance 67
Mini-stuffed Topiaries 68, 69
Ivy Bells 70, 71, 72
Topiary Balls 73
Pre-made Ball 74
Two Halves 75
One Wire Basket 76
Central Pot 76, 77
Suitable plants for balls 78
Basket Variations 79

LARGE-SCALE STUFFED TOPIARIES 81
Atlanta Botanic Gardens 80
Making sketches 81
Workspace and supplies 81
Frame 82
Moss 84
Planting Media and Fillers 84, 85, 86
Plants 81, 86, 87
Fishing Line 88, 89
Fern Pins and wheels 89
Penguin violinist 90, 91
Step-by-Step 92
The Penguin 93, 94
Maintenance and Restoration 94
Tusks, Beaks, Horns – What Harvey does 95

STANDARDS 97
Trained-up standard (most common technique) 97
Fuchsias 97-101
Fuchsia diseases 102
Coleus standards 103, 104
Chrysanthemum standards 105, 106, 107
Ivy 107, 108
Grafted standards 109, 110, 111
Poinsettia 112, 113
Shortcuts and Other techniques 113, 114, 115, 116
Plants grown as standards 117

THE WREATH 118
Stuffed and planted wreath 118, 119
Unrooted – stuffed and stuck 120
Trained-up 120, 121
Oasis® wreath 121
Wire wreath, Kissing balls and May garland 122
Dried wreath 123, 124
Cut greens, 124, 125, 127

SPECIALTY TOPIARIES 128

Topiaries and flowers 128
Basic supplies and tools 128
Floral foam 128
Flowers 129
Floral standards 129, 130, 131, 132
Dried topiary 132, 133, 134
Wire-Frame Floral Topiaries 134, 135, 136
Floral topiary without a frame 136
The Boxwood Tree 137
Topiary as containers 138
Floral umbrella 139, ?
Flowers and foliage names 139
Moss topiary 140, 141, 142
Dried Topiaries 143, 144
Cork trees 144, 145
Flying butterflies 145, 146
Weathermaker Dragon 147
Cut green topiaries 148, 150, 151
Reindeer 149, 150, 151

GOOD IDEAS FROM OTHERS 152

Callaway columns 152, 153, 154, ?
Woven topiaries – Ivy Guild method 155, 156, 157
Grass sculptures 158, 159

FESTIVAL TOPIARIES

Building a carousel 161-166
Creating the Wonderful Garden of Oz 167, 168, 169
Icicles, Snowflakes, Reindeer and Penguins 170, 171, 172, 173, 174
New animals for an African Safari 175, 176, 177
Topiaries for the Dragon's Garden 178-185

TOPIARIES FOR CHILDREN AND THE CHILDREN'S GARDEN 186

Tabletop topiary 187, 188, 189, 190
Pre-made frames 191
Dried topiary 191
Fresh flowers 192
Party topiaries 192, 193
The Children's Garden 194, 195

INTERIORSCAPING, OUTDOOR AND TURN-ABOUT TOPIARIES 196

Planning topiary for interiorscapes 196, 197
Watering systems 198
Transporting topiary 199
Maintenance 199
Outdoor topiary 202, 203, 204, 205
Turn-About topiaries 206-213
Plant list 207

TOPIARY FRAMES 215

Planting guides 215
Pruning guides 215
Shaping 216
Large shaping and support frames 216
Pagoda frame 216
Specialized frames 216
Frame selection 217, 218
Homemade frames 218, 219
Style of frames 219
Topiary Inc. 219, 220
Longwood Manufacturing Corporation 221-223
Step-by-step formula for large topiary 222
Longwood frames 224
Jim Silvia 224, 225
Kenneth Lynch & Sons 225

PLANTS FOR TOPIARY 226

Size and texture 226
Color 227
Leaf shape 227
Flowering habit and timing 227
Growth rate 227
Growth habit 227
Compatibility 228, 229
Plant chart 230-237
Ivy 238
Pierot classification 238
Ivy chart 239, 242-251
American Ivy Society 241